Public Service Information Technology

Public Service Information Technology

The Definitive Manager's Guide to Harnessing Technology for Cost-Effective Operations and Services

Edward Y. Uechi

A PRODUCTIVITY PRESS BOOK

First edition published in 2020
by Routledge/Productivity Press
52 Vanderbilt Avenue, 11th Floor New York, NY 10017
2 Park Square, Milton Park, Abingdon, Oxon OX14 4RN, UK

Printed on acid-free paper

International Standard Book Number-13: 978-0-367-18110-9 (Paperback)
International Standard Book Number-13: 978-0-429-05956-8 (eBook)
International Standard Book Number-13: 978-0-367-40530-4 (Hardback)

Library of Congress Cataloging-in-Publication Data

Names: Uechi, Edward, author.
Title: Public service information technology : the definitive manager's
guide to harnessing technology for cost-effective operations and services / Edward Uechi.
Description: Boca Raton : Taylor & Francis, 2020. | Includes bibliographical references and index.
Identifiers: LCCN 2019036882 (print) | LCCN 2019036883 (ebook) |
ISBN 9780367181109 (paperback) | ISBN 9780367405304 (hardback) |
ISBN 9780429059568 (ebook)
Subjects: LCSH: Information technology—Management. | Project management. |
Strategic planning.
Classification: LCC HD30.2 .U38 2020 (print) | LCC HD30.2 (ebook) | DDC 352.3/80285—dc23
LC record available at https://lccn.loc.gov/2019036882
LC ebook record available at https://lccn.loc.gov/2019036883

Visit the Taylor & Francis Web site at
http://www.taylorandfrancis.com

and the CRC Press Web site at
http://www.crcpress.com

Contents

List of Figures

List of Worksheets

Author

Edward Y. Uechi has worked in the field of Information Technology since 1996, starting as a computer technician and working progressively to an IT manager position. His specialized area is in computer software. He worked at a high-technology international corporation in Silicon Valley for 5 years during the dot-com boom. He then transitioned his career to the nonprofit sector. He managed the IT department at a national nonprofit, public policy organization in Washington, DC. For the last 10 years, he has been advising foreign governments and private companies on paid and non-paid assignments funded mostly by the U.S. Agency for International Development (USAID). A recent project was funded by the World Food Programme (WFP). Current work includes IT technical assistance, organizational development, and management training.

In 2015 and 2018, utility patent applications had been filed in the U.S. Patent and Trademark Office for two computer-based systems that Edward invented to improve agricultural production and payment processing. The novel techniques resulted from observing and analyzing business and operational challenges in developing countries. Through his work in supporting government agencies, Edward has gained functional knowledge of agricultural production with focus on food safety at the farm level and cash transfer payments to social welfare recipients.

Edward earned a Bachelor of Arts degree in International Security and Conflict Resolution from San Diego State University and a Master of Public Administration degree with an Environmental Policy concentration from the Maxwell School of Syracuse University. It is noteworthy to add that he acquired 3 years of training in electronics at Aragon High School in California.

Edward's interests are in IT corporate governance, government contracting, Internet of Things (IoT), data privacy/sharing, and user authentication. He applies these areas in international development/relations with a focus on improving outcomes in developing countries.

Introduction

It is widely known that Information Technology (IT) projects fail more than they succeed in industry. The reasons for a high failure rate stem from various areas. Computer users were not able to articulate their requirements. Software developers had created a software program that did not capture what the organization truly wanted. The time period allocated to implement the work was too short. Financial, human, and material resources had been poorly planned.

This book gets at the reasons why an IT project fails and explains how to get an IT system that you, the government buyer and user, want and deserve. The information in this book can be valuable to contracting officers, technical officers, and inspector general auditors to be able to hold the government contractor in general and the IT provider in particular accountable.

Failures may be tolerated in the private sector. But in the public sector, the same types of failures should be minimized if not avoided completely. The stakes are very high to operate and maintain a computer-based information system that supports a government program. Many programs involve deadlines that individuals and corporations have to submit certain information by, such as filing taxes and reports. Senior citizens, disabled persons, and those who cannot support themselves for reasons beyond their control need to receive social protection payments on a periodic basis, so that a basic level of support can be provided by law. Election ballots and the process of collecting and handling voting information must have security controls and procedures to ensure that the processed and stored data cannot be tampered with. Millions of citizens who want to participate in certain public programs need to be authenticated and verified as real persons. Stored data must be protected and maintained for several years and checked for integrity. A failure in any of the foregoing instances could create a major problem such as an unnecessary delay, a corrupted data source, a fraudulent group of program recipients, or a stolen election by a few unknown groups. Such a failure may be isolated to a certain segment of the population or could have broad implication on an entire country. In any case, the government agency involved has to respond promptly to questions by the news media and the general public. A failure in government in general can result in an outcry by the general public and may serve as motivation by a political party to cut or eliminate a needed public program.

It is therefore critical for public managers to have equally high standards in acquiring and using IT systems, as they do in administering and overseeing government programs. Both are not mutually exclusive. A public program depends on an IT system to have correct information readily accessible at a specified time. An IT system depends on a public program to reference rules to carry out the program in a particular way. Government may be able to deliver a public program without an IT system, but an IT system used in a government program cannot be separated from public administration.

An IT system, which consists of various components, is another kind of tool that the public manager uses to carry out certain work. Like any tool, it must to be managed with care. Neglecting to keep a tool clean and maintained can lead to it being inoperable.

Management of IT is important. And its importance will become increasingly evident, as government agencies adopt advanced technologies to update and modernize their systems.

It can be hard to see the importance of IT management. Under normal operating conditions, computers run smoothly in the background without notice. When a sudden failure occurs such as a software crash, a hardware malfunction, or a network disruption, the IT manager steps in to make necessary repairs. Usually though, instances of system failures are few and infrequent. Nevertheless, the possibility of an IT system failure shows the need for management.

IT management does not just work in the operational area with focus on the technological part but also work on the non-technological part. Different areas are involved in the life of an IT system from its assessment to its disposal. Internal and external organizational dynamics is an area that can influence technical implementation. While fixing a computer malfunction is relatively easy in comparison, resolving an organizational problem is much more difficult. Unawareness of the non-technical issues can cause one or more issues to creep into a project and eventually show itself at some point in time. IT management not only encompasses the technical aspects of operating an IT system but also includes various non-technical aspects that underpin and affect an IT system.

This book will help public managers widen their view of the field of IT. Most people, when they talk about IT, immediately imagine buying a personal computer or developing a software program. A software program and a personal computer are tools, of course. Those who hold this narrow view that IT is just about buying or making tools can become victims in an inadequate IT system that only partially meets organizational needs at best and in an IT project that has gone extremely far over budget at worst. Indeed, such individuals could be prey to a for-profit private contractor that may have another motivation to pursue work with government. As an IT manager who has been dedicated to the ideal of public service since 2005, Edward Y. Uechi writes this book so that all civil servants can use it as a handbook for managing IT and as a guardrail against misaligned IT systems. Above all, all readers will become well-informed consumers of computer technologies.

The scope of this book covers IT management standards and practices in the public sector. This book is from the viewpoint of an IT manager who has worked with governments to improve IT operations. It is not about software development or any kind of specific technology implementation. The book explains how all the areas that go into IT management work together. Building a computer-based information system is like constructing a house; different disciplines are employed and need to be coordinated. In addition to the technical aspects such as computer networking and systems administration, the functional, business, management, and strategic aspects all are equally important. IT is not as simple as expecting to use a software program in 3 months. IT is a complex field that has multiple working parts that have to be managed.

The purpose of this book is to build the capacity of government agencies, so that public managers can fully realize the benefits of using IT systems in achievement of agencies' goals. Inadequate or lack of capacity in IT management exists. In an August 2018 report, the U.S. Government Accountability Office (GAO) had found shortcomings and ineffectiveness in IT management among 24 executive agencies in the U.S. government. In Edward's professional capacity to train and advise personnel in public and nonprofit organizations, he observed similar deficiencies in governments in Iraq, Ghana, and Kenya. In order for government agencies to modernize their operations, government agencies must have the necessary capacity to do so. That means that public managers need to have relevant knowledge and skills.

In alignment with the purpose, this book will achieve the following objectives:

1. To align present and future IT systems with the organization's mission to ensure that program services are delivered to internal and external users in a cost-effective manner.
2. To direct and inform administrative and procurement teams to facilitate the acquisition of IT systems that meet organizational requirements and are operable for several years of productive use.
3. To increase engagement and communication among IT and non-IT managers to work productively in the development of IT systems where requirements are clear and unambiguous to both technical and functional teams.

The primary audience for this book is public managers, those who have responsibility over IT operations and those who work with IT managers, in government agencies. The book is not just for technical IT managers but also for non-technical (non-IT) managers and senior executive leaders. Not only will the Chief Information Officer (CIO), the IT Director, and the IT Manager find this book invaluable to running an effective IT unit, but also the Chief Financial Officer (CFO), the HR Director, and functional managers will understand their roles to cooperate with the technical team. Every manager involved at all levels of the organization has a small yet consequential role to play in developing and managing an IT system.

Other managers who work in nonprofit, non-governmental organizations, foreign governments, inter-governmental organizations, and international organizations will find this book applicable to meeting their IT needs, as they would be managing comparable programs designed to serve the public. Graduate students who major in Public Administration at public and private universities would benefit from reading this book, as the topics will prepare them to be able to manage IT programs and IT projects once they begin their career in public service.

Students should carefully read all the chapters. Current professionals can skim through the chapters and concentrate on particular topics that would be most relevant based on their job function and position. Certain chapters, however, should be read carefully in their entirety by managers with specific roles. Chapter 2 is designed for human resources managers. Chapter 3 is designed for finance managers. Chapter 5 is designed for contracting officers and their technical representatives. Chapter 8 is designed for senior executive leaders and department directors.

As a handbook, public managers can jump to any topic in the book, as the task arises in daily operations to provide practical guidelines. The managers can test their understanding of the topics and concepts with a short quiz at the end of each chapter. Answers are provided after the glossary of terms. Practice worksheets are provided to understand the concepts in Chapters 1–8. Please see the last page of the Manager's Notes for the website address and access code to download the electronic versions of the worksheets and to gain access to some other goodies. The printed worksheets in this book had been designed to conform to page constraints for publication; text had been set larger than normal to ensure legibility on the printed page. While the printed worksheets will aid in understanding the concepts through self-guided practice, the electronic versions can be used in official work. The electronic versions will have additional notes and instructions that are revised from time to time.

The structure of this book follows a logical design. The first chapter begins with summaries of the elements or building blocks of the IT ecosystem, and then, subsequent chapters describe how the elements can be organized, budgeted, selected, managed, and secured. The result culminates in applying all the lessons to develop and execute a long-term IT Strategic Plan, a formal document that specifies IT programs and IT systems in alignment with the government agency's mission. In the end, the public manager will be able to see how all of the necessary parts fit together in a comprehensive view. The conclusion provides a concise summary that leads to three key graphical representations that show the "Big Picture of IT." The public manager can use the graphical representations for business, functional, and technical purposes to manage and implement IT.

A brief description of each chapter follows:

Chapter 1 describes all the elements of the IT ecosystem. Like species in the natural world, the elements can change over time with a new technique, a new method, a new rule, or some other approach that makes an improvement. The elements are broad classifications in which specific technologies and recent developments, such as social media and the Internet-of-Things, fall into. The elements include both technology and non-technology. The chapter enables the public manager to break the latest innovation down to its elements. Chapter 1 concludes with a summary of emerging technology, highlighting challenges that promising computer-related technologies have and will need to be overcome in order to be viable for wide use.

Chapter 2 describes the organization of IT in terms of people and their defined roles. The chapter explains numerous non-IT and IT personnel and IT certifications. The chapter further explains the relationships with other managers and specialists inside and outside of the organization. The chapter describes the Office of the Chief Information Officer. Chapter 2 concludes with defining the organizational structure that would be suitable for the public manager's operating environment.

Chapter 3 describes the mechanics of developing an IT budget for present and future years, accounting for all resources. The chapter explains analytical methods and various cost factors to determine how IT programs and IT systems can be used optimally. Chapter 3 concludes with a method of calculating the return on investment so that the public manager can present to senior executive leaders what will be the benefits of a proposed IT project.

Chapter 4 describes the importance of selecting the right technologies that will best meet organizational needs as opposed to using what is popular or fashionable. The chapter explains how the public manager should examine particular systems and processes with a critical eye. The chapter further describes the process of selecting, controlling, and evaluating IT projects. Budgeting work from the previous chapter is applied to determine whether or not an IT project should be pursued. Chapter 4 concludes with the development of a business case with the factor for social equity.

Chapter 5 describes the difference between contracting and outsourcing and the costs and benefits of each. The impact that outsourcing can have on the government agency's business process is touched upon. If contracting offers the better option, the chapter further describes various agreements with vendors and how the government agency would be able to maximize relationships with vendors. Chapter 5 concludes with turning around a troubled contract.

Chapter 6 describes the process of system development, focusing on important parts of the work to ensure that implementation is managed and controlled while at the same time allowing work to move as quickly as possible. The public manager will understand scope management and change management. The chapter highlights a series of documents that are created in the course of developing and operating an IT system. Emphasis is spent on the principal document that guides software development. Chapter 6 concludes with a practical approach to keeping team members motivated and involved.

Chapter 7 describes the implications and risks of leaving the elements in the IT ecosystem unprotected. A standard three-prong approach (based on managerial controls, operational controls, and technical controls) provides the overall structure for protecting information throughout an organization. The chapter goes into detail in developing an information security program that protects and safeguards an IT system on multiple levels. Chapter 7 concludes with the development of an Information System Security Policy.

Chapter 8 describes the need for and the role of the long-term IT Strategic Plan. The IT Strategic Plan is the keystone that holds together all of the parts laid out in the preceding chapters. The process of developing the strategic plan, starting with a strategic planning committee, is explained. Every department is represented to ensure that the strategy can work for all and in perfect alignment to accomplish the government agency's mission. The chapter goes into the execution of the developed and approved plan. Chapter 8 concludes with monitoring and governance of the IT Strategic Plan.

After reading this book, public managers should be able to accomplish the objectives stated above. Although the objectives are ranked in order of importance, Edward personally places the third objective as a higher priority over the first two. A motivating factor for writing this book is to improve relations between technical teams and functional teams. By including the non-technical aspects and showing how they relate to IT, IT managers will understand the important contributions that non-IT managers make and further understand why their contributions have equal weight in gold – Enterprise Architecture is as valuable as computer source code. Likewise, non-IT managers will understand how much time and labor are involved in developing and operating an IT system. Both groups would then gain a fuller appreciation of each other's work and value each other even more. The outcome would not only produce high morale throughout the organization but also result in high-quality IT systems that everyone involved can be proud to use for several years. In context of public service, this would mean the delivery of effective and timely government programs to citizens.

While the content of this book is written primarily for government agencies, the same content can be applied, where applicable, in nonprofit, non-governmental organizations. Nonprofit managers are considered public managers since they work with the same level of dedication and commitment to serve in the interests of the public. The nonprofit sector has demonstrated to be a strong community to provide charitable support and humanitarian assistance to those in need. As they read the book, nonprofit managers can swap every instance of the term, "government agency," with "nonprofit organization" to check if the corresponding topic would apply. If it does (most topics should), then the nonprofit managers can apply the topic in their organization.

This book shares the author's experience and work so that other public managers can benefit from it and achieve the same level of success in all IT projects. If you need help with any topic or any of the worksheets, feel free to contact Edward via the website: http://www.PublicServiceIT.org/extra/.

Chapter 1

The IT Ecosystem: Elements Described

CMS. CRM. SaaS. PaaS. IaaS. Cloud. These simplified terms have served well to market the latest computer technologies to a wide audience. Sales and marketing teams use these words among others to make Information Technology (IT) easier to understand – or maybe not. Behind these terms are elements that make IT work.

Chapter Summary

The computer has evolved from a single large mainframe that takes up the space of a room to a small mobile device that can be used in the palm of a hand. Changes in the components operating within have led to making the computer more powerful, faster, and smaller. Changes in the components that make an organization function have also had an influence in advancing computer technologies. All of the technological and non-technological components are the elements in the field of IT. The IT ecosystem thrives with all of the elements, changing over time like species in the natural world, in operation to work with each other.

The IT ecosystem is not a fixed system where its elements do not change. An element can be modified by a new technique, a new method, a new rule, or some other approach that improves upon the element. The IT ecosystem can be different for one organization in comparison to another organization. Various elements can be selected to create an IT ecosystem that meets the organization's needs. Public managers can pick and choose those elements.

This chapter enables the public manager to break the latest innovation down to its elements. In doing so, the manager will be able to understand how the product has changed and how it is different from competing brands. In cooperation with the technical team, the functional team can construct a comparable product.

Subsequent chapters will refer to this chapter for descriptions of all elements. Once the elements have been explained, the public manager can then use the elements properly to develop a broad IT program or a specific IT system. The bulk of this book helps the manager to organize, budget, select, manage, and secure all the selected elements in their IT ecosystem.

The End User

Arguably, the most important element is the person or groups of persons who use an IT system. This is the end user, a user who uses a computer product. An end user can be an internal employee who retrieves classified data in a private IT system that operates completely in one building. Another end user can be a civil servant who processes forms. Still another end user can be a citizen who submits personal information to access a government program. End users can be different types of people who work inside a government agency and who benefit from a public program. End users, moreover, can have various roles that allow them to see and do certain things.

The end user can also be a computer machine that performs a task similar to what a person would do. Such a machine user would execute a transaction with another machine user without involvement of a human. A machine user could be programmed to check another machine user and access a specific data record numerous times on a regularly set schedule. This robot or "bot" as an automated end user can free up a civil servant's time. While the robot user carries out routine tasks or tasks requiring intensive computing power, a civil servant can focus on other tasks that require human judgment.

Whether a machine user or a human user, the circumstances surrounding a particular end user can change. The business rule or the time period can change the automated procedure in which the machine user depends on execution. The interests and motivations can change the behavior of a person. A sample of human users can suggest a new way of accomplishing a mundane task. The needs and requirements can change the direction of an organization. The collective group of public managers can decide to move their government agency on a different course.

Since the end user plays an important part in the IT ecosystem, all possible end users who would be using an IT system need to be identified and understood. How the different types of end users (human or machine) will behave have to be considered.

Information Types

The information element is the critical half in the term "Information Technology". Computer technology does something with information. But what exactly is information?

Information can be defined into six basic types:

1. Simple Text
2. Still Image
3. Document File
4. Audio Sound
5. Motion Pictures
6. Multimedia Presentation

Simple text is the simplest type of information. This comes in the form of letters, numbers, and other characters defined in ASCII without any formatting applied such as a particular font size or font style. Typing characters to form a person's name or some other word, phrase, or sentence in an input field is simple text. That submitted combination of characters without any formatting, encoding, or encryption can be transmitted through the network in plain text. The combination of characters without any formatting can be saved or stored in a text file. This basic type of information can be referred to as "raw data."

Simple text can be easily manipulated either by the original first person or by a second or third user who has access to the information. A person can freely enter new characters, delete some characters, and continue typing characters before submitting or saving the information. Other people may be able to access the stored information, change the text, and resave the information as new. An unknown user could intercept the combination of characters in a computer network to capture and save the text in another computer at which point it could be changed or used for some other purpose that the first person never intended. Modifying simple text can be done by a basic text editor tool used in any computer.

Other tools that can be used to create simple text are a typewriter, a fax machine, and a word processor.

Still image is the next type of information. It can be in the form of a simple icon, a data graph, a line drawing, a complex illustration, and a photograph. Any instance of these forms provides a graphical representation of some concept, thing, or person at a particular moment in time. While simple text may not arouse excitement, a still image can evoke a certain type of emotion in an audience. The common saying goes, "A picture says a thousand words." A graphic image can tell a story in a visual way that a writer can in an essay.

Unless it was created by specialized computer software, the original graphic whether it was made by pencil, pen, paint, or film camera will have to be converted into a digital format. A specialized computer hardware device can scan a drawing, a painting, and a photograph for use in a computer. A digital camera that replaces a film camera can create a photograph already in a digital format.

A digital still image can be manipulated or corrupted either accidentally or intentionally. Because it involves a particular process to create and modify, an image requires the use of the same specialized computer software such as Adobe Photoshop or Corel Draw to view and change. A different software program would not be able to open and read the image or it could damage the image if it was forced to read it. A person would need an intermediate software program to convert the image from one format created in Photoshop, for example, to another format that can be read by Corel Draw. The original software program could also resave the image into another digital format such as GIF, TIFF, JPEG, or PNG for viewing in another software program.

Be forewarned that the various image formats come with various image resolutions that can produce loss of quality in the new image. The GIF format generates a low-quality image with significantly reduced colors. It was designed to transmit and display images quickly for the Web. The JPEG format is widely used to save a photographic image with millions of colors and very high quality. The TIFF format is an older digital format that maintains very high image resolution and very high file size. A high-resolution image can be reduced down to a lower resolution format and maintain its original graphical representation as intended by the creator. On the other hand, going from a low-resolution image to a higher-resolution format can distort the graphical representation. The creator of an image has to be aware of the number of times that an image is converted across different formats because each change generates a certain loss of image quality. The manner in which an image is converted or the number of times of changing the digital format could change the image's digital information in ways that make it corrupted.

The document file is a type of information that combines simple text and still images. It can come in a wide range of forms from a simple receipt of goods to a 500-page manuscript that explains a subject in detail. Some common forms that can be found in government are a letter, a policy memorandum, a registration form, and a survey questionnaire. Other forms can be a marketing brochure, a presentation slide, and a training manual. An advantage over simple text is that a document can have formatting with a stylized typeface, a larger font size for the heading and a smaller size for the body, and a different font style such as bold or italics to emphasize certain words. The inclusion of one or more still images can make a document more engaging to read.

Like the image type, any paper-based document has to be converted into a digital format. A specialized computer hardware device can scan a paper document and save it as a still image. If, however, a person would like to edit the text, a specialized computer software program is needed to convert the printed text into digital characters. Without specialized software, the scanned printed material becomes a still image wherein its text cannot be altered.

Numerous specialized computer software programs exist to create a wide range of document files natively in the computer. The business of desktop publishing emerged and quickly flourished in the 1990s. Microsoft, Adobe, and a few other companies produced specialized software for various industries to create letters, brochures, slide presentations, and other documents with less cost and in faster time than it was possible with traditional printing. Once a digital document was saved, a person can open it again and make a change to the text or delete an image or switch an image for a different one.

A digital document file faces a similar problem with an image file. The same software program has to be used for reading and changing the contents. A specialized software could resave a document file in another format that is compatible with a different software program. For example, a WordPerfect document can be exported into a format that is readable in Microsoft Word. Without such an export function, an intermediate software program would be needed to convert the document file.

A document file in a digital format can be changed for good or ill. A group of colleagues can share a digital document among themselves, and each one can add new information or change existing information. Some user could access a certain digital document, insert malicious computer code, save it, and then use the modified document to harm other computers. Specialized software programs can have various degrees of protection against malicious attempts to alter document files.

Audio sound is a type of information that offers a rich experience. Unlike the foregoing information types, audio can provide entertainment on top of just offering information. Forms of audio include a voice recording, a music recording, and a sound recording of natural or artificial objects. Communication from one person to another across a distance is used by a telephone device. Broadcasting audio to a mass audience was typically done (still is today) by using a radio transmitter to send live or recorded audio signals on the Amplitude Modulation (AM) or Frequency Modulation (FM) radio band to a number of radio receivers used by individuals. Other ways of broadcasting audio include transmitters and receivers operating on the Shortwave and Citizens Band (CB) radio bands. Through the use of a satellite operating in space, audio signals can be relayed to reach a larger audience than was not possible with earth-bound radio transmitters. In the past, audio was recorded on magnetic tape. Specialized computer software programs can convert analog audio signals to digital audio files and create new digital audio recordings. Digital audio becomes another type of an electronic file that can be saved in the computer. The digital audio files can then be served on the Internet in Websites and podcasts. With upgraded technology from analog to digital in radio broadcast stations, the same radio station that has been operating for decades can transmit digital audio.

Saved audio sound recordings can be changed and manipulated. With the right equipment, a person can insert a new segment, delete an existing segment, or make edits to change or move segments around. Advanced techniques to enhance or modify audio include increasing or decreasing the volume, obscuring a human voice in a way that makes it sound different, and creating special sound effects such as echo, reverberation, and fade in/out.

Audio sound can be intercepted and recorded by another user. A person could use rudimentary tools to tap into a telephone line and listen in on a phone conversation. A tiny device equipped with a microphone and a transmitter could be planted in a room and start recording any human voice, ambient noise, and other form of sound. Like with any electronic file, digital audio could be intercepted as it is transmitted across the computer network. Once sound has been intercepted in any of these instances, the captured audio could be saved.

Motion pictures is a type of information that involves a rapid succession of still images to create an illusion of people and objects moving through time and space. Typically, motion pictures is projected onto a screen at a speed of 24 frames per second. Another speed rate is 30 frames per second. Each frame presents a single still image. Audio sound is usually added to provide human voice, music, and other sounds synchronized to the movement of the images. Like the audio sound alone, motion pictures also creates a rich experience. Adding images to sound can provide an experience that matches or reflects reality.

Before the advent of video, the production of motion pictures involved costly equipment and supplies and specialized teams. Production companies produced motion pictures on 16 mm, 35 mm, or 70 mm film and distributed their final products to movie theaters. Television news organizations produced motion pictures on 16 mm film and broadcasted their products from radio stations operating on a frequency band different and separate from AM and FM radio.

Transitioning from traditional film to digital video occurred in the 1980s and 1990s. Video cameras replaced film cameras to produce motion pictures for immediate viewing and broadcasting. Video eliminated the need to send rolls of film to a film developer who had to create a positive image from the exposed negative image – a process that can take a day to a week. Analog video was recorded on magnetic tape, either on VHS format or Beta format.

Analog video cameras advanced in development to become digital video cameras. As the components that operate a digital camera have gotten smaller, a digital camera could be installed in a range of devices. Typically, a commercial video camera is a separate device that is connected to a computer. Private companies would use commercial video cameras to monitor their warehouses and other facilities. Specialized government agencies like law enforcement would use commercial video cameras for surveillance of city streets and public areas. The advancement of motion pictures to digital video has dramatically brought the cost of production down.

With digital video motion pictures, specialized computer software programs can make edits to move segments of the footage around, delete a certain segment, or add a new segment from another video file. The audio sound portion can also be added, edited, or deleted. Any archived film footage will have to be converted to digital video. Conversion from film to video requires specialized equipment. Once the film has been converted, the digitized film footage can be added to an existing digital video file.

Digital video can be manipulated. A user could add transitions and subtitles to a digital video. Certain software programs include advanced functions to create special effects. It is possible for the background to be replaced with a different background, while the person who provides voice commentary in the foreground is left unchanged.

Multimedia presentation is the last type of information that can immerse a person into the details of a subject, creating a very rich and engaging experience. It involves combining all of the above information types in an interactive presentation that runs in a computer. It is called "multimedia" because the presentation brings together various types of media (e.g., text, photographs, documents, music, and video footage). Unlike the linear forms of presentation inherent in audio and video, a multimedia presentation includes computer programming to create functions that allow a person to interact with the subject matter in a non-linear way. Rather than simply viewing a presentation from start to end, a user could start in the middle or jump around to whichever content appears more interesting. The multimedia presentation gained popularity in the 1990s and proved effective in an educational environment where participants can learn complex subjects more quickly than through conventional learning methods. While some presentations are delivered and used on the Web, most multimedia presentations continue to be distributed by a CD-ROM or DVD-ROM disc.

In addition to all the software programs described above, another specialized computer software program is needed to combine all the information types and to write the program code to create the user interactivity. Needless to say, all information types must be in a digital format. The completed multimedia presentation becomes a self-contained software application that can be made to run in a computer. Depending on how much information is used, the file size of the multimedia presentation can vary from small to large. Lengthy video footage can make the size very large. The file size is a factor in deciding whether the presentation should be deployed on the Web or distributed by disc.

The risk of manipulating a multimedia presentation is very low for those that are distributed by CD-ROM or DVD-ROM disc. A person would have to be skilled in hacking into the self-contained application and making changes. If successful, the multimedia presentation could be inserted with malicious program code and resaved as a new file. The altered presentation file would then have to be delivered through another channel.

A multimedia presentation deployed on the Web is a likely target for exploitation by an unknown user. A skilled person would have to hack into the presentation, insert malicious code, resave the file, and upload the altered file in its original location. And then the next viewer of the now corrupted multimedia presentation could be harmed by the malicious code.

The ordering of the information types shows the amount of storage and processing needed in a computer. Simple text such as processing a person's name requires the least amount of computing power. A multimedia presentation, on the other end of the scale, needs a significant amount of computing power, since a presentation combines text, image, audio, and video. Motion pictures containing video and audio is a type that can weigh down a multimedia presentation as this type alone requires large storage capacity. Storage and processing capacity can vary for a still image and a document file, based on their size and content.

If information is to be transmitted across the computer network, the speed of the network connection has to be determined to ensure that various information types can be sent without any data loss. Simple text does not require a high-speed network and can be transmitted through networks that rely on dial-up modems. The network speed can vary for a still image, depending on the image dimensions, image resolution, and amount of colors. A GIF or JPEG image of a small to medium size at 72 dpi can be transmitted through a slower network speed. A larger image or a print-quality high-resolution image will need a higher network speed. The network speed can vary as well for a document file, based on its file size. A large document would need a higher network speed. Rich media such as audio, video, and multimedia require a high-speed network *and* a stable network connection. A person can encounter difficulties in viewing rich media when their network connection stops and starts intermittently. A problem that can occur with any information type, if the network connection is not fast enough, is an electronic file that has parts of its contents missing.

The public manager needs to be aware that a particular information type needs a certain amount of storage and processing in a computer and a certain speed in a computer network. Choosing the right computer and network is dependent on the type of information that the government agency will use. The information type needs to be matched in capacity with the selected

IT system. A lightweight IT system will have difficulty in processing a heavy information type such as motion pictures. An organization that uses video teleconferencing (which is motion pictures) over a slow network connection will be unable to communicate with the other party. Failure to understand this fundamental concept can lead to technological issues in the implemented IT solution.

Functional Application

Another element in the IT ecosystem is a functional application. The word, "application", used in this context does not refer to computer software. A "functional application" refers to an organizational activity of significant scope that an organization undertakes, regardless of whether a computer is used. Basic functional applications, which would be found in all organizations, are financial management, human resources management, inventory management, and project management. Contract/grant management and document management are specific applications relevant to government agencies. To a certain degree, a nonprofit organization would use grant management when managing sub grants. More specific functional applications could be undertaken based on the specific work of a particular organization. For example, farm inspection is a functional application used by a government agency that has the mandate to inspect farm production sites. Tax collection is a functional application used by a government agency that has authority to collect taxes. Social security is a functional application used by a government agency that has responsibility to manage recipients of welfare payments. Any one of the functional applications will have its own operating procedure, business process, business rules, decision points, and documentary evidence.

The experts who will know a functional application are those non-IT managers who work in that area. An accountant, a budget analyst, and a finance specialist are experts in the financial management application. An agronomist, an entomologist, a soil chemist, and other agriculture-related specialists are experts in the farm inspection application. These people will know, whether officially documented in a manual or not, the procedures and rules that govern their functional application. They will also know what specific documents need to be collected or how new documents need to be created. Note that a functional expert can be equally technical in their field, as an IT specialist is technical in computers.

Business Process

An important part of a functional application that earns special recognition is a business process. A functional application has activities to deliver or support a service to a group of people. Public managers, civil servants, and private contractors who are involved in any of the activities have tasks and/or decisions that will affect the outcome. All of those involved have to be aware of where their particular task starts and ends. There may be a paper trail – a series of documents that get created from one person and transferred to another person – that helps in moving from one task to the next. All of these tasks, decisions, and documents form a chain of events or a series of steps that create a business process. See Figure 4.1 as an example. The business process provides the underlying structure for how an information system is to function. Thus, a business process is an element in the IT ecosystem.

In many small organizations where team members make up a handful, the business process is usually known implicitly. Everyone understands what needs to be done because small teams tend to share knowledge with each other frequently and work well overall. Thus, the need for documenting the business process does not come up. A new hire could be quickly trained or mentored by showing them how to do the work on the job by another team member.

A large organization with thousands of employees or several offices spread geographically across a far distance can encounter issues related to the business process in a functional application. Everyone may not know what specifically must be performed. It could be cumbersome to communicate knowledge across all the teams, given that there can be layers of bureaucracy. Getting knowledge to team members spread across several locations could also be difficult. The communication problem could lead to one team having an understanding of the process and another team having a different interpretation. Team members who are not clear on the process or have missing information would rely on their own experience and assumptions that may not be in line with the organization. Thus, it becomes critical to have the business process explicitly drawn out on paper.

Regardless of the size of the organization, an organization will have several business processes – at least one process for each functional application. And two or more processes could have places where they join as a result of a decision or the creation of a document. The financial management application is generally one process that has connections in other business processes. It can be hard to know where multiple processes are linked together somehow when all of the business processes are not documented.

Once all of the business processes are drawn on paper, public managers will be in a better position to find areas for improvement. The public manager would realize that some steps in one process can be dropped, creating a new process that is more efficient. Two managers could see that a short series of tasks in their processes are the same and can agree to merge those tasks as a shared sub process. Such a finding where certain series of events are shared among two or more business processes has the potential for consolidating functional applications. The result of any kind of business process improvement can lead to a shorter time in service delivery, a reduction in cost, or a quicker turnaround in making a decision.

Note that an entire business process may neither be feasible nor be desired to be automated in a computer. The level of engineering necessary to create a software program that completely manages all of the steps can be too costly in manpower, equipment, and money. Some areas in the process can be fine left as a manual process. In certain circumstances, specific tasks and decisions can provide appropriate and effective safeguard measures when a human hand is required to provide oversight or judgment. Public programs involve social equity effects that are best left to human users to analyze and decide. For any given business process, there can be parts that are suitable for automation and other parts that should be kept manual.

Government Law

An important element in the IT ecosystem is a government law that can affect any part of an organization. A law and its implementing regulations passed at the national, regional, or local level may direct how a functional application or a government program is to be carried out. It may instruct how certain work in a business process is to be conducted. It may inform how IT resources are to be organized and managed. It may mandate how much information is to be collected and for how long such collection must be stored. A law can be as broad as to govern the protection of a person's identity and personal information. A law can be as specific as to authorize a digital signature as equal to a handwritten signature in all legal matters. The public manager will have to seek out what laws and regulations are applicable in their work, if they currently are not aware already.

Given that there can be several applicable laws in a particular country and that the laws of one country can be different to that of another country, this book does not go into detail of any particular law. To make this book generally accessible to any public manager in any country, the scope of this book does not cover the particulars of government laws. A supplemental edition of this book may be authored to cover applicable laws for a specific country.

The following topics would be of interest to all countries where government laws on the topics may or may not exist:

- Information Technology Management
- Electronic Government or Governance (E-Government)
- Electronic Signature (E-Signature)
- Document Retention and Preservation
- Data Protections Related to Finance, Employment, and Health
- Personal Privacy

Information Security

Information security is a critical element in the IT ecosystem – especially in government operations. The implications of security breaches can be severe and can have wide-reaching effects that extend across a large population. Confidential health records of millions of citizens could be disclosed to computer hackers who break into a public health database. Foreign agents could gain access into an IT system containing classified national security information. Damages that might result include disclosure of sensitive information, corruption in data integrity, downtime in critical operations, disruption of services, loss of government assets, and loss in public confidence.

A security risk can originate from any element in the IT ecosystem. Computer technologies are not the only components that have vulnerabilities. Although a business process has a primary path to follow, there can be a number of alternative paths that a user could take. And a user could exploit an alternative path that was not clearly mapped out. A functional application may have been rapidly developed with not all of the rules and procedures completely thought through. This could leave open the possibility of taking advantage of a government service fraudulently. An end user could do something, either accidently or intentionally, that creates a security issue. While one area of the IT ecosystem can be well protected, the IT ecosystem can still be vulnerable because all other areas have not been reviewed thoroughly for potential security risks.

Technological Elements

Once the non-technological elements described above have been identified, public managers can start thinking about the computer technology. In other words, public managers can begin to identify the technologies that will best manage their identified information. The next half of the chapter deals with the technology part of the term "Information Technology".

While technology improves from one version to the next version, specific technologies made by a particular company can be placed in one of eight technological elements. After reading this chapter, the public manager should be able to know which elements well-known company brands such as Microsoft Windows, Apple iPad, and Cisco Catalyst belong in. The eight technological elements are as follows:

1. Computer Hardware
2. Computer Software
3. Computer Firmware
4. Embedded Technology
5. Computer Network
6. The Internet
7. Telecommunication Infrastructure
8. Emerging Technology

Computer Hardware

Computer hardware is a technological element that provides a set of physical parts to create a complete computer system. All of the hardware components are connected together to process information. This physical device, in essence, accepts information as input in some form, then processes the information according to a set of instructions, and finally releases information as output in another form. The output can be displayed on a monitor screen, printed on paper, or stored on a type of medium. The input can be typed in by using a keyboard, chosen by the click of a cursor icon that moves around the screen, or inserted with a card or file that contains preformatted information. The principal part of the hardware system (the CPU) runs a computer software program to execute instructions that will calculate or process the inputted information. This computer system as a physical machine would be capable of handling a larger amount of information than a person could process manually in the same period of time. Figure 1.1 illustrates the concept that underpins the operation of the computer. More information about the hardware components is described below.

From as early as the late 1950s to as late into the 1980s, government agencies and large private companies used a mainframe computer system to process large amounts of information. A mainframe computer was a physically large system that would take up significant space in a room. This was so because of available technology at the time. Computer design relied on bulky hardware

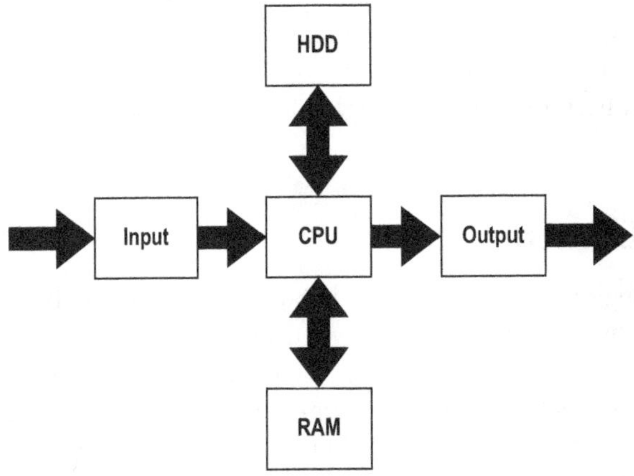

Figure 1.1 Logical computing.

components such as vacuum tubes, electrical relays, large resistors, and magnetic tape reels. The physical wiring itself needed space to allow the wires to be connected between the parts and to not cause problems in the circuit. Earlier mainframe computer systems involved mechanical engineering to make the early electronic parts work.

New materials and advancements in the technology led to making the electronic parts smaller and more reliable. The invention of the transistor replaced the vacuum tube. The invention of the Integrated Circuit chip (IC chip) made it possible to perform numerous logic functions comparable to a number of transistors in a small part that fits on a person's finger, thus replacing the transistor. Copper (or another conductive material) etched on a thin board on which IC chips, smaller resistors, and other parts were mounted provided the connections to create the circuit for all the electronic parts. The amount of physical wires was significantly reduced. The number of mechanical parts was reduced to those hardware components that could not be developed in pure electronic form (e.g., a power supply, a fan, and a plug-in port). Advancements continue to this day to build a newer IC chip that performs more computations than its predecessor.

A microcomputer system uses these smaller electronic parts and IC chips mounted on a thin circuit board. The microcomputer emerged in the 1970s, soon grew in popularity in the 1980s, and is the dominant form in today's computing environment. To differentiate itself from the mainframe computer, the microcomputer was marketed as a "Personal Computer" or a PC since it allowed an individual person to process information from their desk and without being connected to a mainframe. A traditional mainframe computer required people to connect to it through a terminal to send the input and to receive the output. The PC essentially made it possible to do the input, processing, and output in one machine that conveniently shared space on a person's desk.

Although the term Personal Computer is widely used instead of the term microcomputer, the fundamental design of how a microcomputer system is made applies to other computer machines. The latest mainframe computer has evolved to use the microcomputer design. A supercomputer system, which is designed for scientific functional applications, uses the microcomputer design with emphasis on multiple computer processors to carry out intensive calculations in parallel processing. Other specialized applications that use the microcomputer design include a computer server, a computer network device, and a computer peripheral device such as a printer and a scanner. With hardware components getting smaller, a computer designed for a person's desk can be designed thin enough to fit in a briefcase or small enough to fit in a person's palm.

What makes the microcomputer system versatile is its "open architecture" design. Microcomputers depend on the same set of hardware components that can be mixed from different computer manufacturers. Manufacturers would test their hardware products to ensure that they are compatible with other hardware components and with the computer software operating system (OS). The public manager then does not necessarily have to buy a completely pre-configured PC from one manufacturer. Doing so could amount to a very high price tag when the government agency needs to purchase hundreds or thousands of PCs, where each one is assigned to an employee. A cost-effective approach would be to purchase individual hardware components in bulk from various computer vendors and then customize the PCs for each department. Standard hardware components are as follows:

1. A motherboard main circuit board
2. A Central Processing Unit (CPU) microprocessor
3. A Random Access Memory (RAM) memory module
4. A Hard Disk Drive (HDD or HD) storage device
5. A Network Interface Card (NIC) or network adapter

Without getting too technical in how the standard components operate, public managers should at least be familiar with the hardware components inside a microcomputer system. The motherboard is the large main circuit board that contains the connectors for attaching one or more additional circuit boards (a daughter board), the CPU, the memory module, the storage device, the network adapter, and one or more plug-in ports necessary to attach external, peripheral devices such as a monitor screen, a keyboard, and a mouse. The CPU is the "brain of the computer", a microprocessor that executes computer program instructions, processes information, and performs computations. The RAM allows information to be stored temporarily while the computer is running. As the CPU processes information, the CPU is pulling and pushing that information through the RAM. The HDD, which comes in different formats and storage capacities, provides permanent storage of information in the computer. The person's files along with computer software programs are stored in the hard drive. The CPU retrieves information from the hard drive for processing and sends it back for storage. The NIC, which comes in different connection types and connection speeds, allows the computer to be connected to other computers in a computer network.

Depending on the requirements of the end user and the identified non-technological elements, the standard hardware components can be combined in varied system configurations. A functional application that requires intensive computing power, for example, would have two or more CPUs. A requirement to process video to many people on the Internet would have a significant amount of RAM and a very fast NIC. A computer that does not need access to other computers would not need the NIC installed.

Computer Software

Computer software is the intangible technological element that adds value to a computer. Because it cannot be touched and felt like any type of computer hardware, computer software is hard to imagine and thus difficult to define. It is written in a particular format to accomplish a certain task inside the computer. It provides a set of instructions to make computer hardware perform specific functions. Computer software cannot be used without the set of hardware components that make up the computer. Computer hardware would essentially have limited to no use without computer software.

A variety of computer programming languages have been developed to write computer software. Earlier languages include FORTRAN, COBOL, and Assembly. Modern languages include Object-Oriented Languages such as C++, C#, Objective-C, and Java. Other languages used to develop software for the Web include HTML, XML, and JavaScript. Like national languages are written and spoken by using a different grammar structure, computer languages are different in the way in which each language is structured in syntax. All computer languages are designed to process information in some sort of logical manner. The modern languages can be thought of like competing brands, as they can be used to accomplish the same task but would do it with more or less efficiency given their particular format.

Computer software can be divided into four broad categories called (1) operating system (OS), (2) application program, (3) client-server system, and (4) Internet-based application. An OS software program manages the operation of the computer, which covers how each hardware component functions and to a certain extent how each application program interacts. All microcomputer systems must have an OS. The OS works behind the scenes to handle tasks like receiving input from the keyboard, sending information to the screen, and keeping track of files on the disk. Microsoft DOS, all the versions of Microsoft Windows from 3.1 through XP to 10; Apple Macintosh; and Mac OS X are examples of OS software programs used in the PC. Palm OS, Windows CE, Apple iOS, and Google Android are OS software programs used in mobile handheld devices. BSD, HP-UX, IBM AIX, Linux, and Sun Solaris are derivatives of the UNIX OS software program, which are used in high-end computer servers. Note that all the example OS software programs are developed by different companies to market and sell their particular computer systems.

An application program is developed for a specific purpose other than managing general computer operations. The scope of such a software program covers very specific requirements for a functional application, which may cover only a small part of a management program or a small area of operations. Of course, an application program has to be designed to work with a given OS software program. Any number of application programs can be developed for a single microcomputer system. Office productivity programs such as Microsoft Word, Microsoft Excel, Adobe Acrobat, and OpenOffice are application programs used in business. Adobe Illustrator, Adobe Photoshop, and Adobe InDesign are application programs used to create and modify images and documents for desktop publishing. Apple Safari, Microsoft Internet Explorer, Mozilla Firefox, and Google Chrome are application programs designed to browse the World Wide Web (WWW) and to interact with an Internet-based application. The foregoing example application programs are commercial software products developed by different companies. Private companies are not the only developers of application programs, of course. The government agency may have a technical team either employed or contracted to create its own application programs.

A client-server system is a particular application program that involves a pair of software programs. Unlike an OS program and an application program described above that operate in one computer, a client-server system manages a server application program in a computer server and a client application program installed in the end user's computer to work more securely with each other. The end user has to use the proprietary client program as developed in order to connect to the server program. Figure 1.2 shows a model client-server system in which three computers used by end users are connected to a computer server. The client-server system is typically designed and deployed for a large business enterprise that employs hundreds of workers. Moreover, the system usually operates in a private computer network exclusively for one organization. Such a system

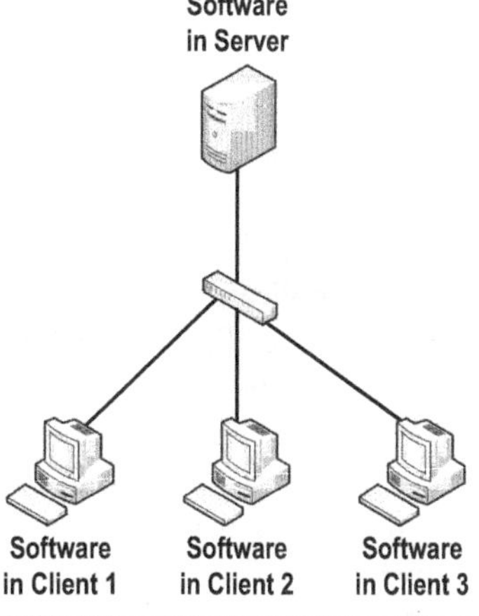

Figure 1.2 Client-server model.

would be more complex than an application program as the system provides functions to automate or facilitate parts of a business process. Example systems include an Enterprise Resource Planning System, a Financial Management Information System, and a Human Resources Management System. These core client-server systems would be supported by and integrated with additional client-server systems such as a Relational Database Management System and a Geographic Information System. Because of the high level of effort involved in developing this kind of software program, the client-server system is usually produced by a private IT company and distributed to a large number of customers. A non-IT organization may not have the resources to develop a client-server system on its own.

An Internet-based application is another particular application program that operates in a similar manner like a client-server system. It too requires a pair of software programs with a server application program and a client application program. For most Internet-based applications, software development does not require the creation of a new client program. End users can use a Web browser application program already available in their computer as the client application program. In some operating environments, however, a proprietary client application program will need to be developed when a Web browser does not exist or would not be appropriate for a given functional application. For instance, a proprietary client application program would be developed for installation and use in a mobile handheld device. Software development concentrates on the server application program to process and handle a high volume of information requests. An Internet-based application can be programmed to automate or facilitate parts of a business process like that in a traditional client-server system.

Although the cost and risk may not decrease as much as compared to a client-server system, a clear advantage of an Internet-based application is in its shorter software development time frame. With a host of programming languages and development tools that are relatively quick to learn, organizations can have an Internet-based application completed fairly rapidly.

Private IT companies that had previously produced client-server systems have redeveloped their systems to perform as Internet-based applications. New technology firms have emerged, introducing a wide range of Internet-based applications that cater to diverse markets for businesses, consumers, and households. In the past where a client-server system operated in a closed computer network, an Internet-based application opens itself up to a global computer network where end users from anywhere in the world can have access. An Internet-based application allows an organization to capture a far-reaching audience faster and inexpensively that was not previously imagined. This is both a blessing and a curse.

Computer Firmware

Computer firmware is a technological element that blends computer hardware and computer software. It is a physical IC chip that has an application program saved inside. One type of firmware chip is called “EEPROM (Electrically Erasable Programmable Read-Only Memory)”. The firmware program, which is usually small in size, provides specific instructions to control the associated computer system in which the firmware chip belongs. Computer firmware can be found in computer peripherals and network devices (e.g., a printer, a scanner, a network router, and a network firewall). The computer manufacturer develops new versions of the firmware program. Saving a new version of the program requires a particular procedure that is done by an engineer or a skilled technician. Designing computer firmware is a specialized field known as ASIC design. ASIC stands for Application Specific Integrated Chip.

Embedded Technology

Embedded technology is a technological element that widens the possibility of converting mechanical and electrical systems into computerized devices. Computer hardware can be incorporated into various machines used to manage production or operation, control the flow of input or output, or collect data. Smaller computer hardware components can be fitted in small mechanical or electrical devices such as a door-locking system, a wristwatch, and a telephone. The motherboard in the devices includes circuitry that provides connections to mechanical components such as a servo motor, an actuator, and a switch. Various sensors, which detect temperature, light, and location, for example, may also be connected to the motherboard. Computer firmware would provide the instructions to manage the connected mechanics and sensors in small devices. Other devices may have adequate storage capacity in a hard drive to operate an OS program and an Internet-based application. The latter computer software program would provide the instructions. A network adapter component would be inside the device to provide a connection to the computer network. An organization can use embedded technology to make a device that traditionally was not viewed as a computer to be a computer. Hence, the term "Internet-of-Things (IoT)" has come about.

Computer Network

Computer network is a technological element that allows an organization to share resources among internal employees, external partners, and other end users. Without a network, each person would have a printer, a scanner, and Internet access all connected directly to their computer. This would be perfectly fine when the person works alone or at home. In a large organization, however, connecting a printer to every computer would be unwieldy to manage – and can be costly. Computer peripherals, network devices, and other resources can be better assigned to a unit, a department, or in some other way the government agency deems effective for allocating IT resources. For example, two high-volume printers are assigned to each of ten floors in a building. There would be a secured facility that operates computer servers and network devices to provide access to functional applications, data storage, and Internet for all the connected end users.

An advantage of a computer network is to employ a client-server model where numerous computer workstations (the clients) can efficiently connect to one or more computer servers (the servers) and use one or more shared resources operating in the servers (see Figure 1.2). The computer servers are located in a secured room completely separated from the end users. In an example client-server model situation: Every employee logs in to their computer workstation. A particular computer server that provides a user authentication service verifies the employee's submitted user name and user password. If verified, the employee is permitted to access certain resources as assigned. The employee would be able to save their documents in another computer server, which runs a file service, for sharing with other employees. When the employee opens an e-mail application program on their computer, the e-mail program connects to another computer server, which runs an electronic mail service, and checks for any new e-mail messages. In all of these instances, the employee is sending a request from their computer client to be fulfilled by a computer server. The computer server, in turn, sends a response to the computer client.

The public manager will often hear the terms: application server and database server. These two specialized computer servers work together to operate a functional application. For any given functional application, the government agency's information is stored in the database server and is accessed through the application server. Depending on the number of end users, the application server and database server could operate in one computer server or could be kept separate in two or more computer servers. The latter form of configuration offers redundancy and capacity to handle a large number of concurrent connections.

Other specific names for computer servers that the public manager should be aware of are as follows:

1. Directory Server
2. File Server
3. Print Server
4. Mail Server
5. Web Server
6. Proxy Server
7. Remote Access Server

In its most basic configuration, a computer network involves a computer and a printer (or another computer) connected to a network switch (see Figure 1.3). The network switch has several ports where one port is connected to the computer and another port is connected to the printer. All available ports would be used to connect to more computers and computer peripherals. The physical connection is an Ethernet cable.

A network switch will have one or more specially designed ports that can be used to connect to a second network switch or a network router. It is possible to connect several network switches to enlarge the computer network beyond a typical size of 24 or 48 computers. This allows the public manager to include a few hundred of computers in the computer network. With the connected router, the computers can have access to the Internet or to another computer network.

A network router is an important device that manages connections in the computer network. It can be thought of like a traffic police officer at a busy street intersection. The network router manages (routes) connections from and to different networks. Security controls could be programmed to block or control users from accessing certain resources. A particular network router could be capable of providing wireless access, which allows more computers to be connected without being physically tied by an Ethernet cable.

Different types of computer networks can be designed. The Local Area Network (LAN) is a common network type used in a house, an office, or a single floor in a building. The LAN can cover up to 500 meters. The Campus Area Network (CAN) serves a college campus or a government

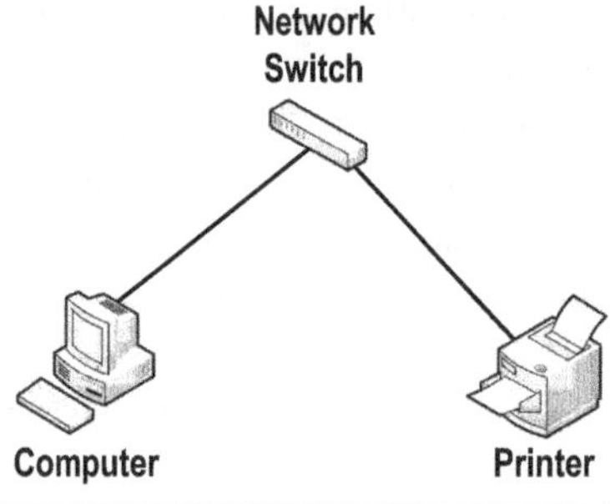

Figure 1.3 Basic networking.

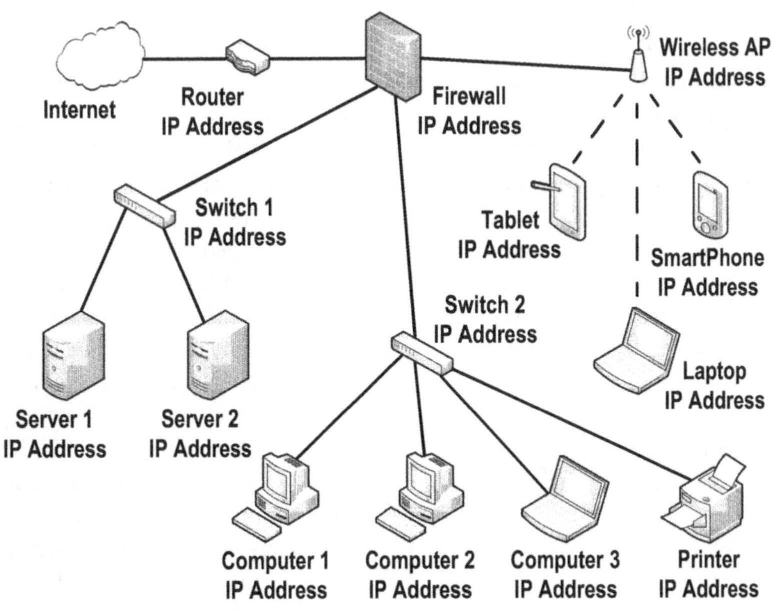

Figure 1.4 Local Area Network (LAN) topology.

complex made up of several buildings within a range of 1,000 meters. Several LANs would be linked together in a CAN. The Metropolitan Area Network (MAN) covers several government offices and other facilities within a city. Several LANs and CANs would be linked together in a MAN. The Wide Area Network (WAN) is a general network type that includes CAN and MAN. It is essentially the linkage of several distinct LANs that allow computers to communicate regardless of physical space. Government offices that are spread across the country or around the world can be linked together through a WAN.

Figure 1.4 shows the network topology for one LAN. This is a standard practice to show what computers and network devices by their machine name and unique IP address are connected and how they are organized. This LAN can be connected to another LAN by configuring the router shown in the figure to register the existence of the additional LAN. An organization will show a connection to its Internet Service Provider's (ISP's) LAN in the router in order to access the Internet. Another route to another LAN will be shown in the router. As a network firewall can have routing functionality, a number of routes can be configured in the network firewall. All of the registered routes create a WAN in which end users in one LAN can access resources in another LAN.

A computer network, however designed, does not necessarily need to access the Internet. If it is a requirement, a LAN, a CAN, a MAN, or a WAN can be a completely closed network where only the connected computers can communicate with each other. A government agency may want to create such a private computer network to ensure that classified information remains within the network. The private computer network isolates internal users from external users who may try to do harm. This also prevents the general public from accessing public services that may be provided on government servers.

The Internet

The Internet is a technological element that enables organizations and individuals to communicate and exchange information with literally anyone around the world. It is one global WAN based on a set of standard protocols. Prior to the Internet, computers were connected in a computer network but they used proprietary, non-standard networking technologies developed by different companies (e.g., IBM's Token Ring and Apple's AppleTalk). A computer network in one organization would not be able to communicate with another organization's network when the two networks used different networking technologies. The Internet had changed that by establishing numerous protocols for computer systems to operate and communicate with each other. Private companies would implement the protocols into their computer products, so that they can work with products produced by other companies. The Internet Protocol (IP) and the Transmission Control Protocol (TCP) are two foundational protocols that provide requirements for how computers operate on the Internet.

Other protocols had been designed to operate specific Internet services. HTTP is a widely known protocol for publishing information on the WWW. FTP is another known protocol for transferring electronic files. SMTP, POP, and IMAP are a group of protocols involved in sending and receiving electronic mail messages. These are just a few common standard protocols. An Internet-based application relies on any one of the Internet protocols to provide its functions to end users.

Telecommunication Infrastructure

Telecommunication infrastructure is a technological element that supports the computer network and the Internet with a backbone connection. This backbone connection provides for a larger capacity through which numerous organizations can pass data simultaneously with minimal loss to that data. An organization would not be able to send and receive information – especially very large electronic files – across far distances that are beyond the limitation of Ethernet. Another networking technology is needed to transmit information from one city to the next city, from one region to the next region, and from one country to the next country. Telephone lines spread across a nation have been relied upon to send all the various types of information, despite the technical limitation of telephony. Fiber-optic cables are being laid down to replace copper cables in the existing infrastructure, allowing for more data to be transmitted at a faster and more reliable rate. Fiber-optic, as a networking technology, is quite expensive to implement, though. Mobile cellular towers, which were constructed to transmit telephonic signals wirelessly between handheld devices, provide an alternative mode to transmit data. The underlying networking technology behind these towers has been gradually upgraded to transmit various types of information at increasingly faster speeds but not as fast or stable as wired infrastructure. Satellite technology is increasingly being used (and relied upon in rural, remote areas), although its network connections can be intermittent due to changing weather conditions. Satellites above the earth relay information in the form of electronic signals from one ground-based station to another ground-based station. Any of these networking technologies can create an infrastructure – the backbone connection – for organizations to send and receive information across a wide geography. Further improvement, though, is clearly needed, especially in the ability to transmit heavier information types such as video and multimedia.

Telecommunication infrastructure requires large-scale capital investment. Construction and maintenance of cables and towers have to be done across a vast range of land. Environmental impact assessments may be required in certain regions before any construction is allowed. Permits would need to be obtained from local and regional government agencies. Towns and populations that lie in the path of new infrastructure designs may object and cause significant delays through legal actions to halt construction. Eventually, those populations would have to be compensated to enable them to relocate elsewhere. This raises a social equity issue in that those groups who are forced to leave are likely to be low income or from minority ethnic backgrounds. In addition to the business and operational costs, establishing new or improving existing telecommunication infrastructure involves political, social, and environmental costs. Private telecommunication operators would be able to handle the business and operational costs, but they may not have the funds, the time, or the patience to deal with the socio-political dimension. The risk overall could be too high for private operators.

Public sector institutions have an inherent interest in overseeing the development of telecommunication infrastructure. A government agency would review environmental impact assessments and grant or deny permits. Zoning laws that guide where cables and towers would be constructed would be passed by government. Government would ensure equitable treatment of certain groups affected by changes to infrastructure. With a balance of laws that provide incentives to accelerate construction further and to reward ongoing maintenance, government agencies would be facilitating development and lowering the risk that private operators would want.

Emerging Technology

Emerging technology is the last technological element that classifies a group of computer-related technologies that have potential and promise. Such technologies may be available in the near or distant future, but in their present form, they are not yet viable for wide, commercial use. A nascent or experimental technology could be too risky or too costly to implement, especially if it involves providing a service to the general public. An emerging technology will have problems or weaknesses that engineers must correct.

There would be components, parts, or other elements that a certain technology would depend on, which limits its potential or constrains its operation. Robotic machine technology depends on the maturity of Artificial Intelligence (AI) for a computerized robot to perform and behave like a real human. Current forms of robotic technology are limited by programmed instructions to make mechanical parts move in certain ways. Self-driving autonomous vehicle technology has to deal with (external constraints) the design of road infrastructure and the regulations that govern the usage of highways and freeways. Self-driving vehicles controlled by the computer would likely start to be used in rural areas where such vehicles can be driven in open fields free from pedestrians and vehicle traffic. Operating self-driving vehicles in urban areas will take a while, as legal and liability issues need to be worked out. Blockchain has to overcome the challenge to ensure that all computers are connected in a stable computer network. Blockchain technology relies on numerous nodes (essentially individual computers) that verify and retain data in an increasingly long chain of connected information. All of the computers used in the blockchain need to be connected and online. AI has to demonstrate its capability to mimic the human brain in ways that enable the computer to generate completely new ideas, insights, and actions on its own and by its volition. Current forms of AI provide very sophisticated statistical analyses that require a substantial amount of data that must be captured and processed by the computer. AI requires substantial data storage capacity and very fast computer processing capability. Quantum computing faces the daunting challenge to handle and manipulate atoms in a controlled operation that in theory offers immense processing capability in a very small form factor. Simply packaging a quantum computer in a physical form poses a great challenge as well.

The public manager should periodically review the progress of the following emerging technologies and evaluate the implications that they may have on society:

- Quantum Computing
- Artificial Intelligence
- Blockchain
- Self-driving Autonomous Vehicle
- Robotic Machine

Chapter 1 Quiz

Question 1: What are the information types in ranked order from least amount of stored data to most amount of stored data?

A. Multimedia, Motion Pictures, Audio, Document, Image, and Text.
B. File, Image, Audio, Motion Pictures, Text, and Multimedia.
C. Text, Image, Document, Audio and Video, Motion Pictures, and Multimedia.
D. Text, Image, Document, Motion Pictures, Audio, and Multimedia.
E. Raw Data, Scanned Photograph, Adobe PDF with Images, Music Sound, Digital Video, and Multimedia.

Question 2: Which one does not include a non-technological element?

A. End User, Text, HR Application, Business Process, Law, and Information Security.
B. End User, Text, Functional Application, Business Process, Regulation, and Information Security.
C. End User, Video, Software Application, Business Process, Law, and Information Security.
D. Person, Text, Functional Application, Business Process, Law, and Security.
E. Multimedia, Finance Application, Person, Information Security, Business Process, and Law.

Question 3: According to the book, which element is the most important?

A. Functional Application and End User
B. Emerging Technology and Computer Software
C. Government Law and Business Process
D. End User and People
E. Information Security and the Internet

Question 4: Which one would have some kind of computer firmware?

A. Telecommunication Infrastructure
B. Embedded Technology
C. Computer Software
D. Computer Hardware
E. Both B and D

Question 5: Why are all the elements brought together called the IT ecosystem?

A. The elements are like species in the natural world
B. An element can be modified by a new technique, a new method, or some other approach
C. An element can be modified by joining it with one or more other elements
D. All of the elements fit perfectly together
E. The elements operate in a fixed system

Worksheets

Info. Type ____			Embedded Tech.	
Functional Application			Computer Firmware	
Business Process	End User	Computer Software	Computer Hardware	Emerging Tech.
	Gov't Law	Info. Security	Computer Network	
		Telecomm. Infrastruct.	Internet	

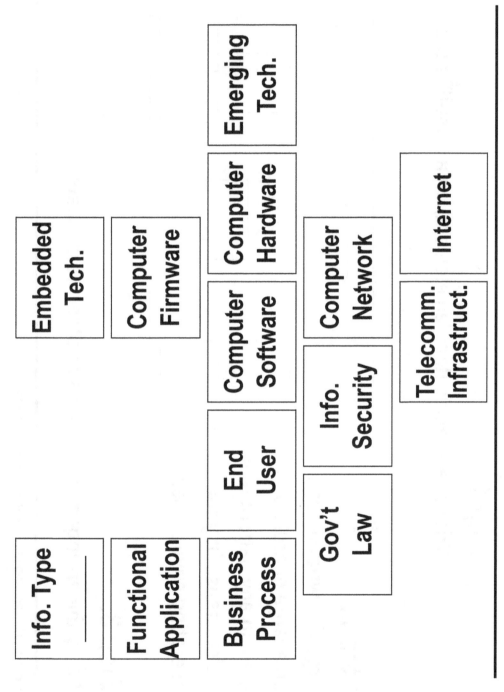

Worksheet 1.1 IT ecosystem puzzle framework.

Step 1:

Write one specific item (an element) on a Post-it® note.

Step 2:

Organize written notes on a large board, sorting them in any pattern that makes sense in your operating environment.

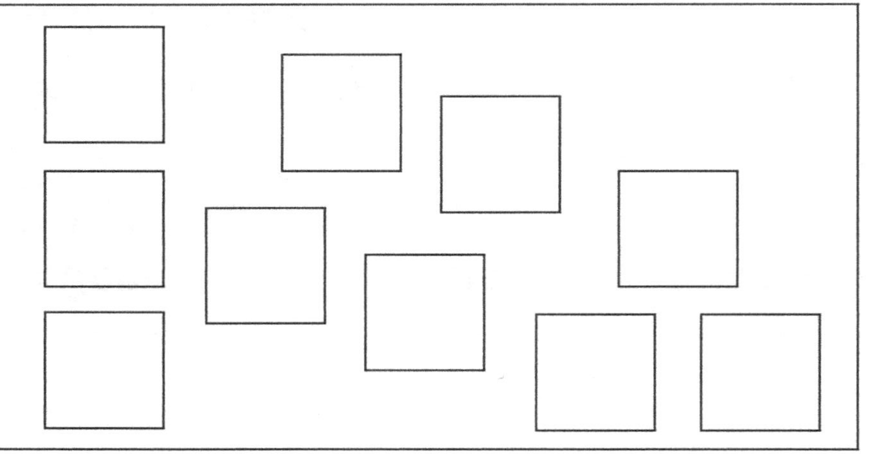

Step 3:

Apply the arrangement of notes to other worksheets.

Worksheet 1.2 IT ecosystem element arrangement exercise.

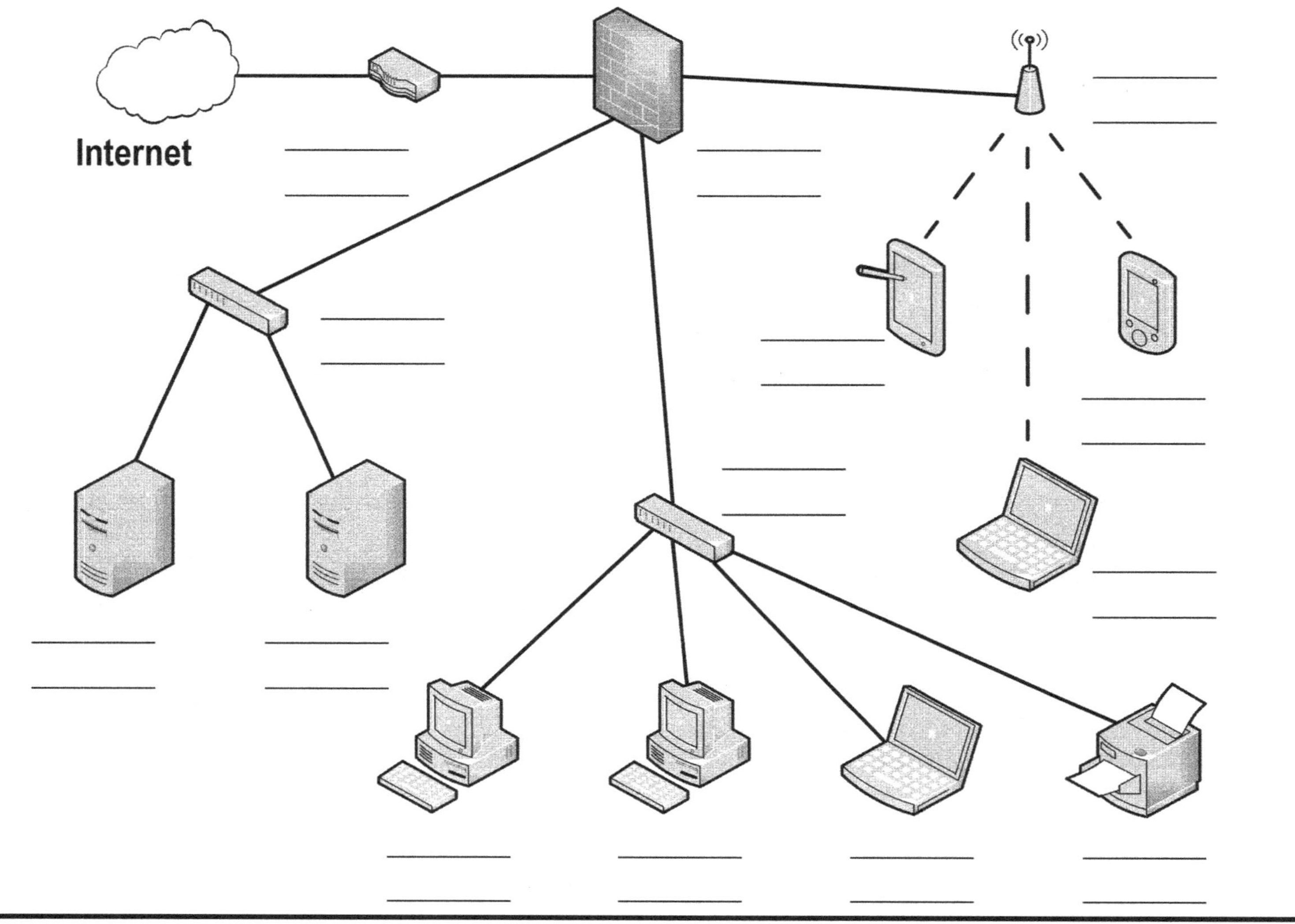

Worksheet 1.3 Network topology.

Chapter 2

IT Organization: People and Roles

This is too technical. Who can advise on what this means in practical terms?
This is too general. Who can define this better to make it technically doable?
Properly organized, you will be able to go to the right person and get the answer.

Chapter Summary

How can so many Information Technology (IT) elements as described in the previous chapter be managed, let alone be deployed?

First of all, it begins with the organization of people in the government agency. And in order to organize, public managers need to know who are the managers, the specialists, and the experts.

This chapter describes all the related personnel, their roles, and where they would be located within an organization. IT specialists could be easily found. But identifying non-IT specialists may not be obvious since they would not be placed in an IT unit. A number of specialists may be employed with an external organization and contracted to the government agency. With non-technological elements involved in the IT ecosystem, the non-IT managers and specialists are not to be discounted and have important roles to play. There can be many non-IT personnel throughout the agency who would provide valuable input into the design and operation of IT systems. This chapter provides a flexible approach to organizing all relevant employees and contractors so that the government agency whether small or large can quickly know who to ask questions or seek support regarding any particular IT system.

IT is a sophisticated field that involves experts from IT and non-IT specialized areas. Specific experts need to know how the organization functions from a business perspective. Specific experts need to know how to develop and test computer software programs. Specific experts need to know how to design and monitor computer networks. Specific experts need to know how to manage customer relationships through the management and repair of computer equipment. Specific experts need to know how to keep government information tightly secured from being accidently or intentionally tampered with.

Numerous specialists and experts will need to be defined in an organizational structure. A large government agency may have a number of IT departments with a tiered leadership structure. A smaller organization could operate adequately with one IT department led by a single IT manager. All of the non-IT specialists would be spread across the organization and would have indirect connections to the IT department. These indirect connections will need to be managed either through a Project Management Office or an Office of the Chief Information Officer. There would be a high-level leader who oversees the indirect connections and can relay issues to the respective managers who have supervisory direct relationships with the specialists involved in the IT systems. A defined organizational structure with clear direct and indirect relationships among all of the IT and non-IT personnel can ensure that IT programs and IT systems are being well spent and well managed in achievement of operational goals.

Organization-Wide Connections

This chapter assumes that the government agency has an organization chart already defined. The public manager should use the existing chart as a starting reference point. With approval by senior executive leaders, the manager can modify the present chart to show how various functions relate to IT. The agency head will need to approve the new organization chart. For the purposes guided by this book, the public manager can at least analyze who are the appropriate people to involve and what will be their roles in an IT system. Worksheet 2.1 provides an exercise in identifying and understanding the various connections and relationships.

Chapter 1 described the elements in the IT ecosystem. As they analyze the organization chart, the public manager should ask the following questions: Who are the end users? Who handles and/or processes the various types of information? Who owns a particular collection of information types in terms of ensuring that the information is accurate? Who has principal authority over the control and use of the functional applications? Who manages the business processes to ensure that all of the steps are carried out properly? Who analyzes the business processes to find improvements? Who interprets the laws and regulations? Who manages and/or supports the various forms of computer technologies? Who keeps all of the elements secure? Answering these questions will lead the public manager to identifying both the IT and non-IT personnel. The questions, moreover, can be used for a specific IT system or for a collection of projects in an IT program.

Once personnel have been identified, the direct connections (i.e., relationships to immediate supervisors) would become known. The indirect connections could vary depending on the context of the project. Unless an IT system affects the entire government agency, oversight may not be necessary at the department level or the senior executive level. There can be flexibility in the indirect reporting structure for specific IT systems operated by isolated units and IT programs that have little to no risk and impact to the organization. A small project, for example, could consist of team members across two departments. The project manager in this case would be a senior manager with the most years of experience in agreement by the two department directors. For most IT programs, a person from an IT unit should be the designated project manager. Depending on the complexity of the project, the project manager could be a senior-level IT specialist, a unit-level IT manager, a department IT director, or a Chief Information Officer.

All of the IT programs and IT systems should have been identified ahead of time and described briefly in an organization-wide IT Strategic Plan. Senior executive leaders will have an awareness of all programs and systems and would be able to intervene when a major problem arises.

The public manager needs to refer to the IT Strategic Plan to understand what is needed in terms of human resources (see Chapter 8 for more information regarding strategic planning).

The next two sections describe numerous job roles that would be involved in any IT system or IT program, distinguished between IT personnel and non-IT personnel. Most of the roles refer to commonly used job titles or job positions. Some roles have their mandate provided by law. A few job roles are broad categories that can encompass a number of job positions that are similar in nature (e.g., senior executive) or that are applied across multiple domains (e.g., functional expert). A job role may be assigned to an existing person who could have an official job position that is different from the name of the role. Referring to Chapter 1, all of the job roles are end users. Based on the level of access, each identified job role would be able to use an IT system.

Non-IT Personnel

The following 12 job roles are generally functional or business related. People who have these roles may have little to no technical skill in IT implementation. Regardless of their level of IT skill, these non-IT personnel will want to be sure that they can use IT systems as intended to accomplish their objectives. And in the context of a public program, the implemented IT system will need to comply with any applicable law. Arguably, the non-IT personnel roles are the most important end users.

General Public

Any organization whether it is public or private would have users who come from the general public. For a government agency, the general public is the citizens with whom the government engages to provide public services. For a nonprofit organization, the general public is the beneficiaries who receive charitable services such as emergency relief and development assistance.

Senior Executive, Political Appointment

A leader and a deputy are appointed by an elected official to lead a government agency. In the United States, this is the Department Secretary and the Assistant Secretary. In other countries, this would be the Minister and the Deputy Minister. Additional persons such as the Director-General or Special Assistant may also be politically appointed. All such positions are written into law. Any political appointment could change after a few years with a new leader being appointed and taking over from where the previous leader had ended. As such, a government agency could be led by a number of different senior leaders during the term of one elected official.

Senior Executive, Non-political, Civil Service

At the highest level of the civil service, a government agency is led by a number of senior executive leaders. These senior leaders are not appointed by an elected official and typically work their way up through career promotions. As career professionals, these senior leaders have accumulated years of experience working in the agency and have gained extensive knowledge of how the agency operates. A few job positions in this category are Chief Financial Officer (CFO) and Chief Operating Officer (COO). Unlike their political appointees, career professional senior executive leaders would remain in their positions for a longer duration.

Information Owner

The Information Owner is a role that is assigned to an existing public manager. This role serves as a point-of-contact to whom inquiries can be forwarded regarding a specific information system. There can be a primary contact and a secondary contact to answer questions. The Information Owner has deep knowledge about what specific information needs to be stored in an IT system. This role bears a degree of responsibility to ensure the accuracy of information in an IT system.

Functional Expert

The Functional Expert is a broad category that encompasses a number of subject-matter experts in different domain areas. Domain areas commonly found in organizations are financial management, human resources management, and inventory management. Specialized domains include, as examples, contracting, health, agriculture, education, and public affairs. The Functional Expert has the technical knowledge for how their specific area operates. The word, "technical", used in this context refers broadly to any scientific or specialized field where the person understands the details of how their field works. An accountant, for example, knows how to keep track of all expenses and revenues in proper order and in balance and is thus technical in financial management. Another example is an agronomist who knows how to manage various inputs, factors, and activities related to farming and is thus technical in agricultural production. The Functional Expert has the capability of carrying out work according to the particular steps of a specific domain area.

Business Analyst

The Business Analyst is a role and a job position that supports one or more domain areas. This role may not have extensive knowledge equal to that of the Functional Expert. The Business Analyst would work alongside the Functional Expert in cooperation. The Business Analyst serves to find ongoing improvements in the manner in which a specific domain area operates. This person would document the business process and operating procedures for a given domain.

Process Owner

The Process Owner is a role that is assigned to an existing public manager. Similar to the Information Owner, the Process Owner serves as a point-of-contact for a specific business process. Any change to a business process has a level of risk and needs to be reviewed and approved. The Process Owner ensures that a business process with periodic modifications can flow smoothly with little to no disruption.

Process Analyst

The Process Analyst is a role and a job position more specific than the Business Analyst. This role focuses on the review, improvement, and documentation of a business process for a specific domain area. The Process Analyst would work alongside the Functional Expert in cooperation.

Data Modeler/Scientist

The Data Modeler or Data Scientist is a role and a job position that would be the functional counterpart to the Database Administrator. This role would work alongside the Functional Expert in cooperation. The Data Modeler shows how the information of a specific domain area is organized by reconnecting all of the precise data fields in numerous relationships. The Data Modeler breaks down information into its specific parts called data. A major output of this work is a logical data model (a diagram) that shows the relationships of all the data fields. With the growth of "Big Data" and Artificial Intelligence in recent years, this position has evolved into a more scientific role. The Data Scientist develops mathematical formulas to analyze the data model and make predictions. This person supports the Functional Expert to analyze issues, connections, and patterns and to draw better conclusions for a specific domain area.

Statistician

The Statistician is a role and a job position that develops the methods, procedures, and equations for conducting large-scale surveys and data analyses. This role has an educational background in econometrics, statistics, and advanced levels of mathematics. The Statistician provides technical support to functional experts in analyzing public programs and the associated data. This role also supports the Data Modeler/Scientist, the Data Architect, and the Database Administrator.

General Counsel

The General Counsel is a role and a job position that provides legal advice and guidance on legal matters related to high-level IT issues (e.g., personal privacy and information security). This role may not have subject-matter expertise in a domain area but rather has broad knowledge of one or more IT issues that would affect the organization. The General Counsel works with senior executive leaders.

Attorney

The Attorney is a role and a job position that supports one or more domain areas. This role may also be a Functional Expert in a particular domain. The Attorney interprets laws and regulations for execution and/or enforcement in public programs. This role may have tasks related to writing and revising rules in conformance with the associated law. The Attorney would provide legal guidance in the design and operation of an IT system.

IT Personnel

The following 25 job roles are related to IT functions and provide support to the non-IT personnel. All of these roles will have knowledge of computer science and electronics or in a field related to IT. These positions would be located in an IT department or a smaller IT unit, or reporting to an IT manager or senior executive leader. Some IT roles may be contracted out to an external organization.

Senior Executive, Non-political, Civil Service

The IT field has its senior executive leaders who have overall responsibility over IT resources. These career professionals are not appointed by political leaders but rather have worked their way up the ranks through promotions. The Chief Technology Officer (CTO), Chief Information Officer (CIO), and Director of Information Technology are common job titles that generally have the same job duties. While these persons would have technical knowledge in computers, primary duties are not to operate IT systems and develop computer software programs. IT leaders provide necessary oversight through management of the IT budget, IT strategy, and IT-related policies. IT leaders work closely with their non-IT senior executive counterparts to ensure that the organization is using IT resources to meet organizational goals. The IT leader would frequently interact on a daily basis with the Chief Operating Officer.

In smaller government agencies and nonprofit organizations where financial resources are limited, the IT senior executive role may be merged with a more technically proficient IT manager role. This two-role-in-one combination allows the IT leader to provide technical assistance when needed to the IT team. Especially in a crisis such as an information security breach or in an electrical power outage, the more technical IT leader can provide rapid and sound analysis to the situation as it is assessed, diagnosed, and resolved.

IT Manager

The IT Manager is a role and a job position that has both managerial and technical responsibilities. This person must be able to balance their time in maintaining specific IT systems and supervising IT staff. The IT Manager role serves in a middle tier position between a senior executive leader and senior technical specialists. This role would lead a unit or a department and would have responsibility over a portion of the total IT budget specifically allocated to their unit. Given the diverse technical areas described below, the IT Manager would likely not have a mastery of all the technical areas but would be highly competent in one or two areas such as computer networking and/or computer software.

Information Security Specialist

The Information Security Specialist is a role and a job position that carries out tasks related to the security of IT systems and the protection of information. This role works with other IT specialists to develop and maintain security controls. This specialist analyzes potential security risks and develops a number of strategies to mitigate the identified risks. The Information Security Specialist may also provide training to end users on how to prevent and manage various security issues.

Telecommunication Specialist

The Telecommunication Specialist is a role and a job position that manages the provisioning and operation of telephonic and data services at the end point of where users are located. Telephonic services cover the use of landline telephones and cellular wireless phones. Data services include Internet connections and mobile data plans. Closed-system communication such as two-way radios may also be included. The Telecommunication Specialist has technical knowledge in how various types of communication equipment operate. This role must work with an external vendor (a telecommunication provider) by communicating and resolving outages and problems that can occur from time to time. The Telecommunication Specialist monitors voice and data services at the organization's end, while a technical counterpart employed at a telecommunication provider monitors services at the provider's end. A telecommunication provider is responsible for the infrastructure that carries voice and data services to the organization's facilities. The Telecommunication Specialist role may be part of the Network Engineer role.

Network Engineer

The Network Engineer is a role and a job position that carries out tasks related to the design, implementation, and operation of the computer network. This role configures and manages various types of network devices and may install wiring throughout a building. As a network can be connected to the Internet, the Network Engineer would assume the tasks of the Telecommunication Specialist.

Systems Administrator

The Systems Administrator is a role and a job position that carries out tasks related to the operation and maintenance of computer servers. This role configures and manages the operating system software programs and server application programs that run in the computer servers. This role also diagnoses and repairs hardware and software issues.

Database Administrator

The Database Administrator is a role and a job position that carries out tasks related to the design, implementation, and operation of database software programs. This role will also analyze data relationships like the Data Modeler. Unlike the non-IT Data Modeler, the Database Administrator has the ability to implement a logical data model into a physical data model (i.e., making sure that the data model operates as designed). With a functioning database, the Database Administrator develops numerous queries that can be used to analyze the data. This role will frequently work with the Software Developer/Engineer to ensure that the computer software program can communicate and perform well with the database program.

Documentation Manager

The Documentation Manager is a role that may be another job position or assigned to an existing technical manager. Numerous kinds of documents that can be created regarding an IT system from functional requirements, technical specifications, process flowcharts to system approvals have to be organized and controlled. The Documentation Manager develops and manages the process and procedures to ensure that every document is accounted for. As an IT system can change from time to time, relevant documents must be updated to reflect the latest change. Certain documents must include a revision history that shows who made changes to what sections and when. The Documentation Manager would be the gatekeeper of the authorized and authoritative source of all previous and current versions of IT-related documents. Although computer-based tools exist to store and manage documents electronically, a person is still required to have management responsibility of all those stored documents.

Configuration Manager

The Configuration Manager is a role that may be another job position or assigned to an existing technical manager. This role carries out tasks related to the control of changes to computer hardware and software configurations in IT systems. A computer software program can be completed and released incrementally in a number of software versions. The Configuration Manager develops and manages the process and procedures to ensure that the newest software version can be configured properly in replacement of the current outgoing software version with minimal risk. This becomes particularly critical when final software releases have passed the testing phase and are ready for the production environment. The Configuration Manager retains copies of all older versions.

Technology Architect

The Technology Architect is one of three major IT architecture roles that may be assigned to an existing IT specialist. This role draws up the design and makes any modifications to the components that will comprise an IT system. Based on needs and requirements, the Technology Architect develops a plan to show how all of the selected technological elements will be connected. The architecture would include the computer network along with the hardware and software. Various types of diagrams may be drawn to suit a particular audience. For instance, senior executive leaders may be provided a high-level abstract diagram that shows selected computer technologies meeting business and functional needs. In another instance, the Network Engineer may be provided a network topology that presents specific devices and computers being connected together. The Technology Architect works with various people – both IT and non-IT – to capture the functional need and the technological solution and to ensure that the functionality aligns with the technology.

Software Application Architect

The Software Application Architect is one of three major IT architecture roles that may be assigned to an existing IT specialist. This role is more specific than the Technology Architect role. This role draws up the design and makes modifications to how a computer software program will function. An example is how data will be entered and processed in the computer. Another example is how a partner organization will be able to access the government's internal computer server and transfer a specific set of data records. Final plans and diagrams provide guidance to the Software Engineer on what needs to be programmed and what should not. The Software Application Architect works with various people – both IT and non-IT – to capture the functional need and the software solution and to ensure that the functionality aligns with the software program.

Data Architect

The Data Architect is one of three major IT architecture roles that may be assigned to an existing IT specialist. This role is also more specific than the Technology Architect role. This role draws up the design and makes modifications to how data will be organized and stored. A logical data model is produced to show the relationships to specific data in a high-level abstract diagram. Following the implementation of the actual database, a physical data model would be produced to show how the relationships have been implemented. The Data Architect works with various people – both IT and non-IT – to capture the functional need and the database solution and to ensure that the functionality aligns with the database program.

Quality Assurance Specialist

The Quality Assurance Specialist is a role and a job position that carries out tasks related to computer software testing. This role writes and implements software test plans and reports the results. The Quality Assurance Specialist would maintain a list of software issues or bugs broken down by status to indicate whether each issue is new, closed, or being worked on by the Software Engineer. The Quality Assurance Specialist works closely with the Software Engineer to follow up on all software bugs.

IT Project Manager

The IT Project Manager is a role and a job position that manages all activities related to the implementation of an IT system across the entire System Development Life Cycle process. This role may have responsibility of a specific budget amount allocated to the IT project. This role may also have supervisory responsibility of IT personnel assigned to the IT project. The IT Project Manager bears overall responsibility for the success or failure of the IT system, managing the risk at each phase of the life cycle process and reporting progress to the IT Manager, non-IT managers, and senior executive leaders.

Software Developer/Engineer, Back-end

The Back-end Software Developer or Software Engineer is a role and a job position that writes and modifies a computer software program with focus on the more complex computer logic. Before the Internet era, this role was simply the Software Developer or Software Engineer who wrote computer code for a desktop personal computer or a mainframe computer. The Internet era differentiates computer code by where the code is executed. A computer program that runs in a computer server is considered the back-end code. A computer program that runs in the end user's computer through a Web application browser is considered the front-end code. The front-end computer code has limited functions and is driven mainly to create a user interface. The back-end computer code, on the other hand, performs the processing for how various functions operate. The Back-end Software Developer would be the principal engineer on a software development team.

Software Developer/Engineer, Front-end

The Front-end Software Developer or Software Engineer is a role and a job position that writes and modifies a computer software program with focus on the user interface. The level of computer programming is not as intense as writing back-end computer code. The Front-end Software Developer creates functions for how the end user will enter and view data on a computer screen. This person works closely with the Back-end counterpart to ensure that both parts of the computer code dovetail seamlessly. The Front-end Software Developer typically would be a junior engineer on a software development team.

Software Developer/Engineer, Mobile

The Mobile Software Developer or Software Engineer is a role and a job position that writes and modifies a computer software program specifically for a computer mobile device. New forms of computing devices (e.g., a smartphone, a tablet, and an embedded device) can run a computer software program. Such a software would have both complex computer logic and user interface functions programmed. In addition, the computer program will have to connect to a computer server where back-end computer code can process data received from and sent to the mobile device. The Mobile Software Developer also works closely with the Back-end counterpart. The Mobile Software Developer would be a member on a software development team, if the IT project requires a mobile software program.

User Interface/Experience (UI/UX) Designer

The User Interface Designer is a role and a job position that designs the layout for all the text and graphics of a computer software program. This role has an educational background in graphics design and/or fine arts. The User Interface Designer creates the icons, graphics, and photographs that the end user will see or interact with on a computer screen. This person works closely with the Front-end Software Developer to understand what can and cannot be programmed in terms of creating a user interface. The User Interface Designer is a member on a software development team.

Systems Analyst

The Systems Analyst is a role and a job position that carries out tasks related to the design and operation of an IT system. This role's closest non-IT counterpart is the Business Analyst. Working with the Business Analyst, the Systems Analyst translates functional requirements into technical specifications as technically practicable. The Systems Analyst analyzes the business process to find parts that can be programmed in the computer. This person frequently communicates with various non-IT personnel to ensure that an IT system is designed according to business needs and functional requirements. The Systems Analyst may assume any one of the IT architecture roles described above.

Technical Writer

The Technical Writer is a role and a job position that carries out tasks related to documenting an IT system and writing and revising all documents throughout the System Development Life Cycle process. This role has adequate technical knowledge of computers *and* adequate knowledge of one or more functional domain areas. The Technical Writer frequently communicates with both IT and non-IT personnel. This role may be combined with the Systems Analyst role, assuming that the person has significant knowledge of computers gained from several years of experience. The Technical Writer is a member on a software development team.

Customer Service Manager

The Customer Service Manager is a role and a job position that manages activities related to technical support. Another name may also be "Technical Support Manager". This role supervises a team of support specialists to answer questions and resolve problems from end user inquiries related to one or more IT systems. This role also has responsibility of a specific budget amount allocated to technical support operations. The Customer Service Manager would operate a dedicated department separate from the IT department.

Level 1 User Support Specialist

The Level 1 User Support Specialist is a role and a job position that handles basic or simple questions or issues related to an IT system. End users who contact technical support for the first time are directed to the Level 1 Specialist. This role documents the support case and resolves the end user's problem. If the issue cannot be resolved, the Level 1 Specialist records the reason and outcome and escalates the support case to the next level. The Level 1 User Support Specialist has basic technical knowledge of computers and is typically an entry-level position.

Level 2–3 User Support Specialist

The Level 2–3 User Support Specialist is a role and a job position that handles unresolved issues that a previous Support Specialist could not complete. Given the complexity of the problem, the Level 2–3 Specialist has advanced technical knowledge of computers and would be proficient or an expert in the specific IT system to which the problem relates. This role reviews the existing support case created by the previous Support Specialist, further documents the support case with a new amendment, and resolves the end user's problem. If the issue cannot be resolved, the Level 2–3 Specialist records the reason and outcome and escalates the support case to the next level. Most support cases can be resolved at the second-tier level. Anomalies, those rare cases occurring in an unusual circumstance, would be escalated to the third-tier level. Unless the volume of third-tier level cases is high, it would not be necessary to split this role into a Level 2 Specialist and a Level 3 Specialist. The Level 2–3 User Support Specialist would be able to handle both second- and third-tier level support cases.

Multimedia/Online Training Specialist

The Multimedia/Online Training Specialist is a role and a job position that develops tutorials, presentations, and courses designed to train end users in how to use an IT system. This role may also have the responsibility of carrying out training in a classroom and/or online setting. This person has the technical skill to create a multimedia interactive presentation that can run in a desktop personal computer or on the Web. The Training Specialist has an educational background in education. This role would work closely with the User Interface Designer. The Training Specialist would work in a technical support team.

Vendor Relationship Manager

The Vendor Relationship Manager is a role that may be another job position or assigned to an existing technical manager. This role carries out tasks related to the management and oversight of vendors and contractors. The Vendor Relationship Manager handles the technical aspect of the contract (i.e., ensuring that a vendor has satisfactorily fulfilled its tasks) in cooperation with the non-IT procurement Functional Expert (e.g., a Contracting Officer). While the non-IT counterpart handles the financial aspect of the contract, the Vendor Relationship Manager takes care of the technical matters. Examples include managing the provision of Internet service by a telecommunication provider, monitoring the work of a contracted software development company, and overseeing operation of an outsourced customer service and technical support unit. The Vendor Relationship Manager must have adequate technical knowledge in the area that they are managing or overseeing to be capable of holding the vendor accountable in meeting the terms of the contract. This role would have the authority to recommend termination of the contractual relationship or to recommend modification to the contract terms.

IT Certifications

All of the IT roles described above should be filled with qualified persons. For any one of the roles, it can be argued what needs to be the minimum qualification. Is it a Bachelor's degree, several years of professional experience, an IT certification in a technical field, or a combination of all three?

The value of an educational degree could lessen over time as a college program may not keep up with changing technology in industry. Requirement of a Bachelor's degree in a field related to computer science or electrical engineering would be suitable for qualifying a person in an entry-level position but may not be a good indicator for a senior-level position. Several years of recent professional experience would provide a stronger indicator of accomplishing tasks relevant to the job role.

As technology changes, certifying organizations would update IT certifications in line with new revisions as directed by computer technology companies. This then would give IT personnel the opportunity to acquire the latest knowledge of a particular technology. Obtaining and renewing one or more IT certifications, however, assume a certain cost to the individual employee or to the employer who may not be willing to pay for it. Practical experience working in the specialty area could be a less expensive way to meeting a qualification.

As a general rule of thumb, entry-level positions should require at least a Bachelor's degree. More weight can be applied to experience as the person moves progressively higher to middle- and senior-level positions within the same field (e.g., a promotion from an entry-level Network Engineer to a mid-level Network Engineer). If a person wishes to move laterally to a different field (e.g., from computer networking to software development), the person should meet an IT certification requirement or perhaps another college degree requirement relevant to that new field.

Computer technology companies have developed highly specific IT certifications for their products. The computer network company, Cisco, has certifications for its Cisco products. As such, a Cisco certification may not be compatible with another network product produced by a competitor. One company-product certification may not be compatible with or transferrable to another company-product certification. Certifying organizations would partner with the technology companies to be authorized in training and certifying individuals. The following are some examples of IT certifications:

- CompTIA A+
- Cisco Certified Network Associate (CCNA)
- Microsoft Certified Systems Administrator (MCSA)
- Microsoft Certified Systems Engineer (MCSE)
- Microsoft Certified Application Developer (MCAD)
- Microsoft Certified Database Administrator
- Oracle Administrator

As mentioned, obtaining an IT certification incurs an added cost. The person would need time to study the training materials and probably purchase materials. There may be a requirement in which the person must have a number of hours of experience. The certifying organization may charge a training fee. An IT certification once earned is valid for a given period of time and must be renewed by an authorized certifying organization. A renewal fee may be charged.

The government agency may want to consider incorporating IT certifications in its professional development program. A budget amount would be allocated to training IT personnel on a periodic basis. This will allow technical staff to stay abreast of latest technologies. The new knowledge would support the staff to solve recurring technical problems that may have been difficult to resolve with older versions of computer technology.

Internal Relationships

Many hired employees will have roles as described above and be spread across different departments and units in an organization. The first challenge then is to figure out who is the right person to talk to or work with when it comes to the design, development, testing, operation, and support of an IT system. The public manager will need to identify all persons who will be involved and organize them in some manner.

Depending on the scope and purpose of an IT system, the number of people could be large or small. A specialized IT system may just require involvement of the IT department and one functional department. For this relatively small IT project, a small team of IT personnel would be able to work effectively with a small team of non-IT personnel. This smaller group of IT and non-IT personnel would see the direct positive impact that the specialized IT system will have and thus be motivated to see the project to a successful completion.

A significantly larger project, in contrast, poses teamwork and communication challenges. A broad IT system that affects the entire organization such as a Financial Management Information System (FMIS) requires involvement from all departments, including senior executive leaders. For this large-scale, organization-wide IT project, numerous relationships up and down and across the organization chart will have to be coordinated. Some personnel may be quicker to accept the initiative and thus easier to work with, while others may be slower to understand the value of the new system and thus can be less motivated to engage.

Regardless of the size of the IT project, managing the internal relationships between the IT and non-IT personnel is key. The public manager must be able to find the right person who can communicate messages back and forth between the various IT and non-IT personnel. A person who speaks too frequently in technical jargon would not be a match with a person who does not understand the very specific terms. The relationship in this case would not go far and can freeze as both parties will fail to understand each other. A person who speaks in overly simplified terms would not be a match with a person who only knows how to implement technology in highly specific ways. The relationship in this case could lead to an unintended consequence where the completed solution takes on a different form that was not envisioned. To bridge the communication gap between IT and non-IT, the manager needs a person who has equal parts understanding of the IT technical aspect and the business functional aspect and can moderate their speech based on whom they are speaking with. Such a technical-functional person can speak with the Functional Expert in highly general terms and then turn around quickly to the Software Developer and speak with the Developer in very specific terms. This middle-man will necessarily have to move back and forth several times until the Software Developer understands exactly what the Functional Expert is asking for. This interlocutor is akin to a language interpreter who translates the words of a foreign-language speaker. The technical-functional person has an ability to translate functional needs into technical specifications. Of all the IT roles, the Technical Writer and the Systems Analyst are better positioned to serve as the moderator between the IT and non-IT groups. The Technical Writer and the Systems Analyst can manage the communication flows so that everyone involved understands the requirements and is in agreement.

As an IT project increases in complexity and necessitates involvement of multiple stakeholders, the Technical Writer and the Systems Analyst could find it difficult to access and engage particular departments. This can slow down work and cause delays. The Functional Experts and other non-IT personnel with whom the Technical Writer and the Systems Analyst have to exchange information might have direct supervisors who are blocking or hindering access, for whatever reason. The supervisors of the Technical Writer and the Systems Analyst would have little authority to break such an impasse. A higher-level director would need to be involved to grant some degree of authority to the IT Manager or the designated IT Project Manager to have IT personnel engage with other personnel across various departments. By mutual agreement with the involved department managers, there would be expressed dotted-line relationships between specific IT personnel and non-IT personnel. These indirect relationships can be temporary according to the needs and time frame of the IT project. At the very least, the relationships are known and agreed upon.

External Relationships

Certain roles with particular focus on the IT functions may not be needed as permanent, long-term employees. The technical support function could be completely outsourced to an external organization that will have the responsibility for hiring and managing all of the support-related IT roles. A fully staffed software development team with all needed roles would only be needed during the time when the computer software program is developed for the first time and subsequently updated with a new version. Once software development has finished, the government agency could reduce the team to a minimum. The completed software would run continuously in an IT system that would be managed by a permanent Systems Administrator. Most of the IT roles could be contracted out and managed by a permanent IT Manager who would serve as the Vendor Relationship Manager.

Some of the non-IT roles could be merged with other positions, contracted out, or reduced to part-time status. The General Counsel may not be needed in a full-time capacity and could be hired to work part time or on an as-needed basis when legal issues arise. The Business Analyst could be contracted out to an external organization when it has been determined that current processes and procedures need to be changed or reexamined. The Statistician role could be combined into the Data Scientist role to create one permanent job position. Another kind of merge could be to combine the Data Modeler, Statistician, and Database Administrator roles into one permanent job position.

Depending on organizational needs, the complexity of IT systems, and financial constraints, the public manager can find ways to reduce the number of people but still have all the needed roles. It will be ideal, however, to retain as much control as possible for all roles. The government agency will lose a certain level of control through contracting and outsourcing. Merging roles together into a smaller group of permanent employees could be a better proposition for the agency that can prove cost-effective.

Contracting of IT projects and particular IT functions is inevitable in public and nonprofit organizations. Thus, the public manager must be prepared to manage the risks and issues that can come from contracting. Chapter 5 describes more about contracting and outsourcing. As it relates to human resources, the public manager must manage the external relationships that are created through contractual agreements. Inadequate management of a government contract in terms of the technical performance of the contractor could create a situation where the government agency is taken advantage of by the contractor whose motivation may not be completely aligned with the work of public service.

Since the contractor is an external organization with its own organization chart and internal relationships, the government agency has little to no control over any personnel employed by the contractor. What control the government agency does have will be described in the contract terms and conditions. The government contract is the principal legal instrument by which the agency can use to hold the contractor accountable.

The Technical Officer who is assigned to manage the technical performance should be the Vendor Relationship Manager. The government agency would want someone who has the IT technical expertise to monitor and oversee the contractor's work. As described above, there could be a major communication problem if a non-IT manager is designated as the Technical Officer. The government agency should not assume that the contractor will not assign an IT counterpart to manage implementation of the IT project. The Technical Officer's knowledge and skills should match or exceed the contractor's knowledge and skills. In this way, the Technical Officer provides an adequate check and balance on the contractor. If the contractor tries to mislead or cheat, the Technical Officer will readily see it and can deal with the issue before it becomes a problem.

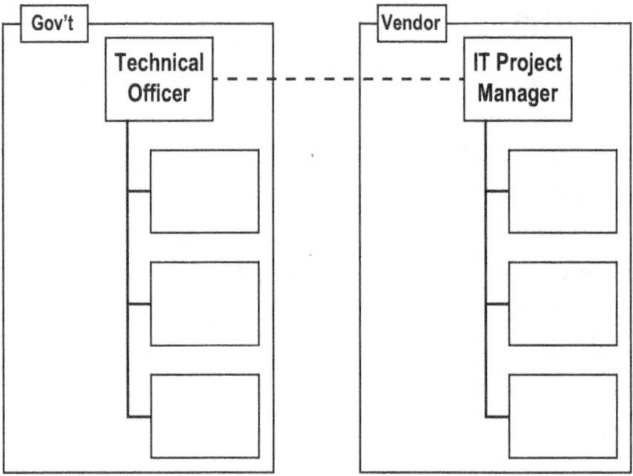

Figure 2.1 External relationship.

The contract terms need to describe the roles and responsibilities of the IT team. Even though the government agency would not have authority over any one of the IT members, the government agency will be aware of the IT roles that will be required to carry out the work. The Technical Officer will be able to direct specific questions or issues to the appropriate roles without direct contact to those roles. The contractor's technical lead will do the necessary follow-up by relaying any such concerns and responding back to the Technical Officer.

Just like with the internal organization of roles, the external roles employed by a contractor need to be identified and organized. The key difference is that the government agency has only one relationship between the Technical Officer and the contractor's technical lead (see Figure 2.1). The Technical Officer would not have any direct or indirect relationships with any of the contractor's team members, unless expressly described in the contract. All of the communication flows from government to contractor and vice versa move between the two technical representatives in the contract.

Leadership and Oversight

With a number of relationships inside and outside the organization and a diversity of roles encompassing business-functional and IT technical areas, how can IT operations and IT projects be effectively led?

The IT leader, at a minimum, should have a Master's degree in computer science, public administration, or in a field related to technology or management. A person who has progressed over the years from a junior specialist to a senior specialist would be the ideal candidate. Such a career professional would have accumulated a rich knowledgebase of previous iterations of computer technologies. That knowledge can aid in determining how risky a new solution may be to implement in the government agency. Moreover, the career professional would have developed rapport with colleagues – both IT and non-IT – across the organization in which the leader has worked. Demonstrated ability to develop and manage IT would have also earned the respect of both IT and non-IT colleagues. A critical part of leadership is the skill in handling both solutions and people.

IT leadership can be divided into three areas: policy and coordination, project management, and daily operations. The IT Manager leads the IT department or IT unit and ensures that all computer equipment and technological elements are operating with minimal disruption. With a high level of technical proficiency, the IT Manager has to monitor IT resources and may have to make necessary repairs. Serving on the frontline of daily operations, the IT Manager will be among the first to hear complaints when an IT system goes down and must be able to work with end users to find workaround, temporary solutions while the downed system is being repaired.

The IT Project Manager leads the implementation of an IT system and ensures that all the components are designed properly according to requirements. This person would need adequate technical proficiency to evaluate the IT system as it is being developed, but the more important skill lies in interacting with various IT and non-IT personnel. The IT Project Manager has to manage the back-and-forth communication between personnel to ensure that business-functional needs are being heard and addressed on one hand, and the technical specifications are indeed meeting those needs on the other hand. Any differences must be reconciled through the leadership ability of the IT Project Manager.

The CIO or the CTO oversees all IT-related activities across the entire organization. This senior executive leader establishes and maintains IT policies, operating procedures, and strategies that provide guidance to downstream work covering all areas of IT. The CIO or the CTO works closely with the CFO, the COO, and other senior leaders to ensure that IT programs and IT systems are meeting agreed-upon objectives and goals as described in the IT Strategic Plan. The more important ability of this leader is to have the "Big Picture" strategic view of IT. The CIO or the CTO regularly reviews the IT Manager's work and the IT Project Manager's work for compliance and reporting. In a larger organization, there can be more than one IT Manager and the CIO or the CTO will have to coordinate all of the managers' work to reduce duplications and inefficiencies. One of many high-level decisions that this senior leader will make is to determine the impact of an IT system on the entire organization. Would such a system be limited to one particular unit or would it bring greater value if all departments had access to it? While all the IT Managers are managing the technical work, the CIO or the CTO can concentrate on how a number of IT systems can best be applied to achieve organizational goals without spending too much money.

In a nonprofit organization or a small government agency, the IT Manager role could be merged with the CIO role to create one job position. It may not be necessary to have multiple tiers of leadership for an organization with less than 500 employees. Such a small organization could manage IT under the leadership of the IT Manager. A Deputy/Assistant IT Manager may be employed to support the lead IT Manager.

A very large government agency with thousands of employees will have a complex organizational structure. In this case, there will be a need for several IT Managers distributed strategically and optimally among several operating units and/or functional departments. To coordinate these IT Managers' work, middle-tier leadership should be in place with one or more IT Directors supervising and coordinating the IT Managers. These IT Directors, in turn, would be overseen by the CIO.

Office of the Chief Information Officer

The "Office of the Chief Information Officer" (OCIO) includes the CIO, the Deputy CIO, and a Secretary. A law may require the establishment of the OCIO in the government agency and may have specific requirements for the OCIO. In general, the OCIO is situated at the highest level of the organization and reports to the agency head (see Figure 2.2). From this vantage point, the CIO has the ability and the authority to coordinate all IT-related activities for consistency, efficiency, and cost-effectiveness. In addition to what has been described above, the CIO would develop

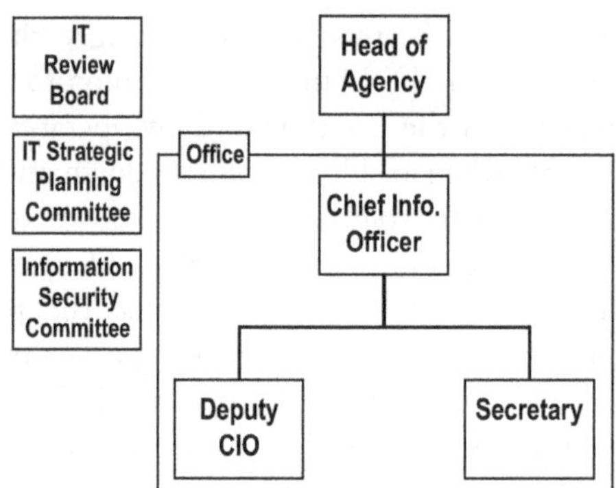

Figure 2.2 Organization chart: office of the CIO.

and oversee strategic planning of all IT programs. In its long-term outlook, the OCIO regularly monitors and reports on the progress and status of those programs with particular attention on IT capital investments.

Organizational Structures

The public manager, by now, should see that the organization of roles is flexible. There is no one fixed organizational structure that must be followed. Based on the size of the organization, the budget, contracting and outsourcing, and business needs, the public manager can design an IT organization chart that fits perfectly. Worksheet 2.1 provides an exercise for the manager to brainstorm ideas for organizing all the needed IT and non-IT roles into job positions. Once the best structure has been determined, the public manager can use Worksheets 2.2 and 2.3 to create the organization chart. The organization chart would then be sent to senior executive leaders, department directors, and other managers for review and approval.

The public manager should bear in mind one overarching aim in finding the right IT structure. IT is a particular function that *supports all other functions* in the government agency. In other words, IT plays a cross-functional role that serves to facilitate and enhance government operations. Other business functions may be able to operate independently and in isolation without IT. Public health, for example, could operate entirely with manual processes, however slow, that may be in the provision of health services. But IT cannot operate without the existence of the business functions. What would be the point of having an IT system if it does not work with a business function?

IT must support all business functions in the following five areas:

1. Ensuring the security and integrity of data and the confidentiality and availability of information
2. Supporting and training end users in how to use IT systems
3. Planning and maintaining essential resources related to computer hardware and software equipment, data storage capacity, and network communication
4. Testing and deploying new computer-based products and services
5. Providing advice and analysis on emerging technological solutions

These IT functional areas can be organized into three general divisions: (1) Network and Telecommunication, (2) Information System, and (3) End User Support. The End User Support division assists employees on how to use IT systems. The Support division covers computer hardware maintenance, computer repair, computer software support, and computer training. The Information System division manages the flow and control of information through manual procedures, automated systems, or a combination of both. The System division covers systems analysis and integration, software program design, software interface design, software engineering, quality assurance, and technical documentation. The Network and Telecommunication division monitors and maintains the IT infrastructure and computer equipment to ensure that employees can communicate with each other and with others outside of the organization. The Network division covers network engineering, telephony management, systems administration, database administration, and information security.

These three divisions are provided as an overall guide. Based on the organization's priorities and needs, the public manager may modify the divisions by splitting a division into more specific units or focusing a division on a core essential service. For example, the government agency could change End User Support to concentrate on "Computer Maintenance and Repair". In this case, computer support and training would be outsourced. "Information Security" may be mission critical and thus would be taken out of the Network division and placed in its own separate division.

Figure 2.3 provides for the basic IT organization chart with three general divisions. As it is led by the IT Manager, this organization chart would represent the IT department for a nonprofit organization or a small government agency.

Figures 2.4 and 2.5 show a full IT organization chart with the IT Manager reporting to the OCIO through the Deputy CIO. Two divisions have been added to bring attention and focus to

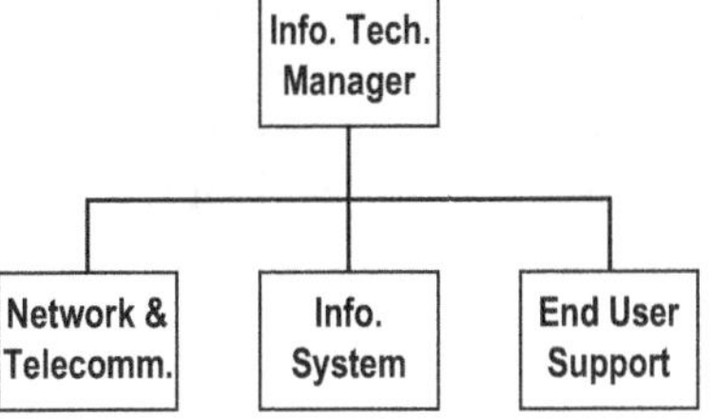

Figure 2.3 Organization chart: IT department.

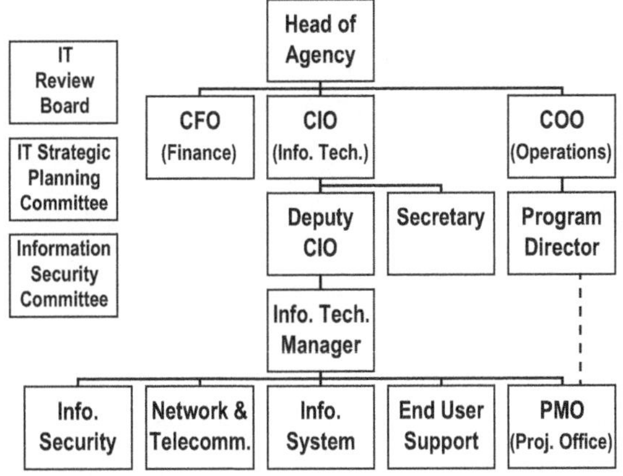

Figure 2.4 Organization chart, part 1 of 2.

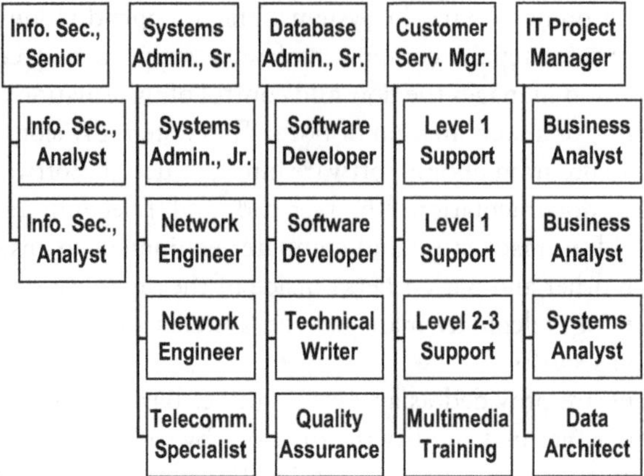

Figure 2.5 Organization chart, part 2 of 2.

information security and project management. The Project Management Office (PMO) reports directly to the IT Manager and has an indirect relationship to the Program Director who in turn reports to the Chief Operating Officer. One or more IT Project Managers may work in the PMO, managing several IT projects for various departments as guided by the Program Director. Chapter 7 provides details about the Information Security Committee. Chapter 8 provides details about the IT Review Board and the IT Strategic Planning Committee.

Figure 2.5 is a continuation of Figure 2.4 and provides examples of teams under each division. The job positions along the top row in Figure 2.5 correspond to the divisions shown in Figure 2.4. These two figures would actually be presented as one continuous chart. A manager or a senior-level specialist would lead a division, supervising the work of specialists. There would be more people under each division. Figure 2.5 displays the general idea to demonstrate the organization of job roles and where roles would fit.

Chapter 2 Quiz

Question 1: Which role could be removed from a software development project that requires a strict following of regulations?

A. Functional Expert
B. Network Engineer
C. Attorney
D. UI/UX Designer
E. Technical Writer

Question 2: In which situation would it be best to use IT certification as a key qualification factor?

A. An external candidate who has been self-employed for the last 2 years has applied to the vacant Network Engineer position.
B. A Mid-level Software Developer is being considered for promotion to Senior-level Software Developer.
C. A Mid-level Network Engineer has found that she enjoys programming and has applied to the vacant Software Developer position.
D. An IT Manager has applied to the vacant Deputy CIO position.
E. Both A and C

Question 3: Of all the IT roles, which role is best positioned to serve as the moderator between the IT and non-IT groups?

A. Multimedia/Online Training Specialist
B. Systems Administrator
C. Systems Analyst
D. Quality Assurance Specialist
E. Information Security Specialist

Question 4: Which pair of project managers would be optimal to ensure that the IT project is successful?

A. Government's Functional Expert and Vendor's Software Developer.
B. Government's Business Analyst and Vendor's Systems Analyst.
C. Government's General Counsel and Vendor's IT Project Manager.
D. Government's Functional Expert Technical Officer and Vendor's IT Project Manager.
E. Government's Chief Financial Officer and Vendor's Customer Service Manager.

Question 5: Which set of divisions would be appropriate to establish the IT department?

A. Information System, Network and Telecommunication, and End User Support.
B. Computer Networking, Information System, Computer Maintenance.
C. Information Security and System Development, and Network and User Support.
D. Network and Computer Repair, Information Security, and Information System.
E. All of the above.

Worksheets

Step 1:
Write one specific item (a job role) on a Post-it® note.

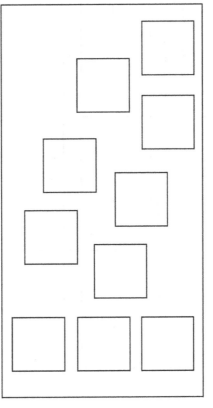

Step 2:
Organize written notes on a large board, sorting them in any pattern that makes sense in your operating environment.

Step 3:
Apply the arrangement of notes to other worksheets.

Worksheet 2.1 Job and team arrangement exercise.

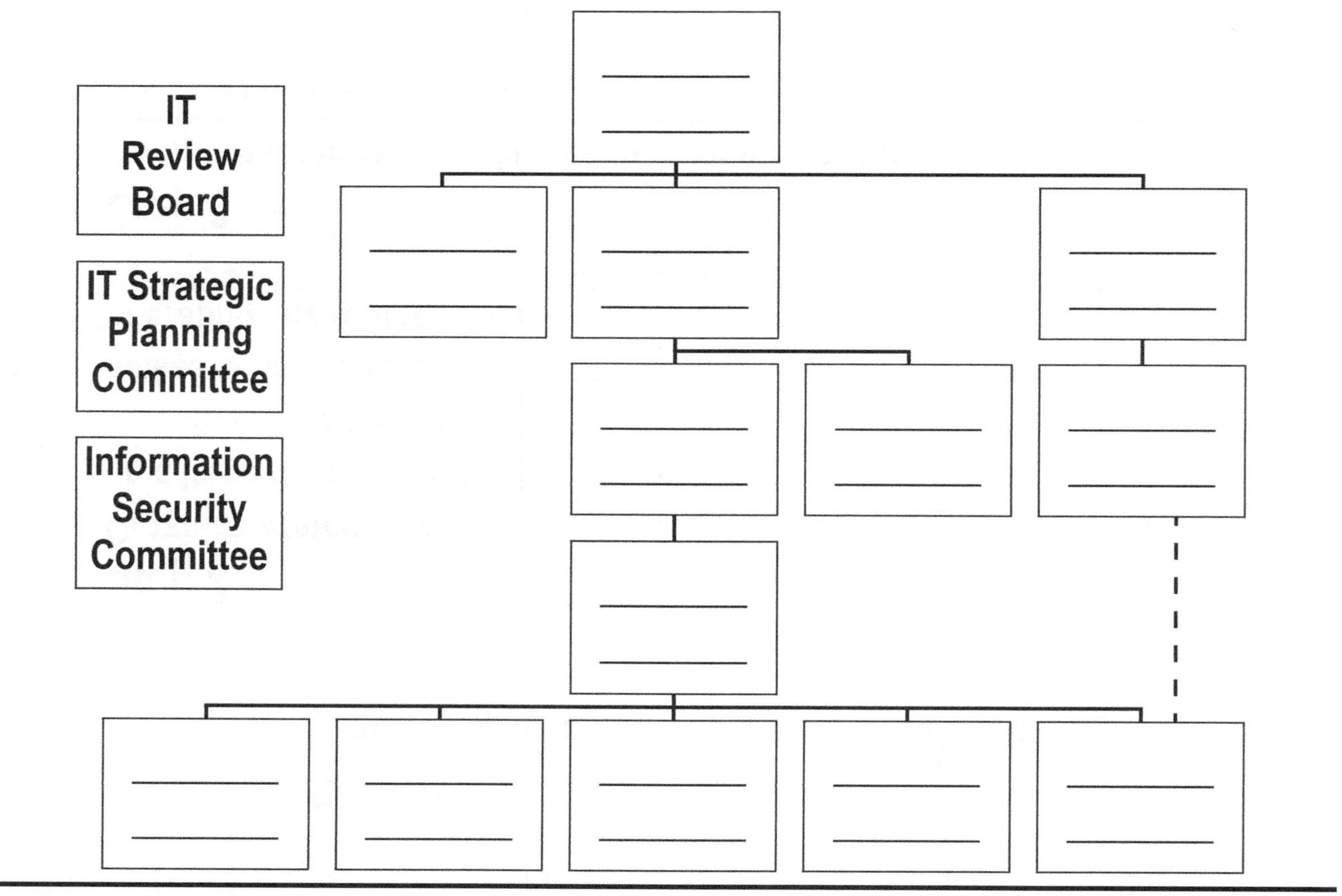

Worksheet 2.2 Organization chart, part 1 of 2.

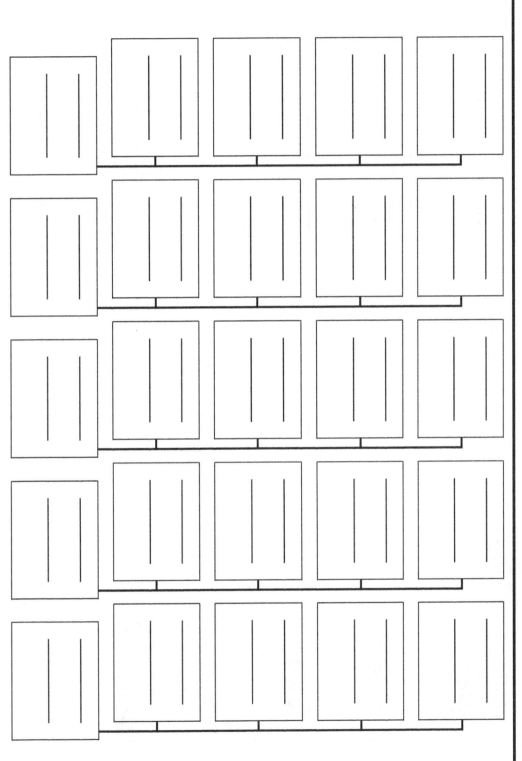

Worksheet 2.3 Organization chart, part 2 of 2.

Department	IT Dept.	________	________	________	________
Mission					
Information					
Application					
Data					
Technology					

Worksheet 2.4 Human resource responsibility matrix.

Chapter 3

IT Budgeting: Realization of Long-Term Benefits

Agency Head says: "I reviewed your proposal to automate the agency. This sounds very interesting. But the cost is too high. And I don't see what this will do *for me*".

As the CIO of the government agency, how will you respond?

Chapter Summary

The previous chapter brought up the point about the role of Information Technology (IT) in supporting a business function within an organization. To build on that further, IT is basically a tool that an organization can use for some purpose. And like with any tool, an IT resource comes at a price. Implementation of an IT system can be expensive.

Fortunately, there is good news. In a private sector market-based economy where competing IT providers can be found, the public manager can select an IT system that matches their budget. With a flexible organizational structure of IT roles, the public manager can further maintain and operate the selected IT system within their allocated budget.

There is bad news, of course. No matter how well the public manager proposes a least costly IT program, the proposal can still be rejected. The reason can vary from misalignment of business needs, an issue related to operational viability or technical feasibility, and a lack of political will.

The public manager then must do more than simply calculate the costs of materials and personnel. The manager needs to evaluate how the new IT system will provide benefits to the government agency and must provide their analysis in a persuasive manner based on available information that can be verified. The public manager has to identify specific changes that the IT system can be attributed to (e.g., cost savings and output performance) and quantify those changes.

Budgeting, in general, is more than an accounting exercise. It is a technical discipline for making decisions on how to meet organizational goals through the allocation of resources. Difficult decisions have to be made on choosing among alternatives, each of which has strengths, weaknesses, and risks. The trade-offs need to be considered. What will be gained by contracting a private company to do all software development work? Can the loss of eliminating permanent IT employees be recovered in equal or more gains through the use of a contractor? Will there be a significant loss of security by migrating all of the data from the government agency's data center facility to a commercial online data storage (cloud) provider? Is the organization receiving more benefits from the reduction of software licensing fees by using Web-based office productivity tools (e.g., Google Docs and Microsoft Office 365) instead of desktop computer software programs? By analyzing the IT budget systematically, the public manager can examine what would be gained or lost from all available IT-related resources and then create a set of resources that would not only be less costly but can also return greater benefits to the government agency.

This chapter describes the mechanics of developing an IT budget for present and future years, accounting for all resources. The public manager will have to factor in a variety of resources that will make IT work – computer technology, equipment, infrastructure, non-IT personnel, IT personnel, and time. IT is more than hardware and software. The chapter explains analytical methods and various cost factors to determine how IT programs and IT systems can be used optimally. The public manager will be able to distinguish which cost factor directly and indirectly relates to a particular IT system. This chapter concludes with a method of calculating the return on investment so that the public manager can present to senior executive leaders what will be the benefits of a proposed IT project. Once an IT system has been developed, the new IT system must generate certain benefits year over year.

Politics in Budgeting

There is a dimension that should not be overlooked in the budgeting process. The government's budget or public budget must serve the purposes of a wider society and for a greater good. Citizens need to see that public programs are working in their interest. IT programs must be aligned with public programs in a way that can facilitate or improve operations to provide services to more people – especially those who do not have the means to obtain services on their own.

But what program should be proposed? Should it be related to health, education, social security, defense, or something else? Priorities will be determined by elected leaders who serve on behalf of their constituencies. A group of citizens from one region may have a different need from another group of citizens. One group may want agricultural development assistance. Another group may want public transportation. Each group's political representative will debate whether each other's program should be funded. Some programs will get funding. Others will be cut or eliminated. The final public budget will be a reflection of what the government values through the eyes of the leaders elected by their constituencies.

Just as elected leaders fight over which public programs will be approved, public managers within the government agency will argue over which department programs should be in the budget. One department will have a project that its director wants funded. Another department will have its own project as well. Each department would have support from their internal employees. If a department program is known to the general public, support would also come from citizens as well.

The financial situation of the IT department is no different from all other departments in the government agency. The IT leader would also have a dream, pet project. There will be essential IT operations that must be funded in order to keep the organization running. Thus, the IT leader must fight among other department directors for a share of the agency's limited budget.

Unlike functional departments, the IT department has an advantage that if played correctly can reap great rewards – and reach an increasingly higher budget amount. All of the functional departments would want some kind of IT system. The IT leader can solicit ideas from other directors and work with them to develop IT plans. Department directors can then incorporate IT into their programs. And while the directors fight to get their respective programs with a computer-based component in the budget, the IT leader can provide background support wherever technical explanation is needed. The IT leader works in collaboration with other directors instead of competing with others for scarce resources. Through this tactical approach of interdepartmental relations, the IT leader works quietly behind the scenes to spread the benefits of IT across the entire government agency.

Budget Principles

A public budget in general and an IT budget in particular should adhere to principles commonly followed in other public organizations. As the budget is drafted and revised, the public manager should answer the following four questions:

1. Was the budget analyzed thoroughly?
2. Is the budget realistic?
3. Does the budget comply with laws and regulations?
4. Does the budget allow the organization to operate within budget?

The IT budget should have undergone a thorough analysis. Every line item should have a specific reason for being in the budget. The public manager should be able to defend how the line item contributes to a specific program, which in turn contributes to an operational goal. The public manager would have worked with colleagues to conduct background research to calculate the monetary amount for every line item. The associated monetary amount for each line item should have been analyzed. Any line item that cannot be defended financially or programmatically should be dropped from the budget.

The IT budget should be realistic, covering what the IT department needs to achieve in a given fiscal year. This assumes that the budget went through a full analysis. Are all the line items reasonable in their justification? Each line item should be attainable within the fiscal year. Any line item that cannot be achieved should be dropped from the budget.

The IT budget must be in compliance with all applicable laws and regulations. This is particularly critical in government as the government agency must be a practitioner of the rule of law. Any line item that goes against a regulation must be dropped from the budget. Compliance with the law can work in favor or against the organization. In other words, the law can either expand or constrict the budget. A regulation that prohibits a certain behavior will force the organization to drop line items from the budget or reduce the monetary amounts of certain line items. A favorable regulation, on the other hand, can encourage the organization to add line items in the budget. By conducting a thorough analysis, the public manager will know what is prohibited and what is not and can operate within the law.

The IT budget needs to allow the IT department to operate within budget. Can the IT department accomplish its tasks in support of public programs and operations? Answering this question assumes that a thorough analysis was done to understand the needs and requirements of the organization. The public manager must be satisfied that the IT department can function properly given what has been drafted in the budget. Absence of an IT budget does not provide any guidance to how the IT department needs to operate. Insufficient funding of the IT department could cause projects to go unfinished, or worse could result in surprises that the government agency is not prepared for.

Based on the limiting factors, the IT budget cannot be perfect, but it can be managed to evolve toward that aim. The IT budget can be used as an instrument that enables the IT department to progress year after year, one fiscal cycle after the other. Seen as a management tool, the IT budget presents a picture of how allocated resources will meet organizational goals. And that picture of one IT budget plan represents what will be carried out in a single fiscal year. Senior executive leaders can review the current fiscal year budget to measure financial performance against the previous fiscal year budget. Changes in operating conditions can be analyzed in the review of current and previous budgets. Those changes and calculated financial performance can be further used to forecast the next fiscal year budget, aiding the public manager to plan for the future.

To be able to measure performance and change accurately, the IT budget must record the estimated amounts *and* the actual amounts. The public manager cannot just enter what *will be spent*. The public manager must capture what *has been spent* in the current fiscal year. Without knowing the actual amounts, the government agency would be stuck in a predicament where the public manager makes estimations based more on theory and less on practice. Knowing what has been spent will provide a realistic view of how the operation is going. The public manager can then rely on the actual amounts to make future estimates that are stronger and more realistic in the next budget.

Government Budget Process

The high degree of rigor inherent in following the budget principles requires a lot of time and effort. The complete government budget process, which consists of four phases, can span a few years, depending on the particular country. In the United States, the budget process can be longer than 3 years (39 months). The lengthy time frame covers the work necessary to manage all of the government agencies' budgets. In addition to the actual year in which the budget is carried out, the budget must be prepared, approved, and audited. The four phases of the budget process are (1) Budget Preparation and Submission, (2) Budget Approval, (3) Budget Execution, and (4) Budget Audit and Evaluation (see Figure 3.1).

In the United States, the first phase (Preparation) requires approximately 9 months. The second phase (Approval) requires approximately 6 months. The third phase (Execution, the fiscal year of the budget process) takes 12 months. And the fourth and final phase (Audit) requires approximately 12 months. The Budget Approval phase involves the legislative branch of government to review the proposed budget plan submitted by all of the executive agencies and to conclude with the final budget plan. The final Audit phase allows government auditors to review all monies spent and to evaluate the effectiveness of programs. The public manager needs to remember that all four phases of the government budget process cover one fiscal year.

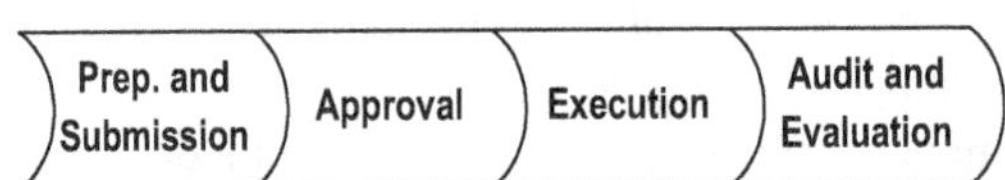

Figure 3.1 Governmental budget process.

Fiscal Year Budget Cycles

The public manager needs to take note that at any given point in the budget process, they would be managing or involved in three or four fiscal year budgets. Figure 3.2 illustrates this for the U.S. government. While the Fiscal Year 2020 budget is being executed, the previous Fiscal Year 2019 budget is being audited and evaluated. Preparation for the Fiscal Year 2021 budget will have been in progress and would be approved at the end of the current year's (FY 2020's) execution phase. Three months before the end of the current year begins the preparation phase for the Fiscal Year 2022 budget. At the end of the current fiscal year budget (2020), the public manager would be in the process of preparing for the fiscal year budget 2 years into the future.

Fixed, Step-Function, and Variable Costs and Other Cost Factors

The IT budget needs to have gone through a full and complete cost analysis of resources. What does the IT department need to operate? What will it take to complete an IT project? It is not enough to calculate the purchase of computer hardware, computer software, and other equipment. IT programs and systems need personnel who will be compensated. If a training program exists, training fees and other related costs need to be added in the budget. Telecommunication usage, electricity usage, and cooling system have to be factored in too.

As the manager writes down all the items and adds up all the costs, the public manager will see the total cost get increasingly larger. The total may become too high, exceeding the limit of the IT department's budget. Reductions will have to be made.

Sorting all resources into cost factors can help in reducing costs. And this could provide a way to save a particular item from being eliminated. The public manager could still keep a resource by adjusting its quantity to an amount that is absolutely needed. By lowering the quantity of the resource, the cost of the resource can be lowered. Most resources can be saved this way. But first, the public manager needs to sort all resources into cost factors. The following method can be applied to sort each resource item:

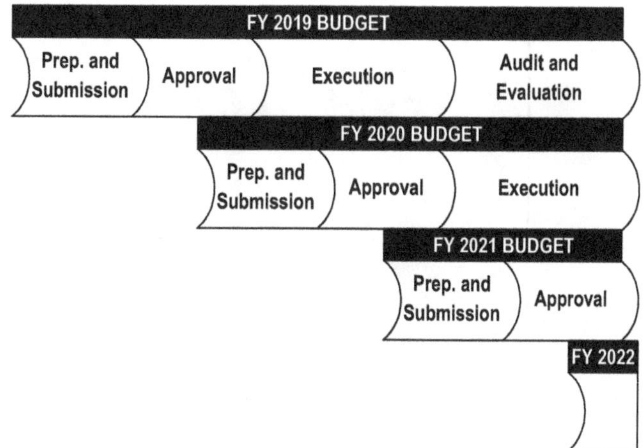

Figure 3.2 Overlapping fiscal year budget cycles. (Adapted from Maxwell School, Department of Public Administration, ed., *PPA 734 Public Budgeting, Summer 2007, Course Reader.*)

1. Does the cost of the resource remain the same regardless of a change in the level of service or in the number of units purchased or used?
   a. If yes, the resource is a "Fixed Cost". Move to the sixth question.
   b. If no, move to the second question.
2. Does the cost of the resource change with every additional unit purchased or used beginning at 1 unit?
   a. If yes, the resource is a "Variable Cost". Move to the sixth question.
   b. If no, move to the third question.
3. Does the cost of the resource first stay the same for a certain number of units and then change with every additional unit purchased or used?
   a. If yes, the resource is a "Semi-variable Cost". Move to the fifth question.
   b. If no, move to the fourth question.
4. Does the cost of the resource stay the same for a certain number of units and then suddenly jump to a new cost at a particular point in a change in quantity?
   a. If yes, the resource is a "Step-function Cost". Move to the fifth question.
   b. If no, return to the first question and try the analysis again. The current resource would be one of the three other cost factors.
5. Simplify the resource further as either a Fixed Cost or a Variable Cost. In the case of a Semi-variable Cost, the resource would be split into both cost factors.
6. Distinguish whether the resource is a "Direct Cost" or an "Indirect Cost".

Ask yourself this first question: Does the cost of the resource remain the same regardless of a change in the level of service or in the number of units purchased or used? If the answer is yes, then the resource is a "Fixed Cost". A fixed cost resource refers to a resource whose price does not change with any given change in quantity. Figure 3.3 provides a graph of what a typical fixed cost resource item would look like. An example of a fixed cost resource is an employee whose compensation remains the same month after month for a year or more.

If the answer to the first question is no, then ask yourself this second question: Does the cost of the resource change with every additional unit purchased or used beginning at one unit? If the answer is yes, then the resource is a "Variable Cost". A variable cost resource refers to a resource

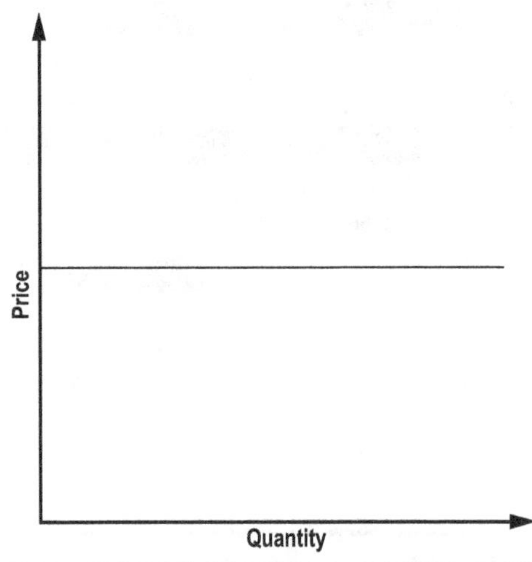

Figure 3.3 Fixed cost.

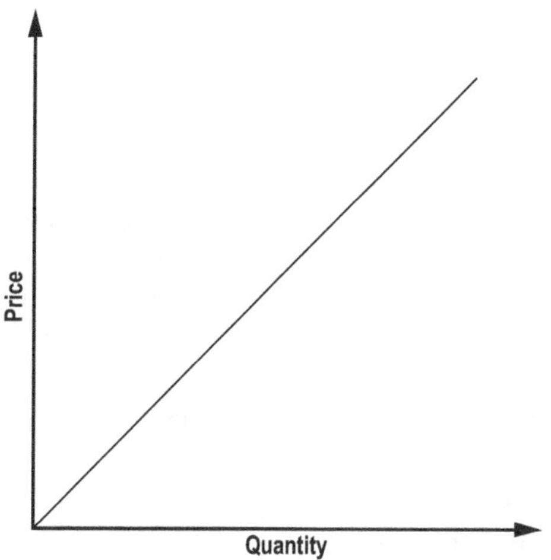

Figure 3.4 Variable cost.

whose price changes at each unit change in quantity. Figure 3.4 provides a graph of what a typical variable cost resource item would look like. An employee who is paid based on the number of hours or days worked is an example of a variable cost. Consumer products are variable cost resource items.

If the answer to the second question is no, then ask yourself this third question: Does the cost of the resource first stay the same for a certain number of units and then change with every additional unit purchased or used? If the answer is yes, then the resource is a "Semi-variable Cost". A semi-variable cost resource refers to a resource whose price initially starts fixed for a given quantity and then changes at each unit change in quantity. This cost factor is not a pure variable cost resource, as it combines attributes of the fixed cost and variable cost factors. Figure 3.5 provides a graph of what a typical semi-variable cost resource item would look like. A Website service that is hosted by an IT provider is an example of a semivariable cost. The organization is charged a fixed price for operating and maintaining a Website with a specified limit of bandwidth. If the amount of bandwidth

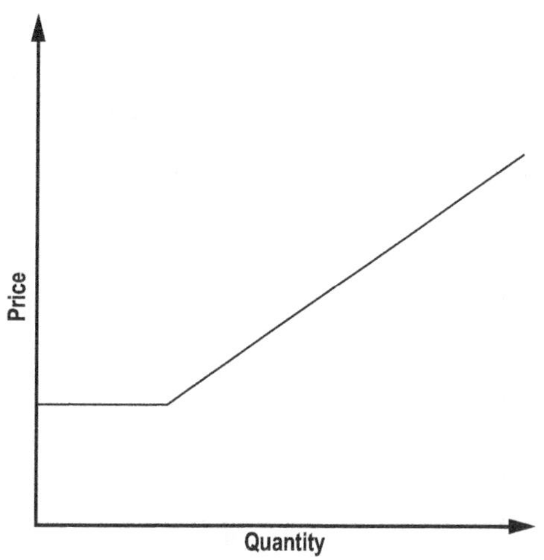

Figure 3.5 Semi-variable cost.

exceeds the limit as a result of high visitor traffic, the organization is charged an additional fee for each megabit per second (Mbps) of bandwidth used in excess of the limit. Data usage is another example where the cost can fluctuate after data usage has exceeded the specified limit.

If the answer to the third question is no, then ask yourself this last question: Does the cost of the resource stay the same for a certain number of units and then suddenly jump to a new cost at a particular point in a change in quantity? In other words, the cost does not change at *every additional unit* but only after a given number of units. For example, the resource's cost starts at $10 at a quantity of 1–100 units. The cost then jumps to $25 at a quantity of 101–250 units. If the answer is yes, then the resource is a "Step-function Cost". A step-function cost resource refers to a resource whose price only changes after a given unit threshold has been reached. Figure 3.6 provides a graph of what a typical step-function cost resource item would look. Volume pricing for a computer software product is an example of a step-function cost.

With further analysis, a step-function cost resource could be defensibly labeled as a variable cost or a fixed cost. If the average difference in price changes from one level to the next is negligible and the specified units in all levels are large, then the step-function cost resource could be a fixed cost resource. This would create a relatively flat line as shown in Figure 3.7, which would resemble a fixed cost line. If the average difference in price changes is large or significant and the specified units in all levels are small, then the step-function cost resource could be a variable cost resource. This would create a relatively steep line as shown in Figure 3.8. The steeper the slope of the step-function cost line, the more variable in cost it appears.

Determining whether a step-function cost factor is variable or fixed can simplify the sorting of resources into two major cost factors. IT resources can either be fixed cost resources or variable cost resources. In the case of a semi-variable cost, a semi-variable cost resource can be split into two cost resources. The initial part of the quantity that does not change in price is the fixed cost resource and the other part of the quantity that does change in price is the variable cost resource.

After IT resources have been sorted, the public manager needs to distinguish whether each cost resource is a "Direct Cost" or an "Indirect Cost". This is a critical step when the budget is divided into several programs. It is important in the evaluation of an IT system. If the public manager simply adds up all cost resources without distinguishing between direct cost and indirect

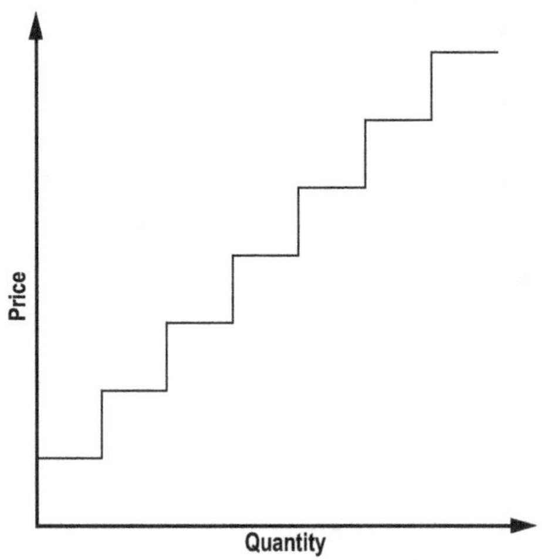

Figure 3.6 Step-function cost.

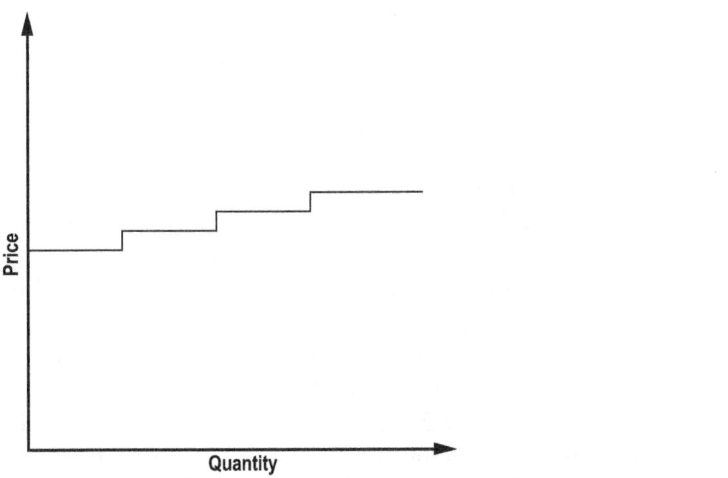

Figure 3.7 Relatively flat step-function cost.

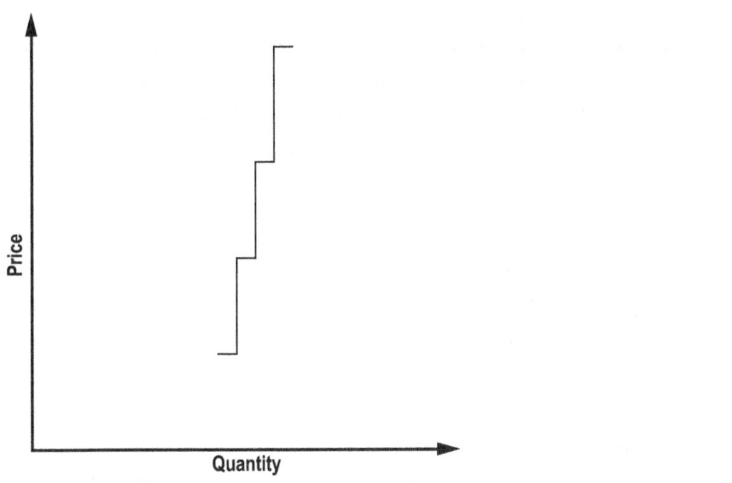

Figure 3.8 Relatively steep step-function cost.

cost, the total cost could lead to an erroneous result. The IT budget could look more expensive than it actually is, or it could appear as though certain resources are being double counted.

A certain resource can be shared among one or more programs or systems. This is an indirect cost. Overhead expenses such as electricity, cooling, and utilities are common indirect cost resources. Every electronic equipment that operates in a building would draw electricity from a central electrical power source. The electrical power source indirectly contributes to the operation of electronic equipment. Administrative personnel who oversee programs would be considered as indirect cost resources.

IT personnel who are not dedicated to a specific program or system are indirect cost resources. In other words, an IT specialist who is not working 100% in one program is not a direct resource. The IT Project Manager, for example, can be managing three IT projects. In this case, it will be double counting to duplicate the IT Project Manager's salary in all three projects. The public manager must allocate a portion of the Manager's salary to each project based on time spent for each project. For example, if 30% of the time is spent in the first project, 30% of the time is spent in the second project, and 40% of the time is spent in the third project, then the Manager's salary will be divided proportionately for each of the three projects (30% of salary for the first, 30% of salary for the second, and 40% of salary for the third). This would also apply to technical specialists such as a Software Developer who develops software programs for multiple projects.

Physical assets such as a computer server and a network device can be indirect cost resources for several projects or systems. One or a few computer servers could be a shared resource for multiple computer software programs. Those computer servers could be operated in one computer network with an infrastructure consisting of network devices. Thus, all the network devices would be shared resources. These physical assets would only need to be purchased one time in the first instance of an IT project. Subsequent IT projects would not include the servers and the network devices because they already exist and had been paid for. There may be some new computer equipment to upgrade existing resources (e.g., hardware components), but such additions would not make a subsequent IT project as costly as the first IT project.

Any cost resource that cannot be shared is a direct cost. Disposable supplies and consumable products are typically direct cost resources needed by a specific project or a team. Certain components that have to be replaced inside a computer would be direct cost resources. Toner or ink cartridges used in a computer printer would be direct cost resources, unless the particular printer is being shared among two or more departments. If a printer is shared making it an indirect cost resource, then the toner or ink cartridge would be an indirect cost resource as well.

The examples of indirect cost resources described above could also be budgeted as direct cost resources. One computer server can be dedicated to run only one computer software program. One Software Developer can work 100% on one IT project. For a large government agency that has numerous office locations, each building can have overhead costs specific to that one location.

Once all of the resources have been organized by cost factors, the public manager will be able to make selective choices on how all of the cost resources can be used optimally at a lower cost. Indirect cost resources can significantly lower the total cost, as those resources can be spread across one or more departments or programs. A telephone system is a common example of an indirect resource where one telephone system is implemented and used by the entire organization. It would be odd that each department would have its own telephone system. In such a case, the organization would be paying for several telephone systems. Direct cost resources are meant for one department, one program, or one system. Other departments could see advantages at using resources dedicated to another department and thus make requests to procure similar resources for their department. This could create duplication of effort as similar direct resources are being used by several departments. The public manager can reclassify those similar resources as indirect cost resources and thus eliminate duplication.

Certain direct cost resources in particular environments may need to remain as they are, however. The government agency would operate a second computer network for transferring classified information. This would be a highly restrictive network for personnel who have security clearance. The first, primary computer network would be available for all employees to transfer unclassified information, access the Internet, and transfer other non-sensitive communication. This example shows that the cost of operating two computer networks is duplicative but warranted, given the need to protect government secrets.

Variable cost resources are those resources that the public manager can use to lower the total cost without having to eliminate those resources. After it has been determined how much of a resource is needed, the public manager can calculate only the quantity that is needed. A little bit extra quantity may be added for contingency purposes. In any case, a variable cost resource allows a degree of flexibility in adjusting the quantity that the department or program will need. In the event that a department must make mandatory budget cuts, the public manager does not necessarily have to drop one or more variable cost resources. The public manager can reexamine those resources and make cuts by adjusting the quantities of those resources.

In contrast, fixed cost resources are difficult to change and justify and may have to be eliminated. The cost will not change by adjusting the quantity. One strategy in finding lower fixed cost resources is to conduct market research on which vendors and suppliers will provide products and services at a lower cost or best value. Different companies in the private sector produce comparable technological resources (e.g., Microsoft Windows computers, Apple computers, Oracle database, and Microsoft database). The technological elements described in Chapter 1 are not specific to any one provider. A number of IT providers would develop similar products and offer their products at different prices. The public manager can research and try out competing products and services and then select those products and services that offer the lower price and yet does not lower quality. Without doing research and due diligence, the public manager could find it difficult to defend why a particular brand of technology needs to be purchased when there are other products that could do the same or higher-quality job.

Another strategy is to convert a fixed cost resource to a variable cost resource. A specific employee, for example, could have their basis of compensation reclassified from a fixed annual salary to a variable daily wage. The public manager can then calculate the number of days of work needed and only pay for those days worked. Another example is to contract an IT provider to operate data services in a remote facility (i.e., a cloud service). In this example, the public manager can convert fixed cost resources needed in an in-house (on-site) IT infrastructure to variable cost resources that would run on demand in a remote facility. The IT infrastructure conversion changes the cost structure to one that is based on the amount of time that those technological resources will be needed to run.

Be forewarned: Any fixed cost resource that is converted to a variable cost resource must be carefully studied. A fixed cost resource inherently is a cost control. A variable cost resource, on the other hand, could lead to an uncontrollable expense. The public manager can find that the cost of a resource is increasing too high, as the quantity consumed increases even more. In certain cases, a resource might be better left as a fixed cost. An example situation to be cautious about is transitioning from a PC-based software program to a subscription-based online software program. In the former, a software program is purchased one time for a specific version and installed in a computer. The purchaser would not have to pay a subsequent time, unless they want to buy the latest software version. The former is a fixed cost resource. In the latter, a software program is purchased for a specified period of time and must be purchased again to renew the service for another specified period of time. Various subscription-based business models would charge annually, monthly, or hourly. The latter is a variable cost resource.

Operational Requirements

Cost resources need to be selected in a way that they are aligned to achieve operational goals. The goals will have been defined in the IT Strategic Plan. Chapter 8 describes the development of the IT Strategic Plan. As it relates to the IT strategy, the public manager needs to analyze the financial part and calculate an estimated total cost of the IT strategy.

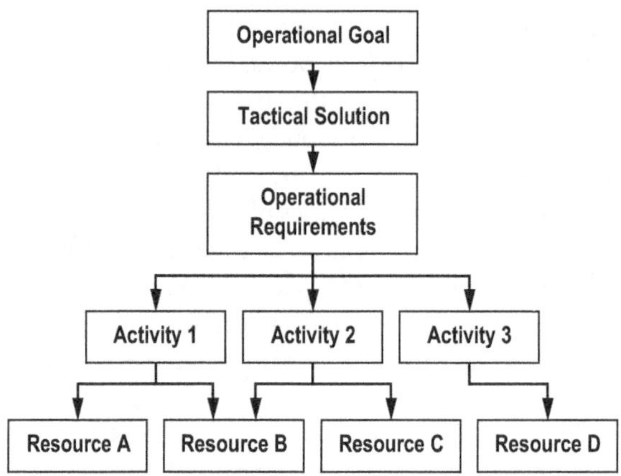

Figure 3.9 Goal-to-cost structure. (Adapted from Maxwell School, Department of Public Administration, ed., *PPA 734 Public Budgeting, Summer 2007, Course Reader.*)

The public manager refers to the operational goals defined in the IT Strategic Plan for guidance. An operational goal will have an associated tactical solution. The tactical solution will have a set of operational requirements. The requirements then are defined as specific work activities. One or more work activities can form the requirements, which make up the tactical solution. Each work activity will need specific resources (cost resources) to carry out the work. If a resource can contribute work to two or more activities, then the resource is an indirect cost (a shared resource). If a resource can only contribute work to one activity, then the resource is a direct cost (a dedicated resource). Figure 3.9 illustrates this structural relationship to associate an operational goal to a cost resource through an associated tactical solution and work activity. Through this structure, the public manager can see which activities and resources contribute to the achievement of operational goals.

By developing work activities and analyzing which cost resources will be needed for those activities, the public manager would be able to optimize operations by arranging resources for a better fit. As an example, one work activity is computer network management. This will need IT personnel who are skilled in managing and monitoring computer networks. A number of Network Engineers and Systems Administrators will be needed as human resources. Various network devices (e.g., a network router, a network switch, and a network firewall) will be needed as equipment resources. Parts, supplies, and tools (e.g., replacement memory, Ethernet wires, and screws) will be needed as material resources. Physical resources for the IT infrastructure (e.g., cabinets, racks, and a secured facility) will be needed. There will also be computer servers and computer software programs. All of these resources are cost resources associated with the network management activity.

Another example is a software development work activity. In this activity, a number of specific IT personnel related to software development will be needed. Material resources to do software development (e.g., development software, documentation tools, and diagraming tools) will be needed. There will also be computer servers and computer software programs to run the developed software program in a testing environment and a production environment.

For the two examples, the computer server and software resources are shared resources associated to both work activities. The software development team needs access to those resources to see how their software program will run. The network management team has the responsibility for configuring and maintaining those same resources. Specific documentation tools and diagramming tools could also be shared among the two activities and perhaps other activities as well. Identifying shared resources will help the public manager to avoid spending more than it is necessary to cover the requirements for every work activity.

Staffing Requirements

A major cost to any organization is labor. The operational requirements just described show that a number of workers will be needed. To be able to manage the cost of every human resource, the public manager should analyze how much time is needed to employ each person. This will enable the manager to decide whether a staff member should be permanent, temporary, or on contract.

A standard metric used to measure labor and time in relation to productivity is "labor-hours per output". Another term for labor-hours is "person-hours", as labor is synonymous to a person who is hired to do some type of work. The term, "man-hours" could be used, but it is archaic since it refers to a specific sex (i.e., man-hours is not gender neutral). The person-hours per output metric can apply to any work activity – not just IT activities. For example, a number of nurses employed for a number of hours can manage 1,000 patients. A number of agricultural extension agents employed for a number of hours can assist 1,000 farmers. A number of data entry clerks employed for a number of hours can process 1,000 forms. A number of computer support specialists employed for a number of hours can process 1,000 support requests. The product of labor (persons) and time supplies the total labor input, which would result in total output. Person-hours per output provides an indicator of the workload necessary to produce a product, a service, or some type of work.

This book derives a mathematical formula from the person-hours per output metric to calculate a staffing requirement for a specific task. This staffing requirement equation requires three variables. The first variable is the number of hours that one person can work. The second variable is the number of hours to complete a specific task that results in an output. This second variable would indicate output efficiency. The third variable is the total output that will be achieved. This last variable would be a given amount based on a need or a goal.

Calculating the first variable requires going through a set of calculations where the number of hours that a person does not work must be taken out. The standard 40 hours per week per person metric represents total hours that is inclusive of breaks and lunches. A person does not work and hence does not produce anything during breaks and lunches. Subtracting out times when a person does not work will produce a more precise measurement called "Working Hours".

The first variable requires the following assumptions for one person:

DHT = Total Hours per Day: _____ (assume 8 hours for most organizations)
DHL = Total Lunch Hours per Day: _____ (assume 1 hour for most organizations)
DHB = Total Break Hours per Day: _____ (assume 1 hour for most organizations)
KDT = Total Days per Week: _____ (assume 5 hours for most organizations)
YKT = Total Weeks per Year: 52
YYT = Total Holiday Days per Year: _____ (assume 10 days for most organizations)
YST = Total Sick Days per Year: _____ (assume 5 days for most organizations)
YVT = Total Vacation Days per Year: _____ (assume 10 days for most organizations)

Based on the foregoing assumptions, the following calculations can be made for the first variable:

YDT = Total Days per Year = KDT · YKT
DHW = Working Hours per Day = DHT – (DHL + DHB)
KHW = Working Hours per Week = DHW · KDT
YDW = Working Days per Year = YDT – (YYT + YST + YVT)
YHW = Working Hours per Year = DHW · YDW

As an example, most organizations would have the following calculations for the first variable:

260 Total Days per Year (YDT)
6 Working Hours per Day (DHW)
30 Working Hours per Week (KHW)
235 Working Days per Year (YDW)
1,410 Working Hours per Year (YHW)

To illustrate the difference between working hours and total hours: A person's "Total Hours per Year" would actually be 2,080, based on the stated assumptions. Factoring in all the days and times that a person does not work reduces the hours by 670 hours or 32.21%. People have to eat, take a break, and take some time off to rest or care for themselves.

Calculating the second variable is specific to a task that results in some output. The unit is "Hours per Output" where output is replaced with the specific thing or result. The calculated value is an estimated average of a number of people of like skill and capacity who do the same specific task. For example, the number of hours that one nurse would need to manage one patient represents the average of a sample of qualified nurses. The number of hours that one support specialist would need to process one technical support request is based on an average of a sample of qualified computer support specialists. Calculating the second variable will depend on performance monitoring records or a sample survey to evaluate human performance. Each specific task, moreover, would have a particular methodology that takes into consideration different factors. Evaluation of the task in question must also remove any unrelated tasks that a person may do. Unless a person is 100% dedicated to one specific task, an employee typically does more than one task in any given day. In the absence of a survey or records for the specific task, the second variable would be an educated guess based on the public manager's knowledge and experience. The more years that the manager has to observe work, the higher the accuracy that would result in the educated guess. In any case, the second variable is an approximated value that is less scientific and more art.

As an example: A particular task is the need to prepare and configure a new computer for one employee. The output is one computer that an employee will use. The question then is how many hours will be needed to configure one computer? Answering this question relies on understanding the details of the work. An IT specialist installs the operating system software and all organization-specific software programs such as for e-mail and office productivity, installs patches and upgrades for all software programs, configures computer security, runs general tests, sets up new user accounts, records the product serial number, and registers the new computer for inventory control. In addition, there will be waiting time for software to download, install, and process. Without using a pre-configured CD-ROM and automated scripts, the total time to complete the task manually can be 3 hours on average. Thus, the answer based on knowledge and experience is 3 hours per computer. The configured computer in this example is the output.

The third variable assumes a given value. It can be an agreed-upon goal written in the IT Strategic Plan. It can also be based on a need determined by consulting relevant teams. The third variable represents the "Target Output" that an organization wants to achieve.

As an example: The government agency has the need to replace all of its aging computers for 10,000 employees within 2 years. The IT Strategic Plan would describe this need and the approaches and solutions to implementing the work. The strategy will have a defined goal of procuring 10,000 computers, each one of which will be distributed to every employee. Thus, the third variable or target output in this example is 10,000 computers.

With all three variables known, the public manager can analyze staffing requirement. The following base equation produces the "Total Working Hours" that would be needed to achieve the Target Output:

$$Ht = \left(\frac{OT}{\frac{DHW}{OH}} \right) DHW$$

where

Ht = Total Working Hours
DHW = Working Hours per Day
OH = Hours per Output
OT = Target Output

The units of the variables in the base equation cancel out, leaving working hours in the result. The result would be a large number that represents the total time needed to produce the total output. To convert the result into days, divide the result by Working Hours per Day.

The example of completing 10,000 configured computers would need 30,000 working hours or 5,000 working days. In years, the work would need 21.28 years! The following base equation substitutes the variables with the values calculated above:

$$Ht = \left(\frac{10{,}000}{\frac{6}{3}} \right) 6$$

The reader may assume that the calculated result is performed completely by one person. This is not true, of course. The Total Working Hours represents the aggregate of multiple persons of like skills and capacity – the work of a team. The public manager will take the calculated result and carry out an additional calculation to analyze how many people should be hired or assigned. The entire work can be divided up among a number of specialists. The following equation will calculate the number of persons based on the average hours that each person will be allotted:

$$Pt = \frac{Ht}{PHm}$$

where

Pt = Total Persons
Ht = Total Working Hours
PHm = Average Working Hours per Person

Alternatively, the average working hours per person can be found, if the total persons variable is known. The following equation can be used in this case:

$$PHm = \frac{Ht}{Pt}$$

Finally, the result will have to be converted into a monetary amount. The total cost of the staffing requirement is the product of total working hours and the average hourly wage per person. Because the staffing requirement equation is based on a specific task, the hourly wage must be a portion of a person's total salary. Total salary represents all duties, responsibilities, and tasks – not just the single task in which the staffing requirement is measuring. The hourly wage for that specific task will be a small amount relative to total salary.

Operating Budget

The selected cost resources are listed in the operating budget. All of these resources (personnel, supplies, equipment, other assets, legal expenses, and overhead) would be spent during one fiscal year. Those resources that are a part of capital investment projects need to be split up appropriately in each year that the resources will be spent. Since a capital project can be implemented across multiple years, it will be wrong to show its total cost in one fiscal year operating budget. An additional item that would be included is depreciation. The sum of all expenses should be equal to or lower than the budget limit of that fiscal year.

The total revenue should be shown in the operating budget. Any fee-for-service program would be listed as a revenue source. In most cases, a general amount would be provided by an authorizing organization. This general amount would represent the budget limit – the total amount that can be spent in one fiscal year.

Capital Budget

IT projects that will be implemented across more than one fiscal year cycle should have its total cost and breakdown listed in the capital budget. Such projects will have cost resources that are very expensive to implement in the immediate term. The sum of the resources can consume a significant percentage of the budget limit, if it were listed in one fiscal year operating budget. Listing multi-year IT projects in the capital budget will treat the projects as long-term investments and may be funded differently.

Certain government agencies may have the ability to obtain funds from the issuance of government bonds. This revenue stream would pay for the long-term capital investment projects. As borrowed money, however, the funds must be paid back to bond-holders. And those bond-holders would want to receive their money equal to or more than the initial purchase amount of the bonds. Bond-holders will want to see a return on their investment. The additional interest amount and the original sale of the bonds will have to be paid at a certain time in the future. This future payment gets recorded and managed as debt.

The government agency needs to take extra care in selecting the right capital investment projects to implement. Investment projects are generally risky. The latest computer technology that has yet to prove its usefulness, arguably, may just be *too* risky for a large established organization. It is critical then that proposals for capital IT projects must be evaluated thoroughly to assess their risk and to ensure that their benefits outweigh their costs. Failure to do the necessary planning and analysis could result in a situation where the implemented IT project is not sustainable or the IT project creates more problems that the organization is not capable of handling. In an example scenario where power generation is continuously intermittent for several months and IT personnel are not adequately trained, a proposed data center that operates numerous computer equipment and stores hundreds of terabytes of data can be problematic to maintain. In another example scenario where new and unproven technology is deployed, the organization can be spending more money and time in constantly upgrading the technology with software patches to resolve issues – especially security issues – that the IT provider did not foresee.

Investment Principles

The public manager needs to be deliberate in the manner in which they make decisions regarding the acquisition of IT projects. The government agency will be spending limited funds on computer technology that could otherwise be spent on something else. After 3 years, the organization may finally realize that the spent technology was not a good idea after all. Hundreds of thousands or millions of dollars later and senior executive leaders would be in shock of where all the money went. The general public would be in an uproar once they hear about the waste.

The following investment principles provide a guide in carefully deciding which IT projects should be funded:

1. IT follows the rule of law.
2. IT is a service to the public.
3. IT is a link to mission.
4. IT is a means, not an end.
5. IT is easy to use.

Follows the Rule of Law

Government passes laws, makes rules, and enforces regulations. There are regulations and standards that govern the acquisition, operation, and use of technology. Technology must comply with applicable regulations. Technology must follow the rule of law.

A Service to the Public

The purpose of government in general is to serve in the best interests of the public at large. The people employed to carry out the government agency's work are servants of the public. By their association through contracts and grants, private organizations that work on behalf of government (i.e., government contractors) also serve the public. Technology then that is deployed in government also works to serve in the interests of the public. Technology that operates for government, therefore, must be a service to the general public.

A Link to Mission

Just because someone *wants* technology does not necessarily mean that they need it. A certain IT system may not serve the government's purpose. Technology must have a link to the organization's mission statement. This would be shown through the connections to goals and objectives defined in the IT Strategic Plan. The relationship between technology and strategy will show where the technology fits into the organization.

A Means, Not an End

Technology should not be implemented for the sake of technology. Technology itself should not be the goal. Like with any tool, mechanical or otherwise, computers and electronics are tools designed to do something. Technology is a means by which an organization can accomplish some kind of objective.

Easy to Use

Technology is inherently complex. Using technology should not be complicated. Government employees should feel comfortable in navigating and using a computer-based financial management information system or some other computer-based management information system. The general public should feel engaged and even empowered when they interact with an e-government Web service or a government Website. Technology as it is presented to people needs to be easy to use.

Return on Investment

Hundreds of thousands to millions of dollars would be spent on selected IT projects. With any project of this size, senior executive leaders will expect to see a return that matches or exceeds what was originally invested. A long-term capital IT project must be able to show what will be returned once the implemented technology is in operation and providing a service to end users.

Calculating the return on investment (ROI) is fairly easy to do in the private sector. The principal metric by which private companies use is profit. The amount in sales revenue that a private company makes provides the key factor in measuring ROI. As soon as a company has made $1 million in selling its product, for example, it will have achieved a matched return on its cost to build a production factory worth $1 million. Subsequent years of selling the product will bring in more sales revenue, and the accumulated total will demonstrably show an increasingly higher return on that initial $1 million investment. This is a simplified example to show how ROI is generally measured.

Unless a fee is collected to use an IT system, calculating the ROI can be difficult. The use of sales revenue is generally not available. Services that are provided to people are free or set at a very low price. The public sector cannot calculate the ROI in the same way as with the private sector.

The government agency then has to find other factors to measure the ROI. What is it that can be credibly linked to or derived from the provided service? In other words, what is being gained by using the service? A factor that is commonly used is people who have benefited from the service. For example, a number of persons were immunized. A number of persons used a mobile software program. In the context of IT, the public manager needs to examine what is the change that results in using or operating an IT system. Such IT effects directly relate to output efficiency, cost savings, and time savings. For example, a computer-based motor vehicle registration system can reduce the time of registering a vehicle per person by a certain percentage. A higher number of documents can be processed and certified after a computer-based information system has been put into operation.

Whatever gains and benefits that can be derived, the public manager needs to quantify the gains in financial terms. Here is the difficult part and an area that can be contentious. People may not agree on the value applied to a particular benefit. For example, how can a number of persons metric be converted into a monetary amount that everyone will agree? This will entail calculating the value of a human life, and that involves drawing on societal norms and philosophy. In order for a quantified gain to be widely accepted, the methodology must be presented to explain how the gain was calculated. The methodology must be clear and logical, so that others can reproduce the calculation. The resultant value, moreover, should be reasonable. Other public managers and the general public need to be able to follow the logic behind how the gain or social benefit was converted into a monetary amount.

The method that this book uses to calculate the ROI is Net Present Value (NPV), a standard method used to analyze cash flow in accounting. The NPV is the difference between the present value benefits and the present value costs. The cost side of the equation is the calculation of funds going out (i.e., expenses) in a number of future years. The benefit side of the equation is the calculation of funds coming in (i.e., revenues) in a number of future years. The net calculation will show whether the result is a positive amount, a negative amount, or zero for all the future years in the equation. This calculated net value provides an indicator of the return.

Any amount whether it is a cost or a benefit that would be spent or received in a future year needs to be converted in today's terms. Money that is spent or received in the future does not have equal value to money spent or received today. In other words, the use of money in the future is treated differently than if it were used in the present year. Because the future has not happened yet, the future value is worth less than the value in the present. And the future value will increasingly diminish with each year into the future. The present value equations below will show this.

For each year that costs are expended and benefits are received, the public manager needs to calculate the present value of the future amount. The manager then has to add up all of the years' present values to arrive at the total present value. This procedure is carried out one for the benefits and the other for the costs – two present value equations.

$$PVB = \sum_{n=1}^{N} \frac{FBn}{(1+r)^n}$$

$$PVC = \sum_{n=1}^{N} \frac{FCn}{(1+r)^n}$$

where

PVB = Total Present Value of Benefit Amounts in All Years
PVC = Total Present Value of Cost Amounts in All Years
FBn = Future Benefit Amount in Year n
FCn = Future Cost Amount in Year n
N = Total of All Years
n = Year Number (Individual Year)
r = Interest Rate or Discount Rate

With the benefit sside and the cost side calculated, the public manager can finally calculate the NPV.

$$NPV = PVB - PVC$$

Figure 3.10 shows the long-term costs and benefits for developing and operating a computer-based farm inspection information system. In this project, a government agency is considering outsourcing its farm inspection program to a private company. The private company will handle all of the field work necessary to inspect 1 million farm production sites throughout the country, hiring and managing food safety inspectors and agriculture-related specialists. The private company will operate and maintain the system and provide technical support to all end users. The government agency will rely on the IT system to ensure that farmers' operations are in compliance with the national food safety law.

The computer-based farm inspection information system is estimated to cost \$3 million and will be paid for over 3 years at \$1 million per year starting in year 1. Operating the system is estimated to cost \$10 million per year, starting in year 2 and ending in year 10. Half of the estimated operating cost is required to start up the project in the first year. The total costs spread across 10 years will be \$6 million in year 1, \$11 million in years 2 and 3, and \$10 million from years 4 to 10. Figure 3.10 shows the costs for each year.

The government agency is authorized to charge an inspection fee at \$25 per farmer. Farm inspection is required once every 2 years. The government agency can expect to begin using the new system in year 2 with 250,000 farmers. The number of farmers will increase to 1 million in year 4 and will remain at that level every year thereafter, meeting the agency's target goal of inspecting 1 million farms. The total benefits spread across 10 years will be \$6.25 million in year 2 and \$25 million every 2 years in years 4, 6, 8, and 10. Figure 3.10 shows the benefits for each year.

The discount rate in this project is fixed at 6% for all years.

What is the NPV of this project? Should the government agency pursue this project?

By using the present value equations described above, the answer will be

PVB = \$72,634,011.55
PVC = \$71,556,901.33
NPV = \$1,077,110.22

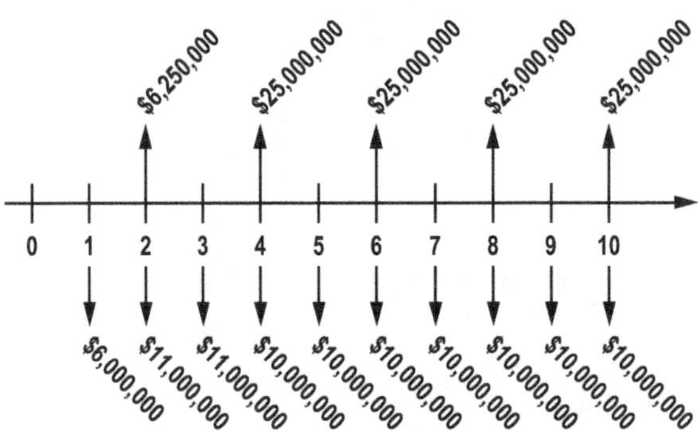

Figure 3.10 Long-term operation of a farm inspection information system. (Use of the timeline and arrows adapted from Peter J. Wilcoxen)

The NPV is a positive value. The total benefits exceed the total costs. As such, this project can be pursued.

As a caveat, the low NPV value may be a concern. In terms of cash flow, the long-term return will be modest. Fees received in the even years will have to be used to cover expenses in the odd years. No benefits are received in the odd years. This project could result in a break-even financial situation. A private investment firm would likely not pursue this project since the return is not substantially large. A high NPV value, however, is not an issue in the public sector. As long as expenses can be covered over several years of continued operation, then the project would still be pursued. The main issue that the public manager needs to avoid is a project whose benefits fall short year after year, leading to a financial situation where the costs cannot be recovered. This would be reflected by a negative NPV value.

A little note about Figure 3.10: It illustrates a cash flow diagram. The numbers along the horizontal line represent years. The timeline always begins with zero. This marker represents today (the current year) or the present value in technical terms. The next marker is year 1, representing the end of the first year. The next marker is year 2, representing the end of the second year. Subsequent markers follow this convention. Upward arrows stemming from any given marker represent cash flowing in. In other words, an upward arrow represents the benefits. Downward arrows stemming from any given marker represent cash flowing out. In other words, a downward arrow represents the costs. Amounts in any years except the zero marker are future amounts.

Now that an equation is found to calculate the ROI, the benefits need to be analyzed and converted into monetary amounts. For each identified benefit factor, the public manager needs to calculate the amount of benefit received before and after a new IT project or IT system is implemented and then calculate the difference between the two scenarios. What will be more important to know is what was the change in implementing an IT project or an IT system.

To do this, the current amount of benefit needs to be known. This is the scenario before the introduction of anything new. For example, the government agency processes registrations at a rate of 1 hour per registration.

After a computer-based information system is deployed, the government agency could process registrations at a rate of 15 minutes (a quarter of an hour) per registration. This future benefit is the scenario after implementing something new.

The Hours per Output result in each scenario needs to be entered into the staffing requirement equation described above to arrive at the Total Working Hours for each scenario. The public manager should bear in mind that the target output may change for each scenario. And then, Total Working Hours in each scenario is converted to a monetary amount by multiplying it with the average hourly wage as previously described.

Finally, the monetary amount of the after scenario is subtracted from the monetary amount of the before scenario. The calculated difference will provide the value to be used in the present value benefit equation. The calculated difference can be a positive amount, a negative amount, or zero. The equation for calculating the difference between the before and after scenarios for each benefit factor is shown below.

$$\Delta S = SB0 - SAn$$

where:

ΔS = Change in Benefit (Difference between Before and After Scenarios)

SB0 = Scenario Benefit Before Implementation

SAn = Scenario Benefit After Implementation in Year n

The foregoing benefit calculation is for one identified benefit factor in 1 year. As the amount of benefit can fluctuate year to year, the public manager would need to run the calculation for each year of a number of years. Also, there can be a number of benefit factors that would have a direct impact on the IT system. The public manager, thus, needs to calculate the amount of benefit for each identified benefit factor. The sum of all benefit amounts identified in a given year will then be the total benefit for that year.

There may be benefit factors that already have monetary amounts, such as in purchases in equipment and supplies. The public manager would want to capture any savings that would result in reducing the costs of resources. In the before scenario, for example, the IT department may be spending $500 in supplies. In the after scenario, this spending on supplies could be reduced to $300. Thus, the calculated difference would be a benefit.

Calculating the total cost for each year is straightforward. Additional cost items that are directly and indirectly related to the IT project or IT system will have to be included. Remember, the amount of an indirect cost resource has to be added in proportion to the project or system. The sum of all cost amounts identified in a given year will be the total cost for that year.

With all cost factors identified and calculated and all benefit factors identified and calculated, the public manager can calculate the NPV.

Chapter 3 Quiz

Question 1: What type of cost factor is it when you can choose to purchase a software program at $100 per user for 1–100 people, $175 per user for 101–200 people, and $285 per user for 201–300 people?

A. Semi-variable Cost
B. Fixed Cost
C. Variable Cost
D. Step-function Cost
E. Both B and C

Question 2: The cost to operate and maintain an IT system is apportioned to contribute to the goals of four public programs. What type of cost factor is this?

A. Fixed Cost
B. Direct Cost
C. Indirect Cost
D. Variable Cost
E. Both A and C

Question 3: After a careful study, you have two options to operate an IT system: You can (1) operate the system internally at a total cost of $25,000 in year 1 and for negligible minor costs in subsequent years, or (2) use an IT provider that will charge a variable rate at $2.90 per hour to operate the system 24 hours per day for 365 days per year in perpetuity. The IT system must operate continuously for 3 years. Which option should be pursued and why?

A. Option 1, because the cost is controlled.
B. Option 2, because the service rate is low and seemingly affordable.
C. Either option 1 or 2, because the cost of a full year is about the same.

Question 4: Money that is planned to be spent 3 years into the future is converted into a value that is equivalent in today's terms. Why is this conversion performed?

A. Present value of money is the reference point by which all money is judged.
B. Future value of money has not been spent yet.
C. The mathematical calculation is worth the time and effort.
D. Future value of money is not worth the same as the present value of money.
E. Future value of money is worth more than the present value of money.

Question 5: What can be used to show benefits and thus a return on investment in a proposed project?

A. Revenue generated from service fees
B. Reduction in hours spent on routine tasks
C. Increased output per person-hours
D. All of the above
E. Only A

Worksheets

Step 1:

Write one specific item (a resource) on a Post-it® note.

Step 2:

Organize written notes on a large board, sorting them in any pattern that makes sense in your operating environment.

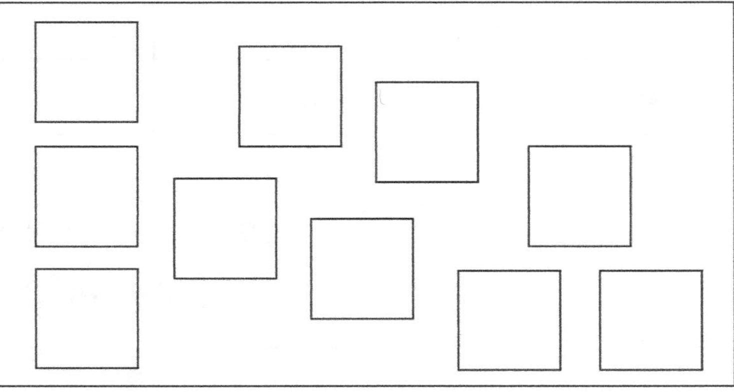

Step 3:

Apply the arrangement of notes to other worksheets.

Worksheet 3.1 Resource arrangement for budgeting exercise.

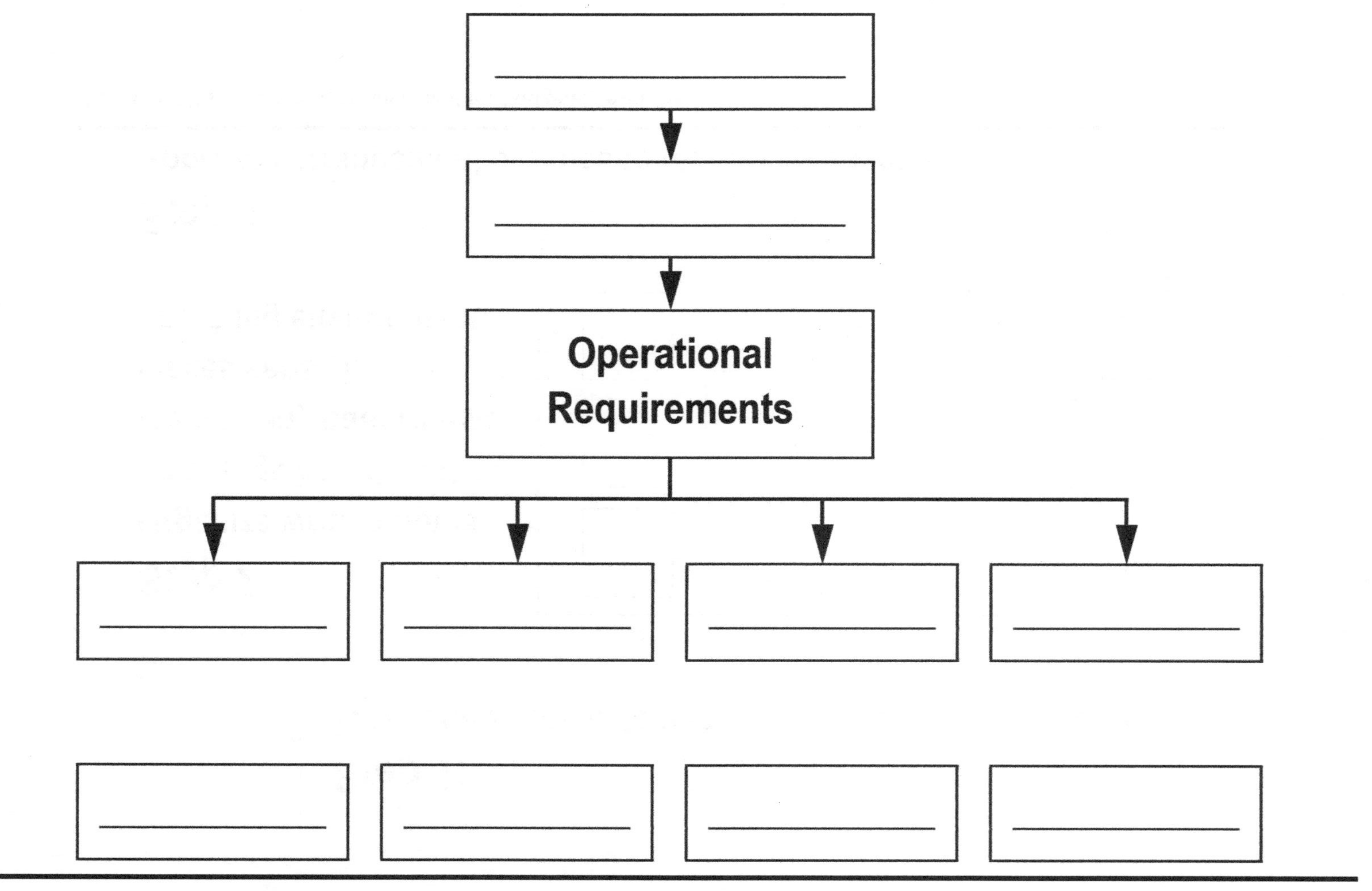

Worksheet 3.2 Goal-to-Cost structure.

Project: ______________________ Manager: ______________________

No.	Description	Indirect %	Fixed	Variable	Total

Estimated Total Cost:

Worksheet 3.3 Cost analysis.

Project: ____________________ **Manager:** ____________________

Account No.	Description	Estimated	Actual	Difference
	Total:			

Project Limit: ____________

Worksheet 3.4 Project budget.

Fiscal Year 20___ ___ Revenue ___ Expenditure

Account No.	Description	Month: ___	Total	Average
	Total:			

Budget Limit: ______________ Surplus (Deficit): ______________

Worksheet 3.5 Fiscal year, annual budget.

Fiscal Years 20___ to 20___ ___ Revenue ___ Expenditure

Account No.	Description	FY 20___	Total	Average
	Total Future Amount:			
	Year Number:			
	Discount Rate:			
	Total Present Value:			

Funding Request: ______________ **Net Present Value:** ______________

Worksheet 3.6 Several years of budget planning.

Chapter 4

IT System Selection: Moving Past Hype and Brand

The words, "innovation" and "transformation", are in vogue today and have been used to promote many things in recent years. Is that program boasted by a government contractor really transformative that it completely changes the status quo? Is that system so innovative, so new, that it creates a whole new category for doing things or that it sets itself apart from the rest?

Chapter Summary

Public managers should be cautious when they hear that a product is innovative. They should be very suspicious when a proposed program claims to transform a certain aspect of society. The way in which a product or a program is designed and used will reveal whether it is truly innovative or transformative. A new solution does not need to be labeled as such. The innovation will show itself in the product or program.

Government agencies and nonprofit organizations tend to be risk-adverse – and for good reason. Whatever new solution is implemented, the effect should not make the situation worse. Since public programs are designed to help people, the lives of people could be harmed by a program intervention. Any program whether or not an Information Technology (IT) component is a part needs to be carefully planned. Given the potential for improvement in efficiency, an IT system needs to be examined with a higher degree of scrutiny. The increases in speed through which automation, in general, and decisions, in particular, can be made by the computer could lead to a haphazard or biased output that would otherwise might have been prevented through a human-based decision-making process. An IT system can certainly do good, but it can potentially do ill.

This chapter describes the importance of selecting the right technologies that will best meet organizational needs as opposed to using what is popular or fashionable. This chapter explains how the manager should examine particular systems and processes with a critical eye. How much of the business process should be automated? Are there specific decision points that ought to be left for a person to make? This chapter further describes the process of selecting, controlling, and evaluating IT projects. Budgeting work from the previous chapter is applied to determine whether or not an IT project should be pursued. This chapter provides some practice to calculate benefits and costs. This chapter concludes with the development of a business case with the factor for social equity.

"The Right System" versus "A Popular System"

An IT system that has lots of people using it or has many likes in the consumer ratings does not mean that you should use it too. Along a similar vein, a company that is simply known for its marketing brand name does not mean that you have to buy and use the company's product. Popularity should not be the primary criterion for selecting an IT system. A popular IT system may not have any bearing on the specificity of needs and requirements inherent to a particular organization. In other words, an IT system that is popular and touted may not work in the government agency that has a unique mission to fulfill.

Implementing a system simply because it is popular and that it may not be aligned with needs or even fit properly with existing programs will add overhead that has to be managed. It could create new issues – especially security issues – that will have to be resolved. The public manager could realize that the popular system does not fit after all and then must spend extra money to procure another system.

The public manager needs to find the right IT system that matches their organization's requirements and operating environment. Underneath the popular system or well-known brand is a technological element that could be similar or identical to another lesser known system. This lesser known system would accomplish the same functions and may be priced lower than its popular, competing product. A database software program is an example. Different IT companies provide a database software package with more or less the same functions. Although each IT provider would have a particular programming syntax to organize data, all of the database packages would be following the same standard known as Structured Query Language (SQL). Specific IT personnel would need to be hired to manage a particular IT provider's database package, although existing technical staff could quickly learn through professional development.

An organization's operating environment can be unique or homogenous that the introduction of a popular system may be problematic. An organization may operate with all Microsoft products, and the deployment of an Oracle database may not perform well in that Microsoft environment. In the past, IT managers cringed at the thought of connecting Apple computers to the enterprise computer network because of the additional work needed to support the different software operating system and to back up and restore data from Apple's unique file system. This is not to say that an environment with different systems should be prohibited. A heterogenous environment with varied IT systems can operate fine. But the addition of a new system with unique or particular functions brings in new issues that leaders must be aware of. At the very least, all of the different systems must be coordinated.

The main point is for the public manager to step back from the craze of jumping too soon into accepting a new IT system. The manager's decision should be sober and deliberate. Chapter 1 described the elements that can be used to evaluate competing products and services on how each one compares against the other. Once a decision is made, the new IT system will have to operate for several years. The public manager will want to be certain that the IT system is the right one for their organization.

Stand-alone versus Integration

Should an IT system be integrated with existing systems or should it operate separately as a stand-alone system?

There can be cases where stand-alone systems are warranted. Because of its unique mission, the government agency will need a highly specialized IT system. An agency focused on environmental protection, for example, will need a very different system from one that another agency that provides health services will need. Information security can be an overriding concern that dictates certain IT systems must be kept separate in another computer network. Public Websites that exchange information with the general public and external organizations will need to operate separately from the government's internal network. The computer network itself may need to operate as a completely separate network.

In areas where services have to reach multiple departments across the agency or where numerous employees spread throughout the agency are involved, integrated IT systems would be preferred. A user management system is an example that allows for all employees to log in to the internal network and access shared agency resources. Administrative functions standard to any organization such as financial management, human resources, and inventory management provide cases for an integrated system. The government agency will need to ensure that records related to finances, human resources, equipment, and supplies are consistent from all departments. Stand-alone financial systems deployed separately in every department could create problems in reconciling accounts.

In general, an integrated IT system provides a higher level of efficiency for an organization to manage administrative functions. There will be special cases where an organization needs stand-alone IT systems. But a stand-alone system is an exception and not the rule. Regardless of whether an IT system is integrated or stand-alone, all systems must still be managed. Having too many stand-alone systems can place excessive burden on IT personnel to manage. It could create additional pathways in which security issues could find their way to exploit. While a stand-alone system can meet very specific needs that an integrated system cannot, a stand-alone IT system adds another layer of overhead.

Senior executive leaders would want to draw the line on what needs to be integrated and what can be left as stand-alone, finding the right mix of both types of systems. This would be done in strategic planning where public managers discuss their needs and requirements and work toward finding commonalities on where needs and interests are shared. Through these shared interests, an integrated IT system can be identified. The IT Strategic Plan will describe all possible IT systems – integrated and stand-alone – that will be implemented along with approaches and solutions for management and operation.

Business Process Analysis for Automation/Programming

A major part of selecting the right system and determining whether to implement a stand-alone or integrated system involves a review of the business process. Any complex work from an administrative function to a highly specialized field has a series of steps to follow. The steps consisting of tasks, decisions, and documents form a path by which teams use to accomplish a certain program. This business process would have a main path where most activities flow. At a number of decision points, the main path can split into different directions. Some would loop back to the main path. Others would create an alternate, secondary path. Figure 4.1 provides a simple and generic example of a business process that encompasses a main path, a loop back, and an alternate path.

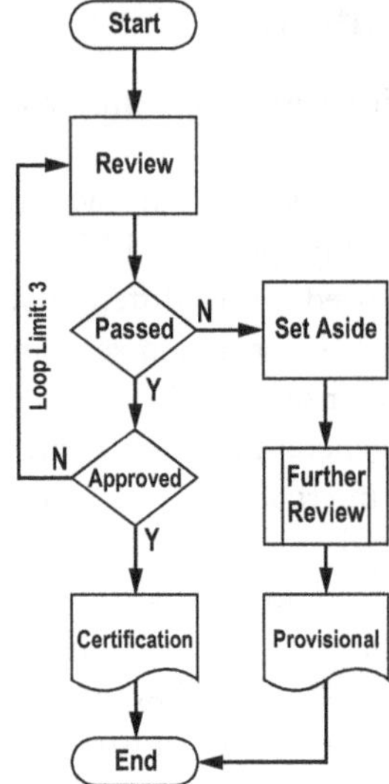

Figure 4.1 Business process example.

It is critical to note that the layout of the flowchart needs to be straight and even as possible so as to allow any reader to follow the flow. The flowchart provides a visual diagram in which the reader's eye should easily move through the steps in a straight line. Any change in direction should be at a 90° angle. Steps that are uneven, placed at various angles, and/or arbitrarily set create clutter and a visual eyesore that defeat the purpose of communicating the intent and purpose of the business process. The business process flowchart must be clear and easy to read.

The shapes used in the flowchart are standardized so that the Business Analyst, Systems Analyst, and others can understand. The five major shapes commonly used are described in the following.

Elongated Oval

The elongated oval shape represents a terminator that ends a process. It can also be used to show where the process starts (Figure 4.2).

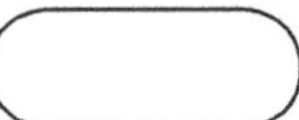

Figure 4.2 Terminator symbol shape.

Empty Rectangle

The empty rectangle shape represents a specific task that is performed. This is the most common and widely used shape in the process, since there will be a series of tasks to be performed (Figure 4.3).

Figure 4.3 Task symbol shape.

Rectangle with Narrow Divided Sections

The modified rectangle with narrow divided sections shape represents a predefined process that refers to another process or a sub process. This may be a number of specific tasks grouped together to provide coherence for a sub process. In a certain case, it may not be relevant to show all the tasks of a particular group. Moreover, the inclusion of too many tasks can make the process look cluttered and difficult to read. The placement of the predefined process shape would be a reference to another flowchart, which is displayed on another page (Figure 4.4).

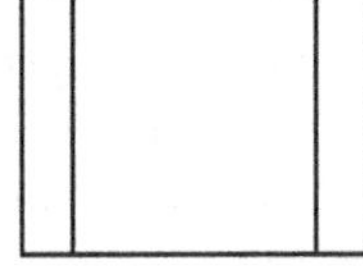

Figure 4.4 Predefined process symbol shape.

Rectangle with Curved Bottom

The rectangle with curved bottom shape represents a document that is involved in the process. This could be a form, a certificate, a report, or some other kind of document that is collected, reviewed, inputted, or outputted. The document shape shows where evidence or artifacts will be found along the process (Figure 4.5).

Figure 4.5 Document symbol shape.

Diamond

The diamond shape represents a decision that is made in the process. This particular shape can have an alternate path that splits off from the main path. A commonly used decision question is yes or no. The notation of a yes or no decision would be abbreviated as Y or N, respectively. The specific answer will lead to a different path. Unlike the other shapes, the diamond shape is the one that technically can have more than one arrow that points outward, leading to more than one path (Figure 4.6).

There are more shapes that can be used in a process flowchart, but the foregoing five shapes are the most important for everyone to understand. The shapes are connected together by arrows that lead from one shape to the next. All of the shapes except for the diamond shape have one path that

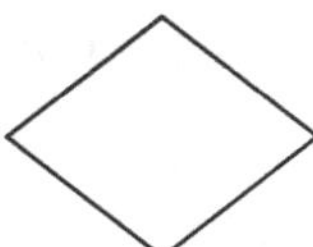

Figure 4.6 Decision symbol shape.

flows through. In a particular circumstance, another arrow may go directly *in* toward a rectangle shape. A typical example is a loop in the process. This rectangle shape shows an arrow *pointing in*, not pointing out. A diamond shape, on the other hand, shows at least two arrows *pointing out*.

With the business process documented, the public manager can analyze areas for improvement. Does one section seem like there are too many tasks? Could it operate better with a few steps eliminated? Does another section have not enough steps? Could a particular area use a decision step? Should the process require more or less documents? These are just some of the questions that the public manager will ask to make the business process more effective or efficient.

The public manager can further analyze areas for integration. The business processes of two or more functional domains can be reviewed. As the manager goes through the flowchart of each one, the public manager may see similar or identical steps. The multiple domains may flow to the same document. Similar or identical steps shared by different functional domains could be an area for integration. If more and more sections of the processes are found to be identical, the public manager may want to consider combining the functional domains' business processes. Depending on the number of shared steps, the scope of integration can be very small to full coverage. In terms of IT, the scope can be as small as a data exchange interface or as large as folding one functional domain into another.

Specific to an IT system, analyzing the business process becomes critical to knowing which areas need to be and can be automated or programmed in the computer. Current technology may not be capable of automating the entire flow of a business process from start to end. If it could, implementation would likely be costly, consume a lot of time, and involve many people, some of whom will no doubt push back against any such effort. Given available technologies and resources, non-IT personnel should consult with IT personnel to understand what can and cannot be programmed in the computer. IT personnel can and should provide assistance in analyzing the technical feasibility of automating the business process. The public manager can then prioritize sections of the business process for automation and programming. Through an iterative method of software development, each section could be planned in a schedule for development and release in a future software version.

Certain areas in the business process may be undesirable for allowing the computer to do the work. In other words, there may be specific steps that should be left alone for a human to carry out. There can be a major decision that only a human can make. And in the context of a public program, a major decision can have ramifications that affect a large population of people to whom the program is intended to serve or protect. There can be work-related activities and documents that would need to be verified and corroborated by another team or by a third-party investigator or auditor. In this instance, a human is needed to review what had been inputted and to provide confirmation in a verifiable way that the necessary check had been made. It is perfectly fine (and in some cases necessary) to have parts of the business process in a manual form.

A thorough analysis of the business process will allow the public manager to see what can be automated, what needs to be left manual, and where there are points for integration. This information can aid in selecting the right IT system.

Management of Selection and Control

Selecting, controlling, and generally implementing IT projects requires three broad groups of experts: management experts, technical experts, and end-user experts. Each group brings deep knowledge from their vantage point to contribute to IT selection and implementation. Based on the provided advice, guidance, and feedback, all of the groups can be considered experts in their own right. As will be further described in Chapter 6, all of the groups have a role to play in the design of an IT system. Management experts (both non-IT and IT leaders and managers) contribute at the higher level of project implementation through selection, control, and evaluation. This means reviewing and analyzing technical solutions so that they are linked to, aligned with, and in accordance with strategic plans, capital investments, maturity models, IT architectural frameworks, and organizational policies. Technical experts (IT personnel) contribute at the lower level of project implementation through design, development, and operation. This means defining the technical requirements based on understanding the objectives and goals provided by the management experts and gathering needed information from the end-user experts. End-user experts (users who understand how specific functions work with or without a computer) contribute to ensure that the deployed IT system works as designed for them. This means submitting input and feedback to and sharing information with the management experts and the technical experts on how an IT system is to be used, how specific functions are to be navigated, and how activities are to flow properly from start to end in a business process. All three groups provide information for each other to learn and apply.

Communication between the three groups is essential to ensure that an IT system is selected and implemented in accordance with everyone's respective knowledge area. The management group takes the lead in overseeing discussions, facilitating the communication process among various teams and reconciling differing views of opinions. Management experts must be able to say no or make a rejection when a certain part does not comply or is not aligned with an agreed-upon policy or strategy. The management group, overall, has the responsibility to ensure that an IT system and all related work that make up an IT project are carefully selected and controlled.

Proper control of an IT project goes through the following four phases (Figure 4.7):

1. Project Pre-Selection
2. Project Selection
3. Project Control
4. Project Evaluation

Project Pre-Selection

The Project Pre-Selection phase establishes the policies and criteria for deciding on what IT projects will be implemented. In this phase, a discipline is created to ensure that the public manager only spends funds on projects that meet established policies. The policies need to reflect the organization's goals and priorities, which in turn should achieve the wider mission. As this part starts the process of engaging with IT personnel, guardrails must be in place to provide guidance in how IT projects are to be funded and accepted. The following rules and process need to be clearly described and communicated to all personnel:

1. Definition and Composition of an IT Project
2. Funding Requirements

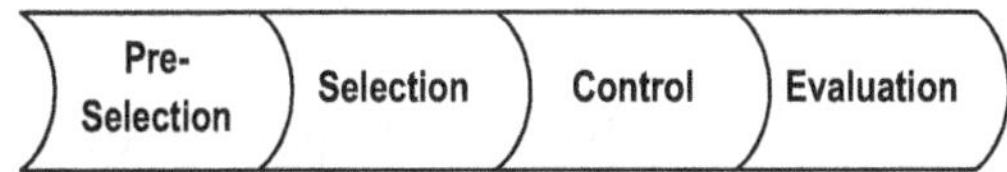

Figure 4.7 Project control process.

3. Business Process Requirements
4. Financial Metrics and Thresholds
5. Qualitative Factors
6. Risk Assessment
7. Screening Criteria
8. Screening Process
9. Allowable Exceptions

Definition and Composition of an IT Project

How is an IT project to be defined? What must be included in an IT project? This rule must stipulate how an IT project will be implemented in terms of human resources (i.e., roles and responsibilities of key personnel) – not just in regard to technological resources.

Funding Requirements

What must an IT project have in order to be funded?

Business Process Requirements

What requirements or guidelines must an IT project follow when automating or programming a part or the whole of a business process?

Financial Metrics and Thresholds

What are the financial metrics (e.g., return on investment value and cost-benefit ratio) that an IT project will be measured by? The values of the metrics must be specified.

Qualitative Factors

What are the qualitative factors (e.g., system outage, failure rate, and ease-of-use) that an IT project will be evaluated or measured by? Methods for how such factors need to be quantified should be provided. In any case, it must be clear how qualitative factors will be evaluated.

Risk Assessment

What is the level of risk that will be acceptable for an IT project? Are there different levels of risk and what are the risk levels based on the composition of an IT project? The definition of the risk scale and the risk assessment methodology need to be clearly described.

Screening Criteria

How will an IT project be judged and selected? Are the requirements evaluated on a weighted scale? Who will evaluate an IT project and what are their roles and responsibilities?

Screening Process

What is the process of screening an IT project from first being introduced to making a final decision? How long will the process take? Is there a set schedule?

Allowable Exceptions

What can be tolerated in the case that certain requirements are missing or inadequate? The policy must clearly describe when such exceptions are permitted and how they will be managed and handled. Any exception to be allowed needs to be adequately justified.

Project Selection

The Project Selection phase evaluates IT projects in accordance with established policies, procedures, and criteria. This phase executes the screening process. By this time, there should be a small number of projects that will go through the screening process. The majority of projects would have been weeded out in the Pre-Selection phase, as project teams would have done their own evaluation and decided on whether or not to develop a full project proposal. Acceptable IT projects must follow the rules described above, meeting specified requirements, thresholds, and risk level. Any IT project that does not comply with established policies and criteria will be screened out (rejected).

Accepting and rejecting IT projects should be transparent and fair. Wherever possible, criteria including qualitative factors should be quantified. All of the projects should be listed in a spreadsheet and scored based on the criteria. IT projects can then be ranked from those that meet all requirements to those that are least compliant. The top five or ten projects would then be selected for implementation. For all other projects that do not satisfy established policies, project teams will know which areas are inadequate and can rework their proposals for another review.

Project Control

The Project Control phase runs in parallel with the System Development Life Cycle process (see Figure 6.1), which will be described in Chapter 6. During this phase, a selected IT project is being implemented. Periodic monitoring is conducted to ensure that the project is developed according to specifications, scheduling, and budget. Actual costs are recorded and reviewed against what was initially estimated. The actual dates and times that activities start and end are also recorded and reviewed against the estimated schedule. Differences in schedule and budget are analyzed and reported, the information of which can be used to evaluate future projects. Any issue, unexpected, technical, or otherwise, is reported and followed up on for resolution. The risk assessment is reviewed and adjusted accordingly with the introduction of new issues and risks. An updated level of risk may be made based on a subsequent risk assessment review. The overall status of the IT project is monitored and updated based on all reviews and reports.

One or more evaluations will be conducted to assess the technical performance of the IT project and delivery of project outputs. An evaluation may be conducted by the internal management experts, the agency's auditor, or a third-party independent evaluator. If involved, a contractor would be evaluated in accordance with the provisions of their contract. In any case, all activities related to the project that had been carried out are reviewed, analyzing the level of quality, level of output, and any change or deviation from the original proposal. When available at the earliest possible time, actual outcomes and metrics are recorded and reviewed against what was initially measured or estimated. Differences in outcomes and metrics are reported.

Monitoring and evaluation will provide information to follow the progress of the selected IT project as it is implemented. Comparing the actuals and the estimates will indicate changes and by how much change. The management experts can then effectively control the IT project. If differences become too wide, the project may need to be amended. If issues have arisen that cannot be resolved, halting or terminating the project may be warranted.

Project Evaluation

The Project Evaluation phase concludes the process, providing a fair evaluation of a selected IT project as it is now finished. The management experts will want to know what is the result. Is the completed IT system working as intended and designed? Would further changes or modifications be necessary? What is the status of the IT system (e.g., operational, put aside, or discarded)? If failed, what happened and why?

In addition to technical questions, the management experts would want to ask business questions about the concluded IT project. Did the business assumptions hold up as valid for justifying the project? If not, how should those assumptions be revised? Did the project effectively meet the objectives and goals? Are the objectives still valid? If not, how should the objectives be revised?

This final phase would provide a period of time to reflect on the success or failure of the IT project. With regard to project failure, the management experts will want to know what can be improved to evaluate future IT projects. Was it the project itself that caused failure or was it the objective that drove failure? An objective overly broad and ambitious may have been the cause. A thorough evaluation would identify the cause-and-effect relationship. Feedback about the completed project will inform the management experts to make any needed changes and to revise established policies and criteria accordingly.

Cost-Benefit Analysis

A standard method for analyzing a public program or an IT system is to conduct a cost-benefit analysis. Another term that is used is "benefit-cost" analysis. Both terms, cost-benefit and benefit-cost, refer to the same standard. This method presents the costs, the benefits, and equity impacts of a public program or an IT system in a clear and efficient manner that facilitates project selection.

While the narrative part of the proposed solution provides the details, the cost-benefit part offers a concise summary of essential values that can be quickly viewed and easily judged. The cost-benefit of one system can be compared against other systems and alternative solutions. If a question arises about a particular value or there is a concern regarding an included factor, the public manager can refer to the narrative for an explanation. If conducted properly, the cost-benefit analysis provides a high degree of objectivity. While the narrative could reveal internal bias in the way the text is written, the cost-benefit part would not have the same level of internal bias. The calculated amounts in a cost-benefit analysis can be checked and verified by other analysts, if the methodology behind the analysis is described in a transparent manner.

There has been criticism on the use and abuse of cost-benefit analysis, particularly in the social sciences field. Chapter 3 highlighted the problem and has put forth a method for calculating benefits. It cannot be emphasized enough that much of the debate about questionable numbers that spark controversy revolves around the underlining analytical methodology. How did the analyst arrive at that figure? What information was used to calculate the number? If the methodology were laid out for others to follow, other analysts and external reviewers can understand the context, follow the logic, and try to replicate the calculation to arrive at a similar result. With no methodology included, the calculated values would not have a foundation of support and backing to prove the numbers.

Development and execution of a sound analytical methodology require established procedures and skilled persons. The public manager who conducts the analysis needs to have an aptitude for quantitative analysis, qualitative analysis, or both forms of analyses. Strong knowledge and practice in statistics, microeconomics, and research methods are essential. Additional knowledge in econometrics and advanced mathematics would be beneficial. The public manager needs to have skills in data management, if the person will be processing hundreds or thousands of records. The analyst must have an understanding of information management to be able to sort through documents and synthesize different and varied parts of information. The manner in which information and data are collected, stored, handled, and reviewed must be formalized in a set of procedures and protocols. The established procedures for data collection and data analysis must be followed consistently for accurate reporting of results. Safeguards must be in place to control and minimize various kinds of biases and to distinguish between credible sources of information and false or faulty data. All of the tools (e.g., a survey instrument, a statistical software program, and a mathematical formula) must be designed and used according to established procedures.

Chapter 3 described the methods for identifying and calculating the costs and benefits. One thing that the public manager must remember is that all amounts need to be shown in present value terms. The calculation will involve a number of years in which the IT system will be implemented, operated, and used. This means estimating the costs and benefits of future years and converting the future amounts into present values. The total benefit amount will be shown along with a breakdown of individual benefit factors. The total cost amount will also be shown along with a breakdown of individual cost resources.

An additional cost is the inclusion of equity impacts. This makes the public sector distinctly different from the private sector. The public manager must identify any potential concern or issue that could create a loss for or otherwise harm a certain population or a natural resource. A public program, in general, could displace a local community or cause a change to the environment that would not be beneficial to society. A hydroelectric public works project, for instance, forces many families to relocate elsewhere, as their present location will be flooded and filled up with water when the dam is constructed. An IT system could negatively affect a certain population. The implementation of new telecommunication infrastructure could disrupt the lives of people who reside in the area. New infrastructure such as fiber-optic cables and radio towers would go through land that may not be owned by the government. Private businesses that operate in the path of planned infrastructure could lose revenues as construction would disrupt or limit commerce. The implementation of electronic record keeping raises a personal privacy concern that could prevent certain groups such as people with disabilities, people with a bankruptcy record, and people with a criminal record from gaining employment or obtaining housing. Disclosures of personally confidential information whether accidental or intentional can harm persons who are the subject of the disclosures. In all of these examples of equity impacts, the affected groups would have to be compensated for their loss, damage, or harm.

The cost of an equity impact could vary depending on the particular concern or issue identified. The public manager in cooperation with management experts and attorneys will have to evaluate and select the appropriate remedy. There may be a law that provides a specific remedy. One remedy may be a one-time fixed amount provided to each person or household affected by the impact. Another remedy may be a number of lump sum amounts disbursed periodically over a specified time limit to assist each affected household in the transition of the change that results in the project. Another remedy may be to pay out an agreed award amount to a claimant who files a legal claim for a harm that was caused. In addition to the amount paid to citizens, other costs that will involve administering the remedy must be included. For instance, personnel will be needed to review cases and claims. There would be time and labor to investigate every case. There may be legal costs. There may be a cost for distributing the payments. The public manager has to calculate all possible costs that will be involved in correcting each identified equity impact.

The following method should be applied for each IT system:

1. State the objective to be achieved. (This will be previously agreed upon in the IT Strategic Plan.)
2. Establish business assumptions.
3. Develop the analytical methodology.
4. Identify all possible benefits.
5. Quantify and calculate all possible benefits and convert into present values.
6. Identify all possible costs.
7. Calculate all possible costs and convert into present values.
8. Identify all possible equity impacts.
9. Calculate the costs of all possible equity impacts and convert into present values.
10. Calculate the difference of the costs and benefits, using Net Present Value.
11. Evaluate the identified benefits, costs, and equity impacts in relation to the stated objective.
12. Return to the second step and repeat the steps, making any revisions as needed.

Steps 2 through 11 should be repeated a number of times. Conducting a cost-benefit analysis only once is like the first draft of a written document. The first attempt could be filled with errors and faulty items. The public manager should consider the first few iterations as generating ideas. As the analysis is evaluated several times, all the factors and calculations would be clearer and tighter, resulting in a more persuasive argument for why the IT system should be implemented.

The result of the analysis should be displayed in a table format that lists the benefits, costs, and equity impacts along with the respective calculated values. Worksheet 4.5 provides a template to use. Separating the equity impacts from the general costs will highlight what would be the concerns that senior executive leaders need to be aware of. The calculated difference should be shown in the table. The cost-benefit table should be kept to a few pages, if not in one page. The factors, calculations, assumptions, methodology, and other details related to the cost-benefit analysis need to be described and explained in a longer narrative. The cost-benefit narrative and table would be parts of the IT project proposal.

In addition to conducting the analysis on the proposed IT system, a cost-benefit analysis should be done on the *status quo* and on a number of alternative solutions. How does the proposed system compare to other similar systems? What is the effect of *not implementing* the new system? In other words, what are the costs and benefits of maintaining the current system? The results of the *status quo* and alternative solutions can be included and used to illustrate how the new IT system stands up against the alternatives.

Full-Scale Deployment versus Pilot Deployment

The result of the cost-benefit analysis could reveal that the benefits are not enough to select the IT system. Implementation may be too disruptive or highly risky, especially for the government agency or a large organization with thousands of employees and numerous office locations. An approach to overcome this challenge and to make the IT project more attractive is to scale down the effort to a smaller project. Instead of deploying the IT system at full-scale immediately, the IT system can be deployed as a pilot first. Senior executive leaders would be able to see how the system operates at a smaller scale without having to spend the full cost. Management experts would be able to collect sample data on the system's true value in a real-world setting. Technical experts would be able to have a live production system in existence to conduct real-world test scenarios as opposed to a development, hypothetical system where simulated tests would be produced. End-user experts would be able try out the functions and submit feedback to the management and technical experts. If the pilot system proves successful, then the full-scale version can be implemented.

To ensure that the pilot IT system reflects its full-scale version, the pilot IT system must be reconfigured so that all of its components and features can demonstrate the capabilities of its full-size model. It is not sufficient to create a system with only a few features that capture a part of the full system. That is not a true pilot system. Designing the pilot system is similar in theory to designing a sample frame to capture the average of the larger population. The pilot IT system needs to represent the full-scale system at a smaller size. A full-scale IT system, for instance, would be operable in all office locations to provide a specific service to all end users throughout the country. A pilot IT system would be a reconfiguration to operate in a few strategic locations, providing the same service to a selected group of end users. End users could be randomly selected to use the pilot IT system. The public manager would adjust the original project budget, reducing the time, schedule, and costs necessary to produce a smaller system in scale.

Business Case with Social Equity

After the analysis has completed, the public manager should present a summary to senior executive leaders and other key decision-makers. A business case is a standard document for proposing a technology-related project. It lays out the case for why the IT system is needed. The business case document provides a succinct description of what the system is, will do, and will achieve. The document states an estimated total cost of the project along with how much is needed to spend immediately, significant cost resources involved, an estimated return on investment, and major benefits to substantiate the return. The document outlines the implications of what may happen if the project is implemented or not implemented. Decision-makers would want to know if anything could happen when the project is rejected. For example, the current IT system, if left unchanged, could be vulnerable to new forms of security attacks. The business case further describes the risks and uncertainties in the IT project.

The principal aim is to explain what will be improved in terms of changing the way the government agency operates. The proposed IT system must do something to have an effect on business operations. What part of the business or more specifically which areas of the business process will be involved? The business case needs to describe an existing business problem. For example, the current registration process takes too long, making it a hassle for private business owners. Several reports from the Inspector General's office had revealed that persons can subvert the government agency's main process to create fake documents for products that have not been tested for sale and consumption. The business case then links the proposed IT system to the business problem, describing how the technology will solve the problem. For example, a computer-based information system will reduce the time and data entry errors in the registration process, since government employees will be able to review previously submitted data instead of entering the same data over and over again. In another example, the proposed IT system outputs a unique certified document that cannot be reproduced and enforces tightened measures and controls to verify and document the person who submits information, the person who reviews information, the person who approves the certification, and the product that is the subject of certification. By linking the proposed IT system to the business problem, decision-makers will be able to see the organizational value of the technological solution. In other words, senior executive leaders will see the technology's worth to the organization through non-financial, intangible rewards.

For proposing an IT system in the public sector, a description of social equity needs to be included in the business case. The public manager will have examined the equity impacts in the cost-benefit analysis. All of those impacts need to be briefly highlighted, stating the costs to provide remedies to correct the situations. The implemented IT system, especially a large-scale IT infrastructure project, could displace local communities. Decision-makers need to be aware of any kind of displacement or social change that may have a negative impact. The proposed IT system will not only have a financial cost, but there may also be a societal cost.

The business case document should include the following parts written for non-IT personnel in general and senior executive leaders in particular:

1. Executive Summary
2. Description of the IT System
3. Restatement of the Objective
4. Description of the Business Problem
5. Description of the Affected Business Operation and/or Business Process
6. Description of Improvements to the Affected Business Areas
7. List of Key Financial Metrics:
   a. Total Cost
   b. Immediate Cost
   c. Return on Investment Value
8. List of Major Benefits
9. List of Significant Cost Resources
10. Long-term Costs

11. Risks and Uncertainties
12. Implications of Project Implementation
13. Implications of Not Implementing (Project Rejection)
14. List of Equity Impacts
15. Description of Remedies and Costs to Correct the Equity Impacts

Chapter 4 Quiz

Question 1: You analyzed a finance business process, an HR business process, an inspection business process, and two project management (PM) business processes, and conclude that the two PM processes are nearly identical and all of the processes share a small segment in common related to payments. What should you do next?

A. Do nothing.
B. Analyze further on the shared segment found.
C. Consolidate the two PM processes as one process.
D. Design a larger flowchart diagram that shows the connection of the shared segment with all processes and a consolidation of the two PM processes.
E. Both B and D

Question 2: You analyzed a long business process and found that there are two critical decisions (one at the start and the other at the end) that if they are not made carefully could result in a negative outcome. What should you do?

A. Do nothing.
B. The decisions can be dropped or ignored, since the computer can be programmed to make those decisions.
C. Go ahead and plan to automate the entire business process.
D. Plan to automate the middle portion of the process and leave the ends of the process for a human decision-maker.
E. Break up the lengthy process into three separate processes.

Question 3: Why should equity impacts be analyzed and included in a cost-benefit analysis?

A. The inclusion of equity impacts is optional.
B. Any negative implications that may result from a proposed project need to be identified.
C. Equity impacts could raise the costs higher.
D. Equity impacts are hidden costs that would eventually reveal themselves in the course of project implementation.
E. All of the above except A.

Question 4: Your IT system is not selected, but you feel confident that it should be implemented. What should you do next?

A. Accept the rejection and move on.
B. Propose a pilot project of the IT system.
C. Submit the proposal to the decision-makers' supervisors, overriding the rejection.
D. Scale down the project proportionately (the budget, the scope of work, the scheduling, the components, and the roll-out) to 35% of size and propose this scaled-down version as a pilot project.
E. Change the configuration of the IT system and submit a new proposal.

Question 5: What needs to be included in the business case?

A. Implications of Not Implementing
B. Long-term Costs
C. Affected Business Process
D. Total Cost, Immediate Cost, and Return on Investment Value
E. All of the above.

Worksheets

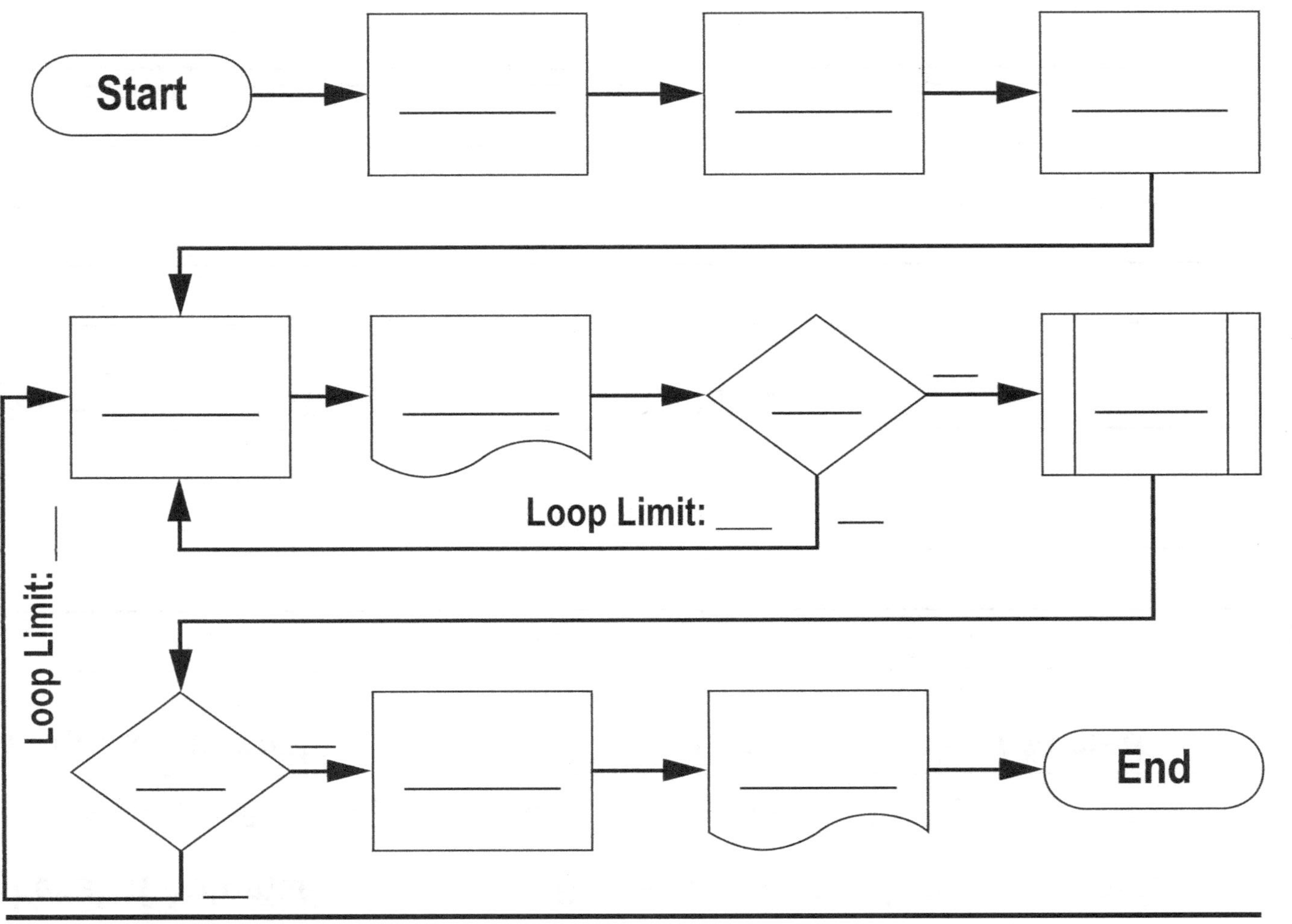

Worksheet 4.1 Business process flowchart.

Business Process: ______________ In Department: _________________

Level of Automation: __ Entire Process __ Partial Process __ None

Impact (On Failure): __ Severe __ High __ Moderate __ Low __ None

Area(s) to Automate	Critical Decision(s), Affected
____________________ ____________________ ____________________ ____________________	____________________ ____________________ ____________________ ____________________
Risk(s)	**Liability**
____________________ ____________________ ____________________ ____________________	____________________ ____________________ ____________________ ____________________

Worksheet 4.2 Business process analysis for automation.

IT System: ____________________ Vendor/Provider: ______________

Class: __ Commercial Product __ Contracted Build __ Internal Build

Key Feature(s)	Strength(s)
______________________________	______________________________
______________________________	______________________________
______________________________	______________________________
______________________________	______________________________
______________________________	______________________________
Weakness(es)	**Risk(s)**
______________________________	______________________________
______________________________	______________________________
______________________________	______________________________
______________________________	______________________________
______________________________	______________________________

Worksheet 4.3 **IT system strength and weakness.**

Step 1:

Write one item (a vendor's product) on a Post-it® note.

Step 2:

Organize written notes on a large board, sorting them in any pattern that makes sense in your operating environment.

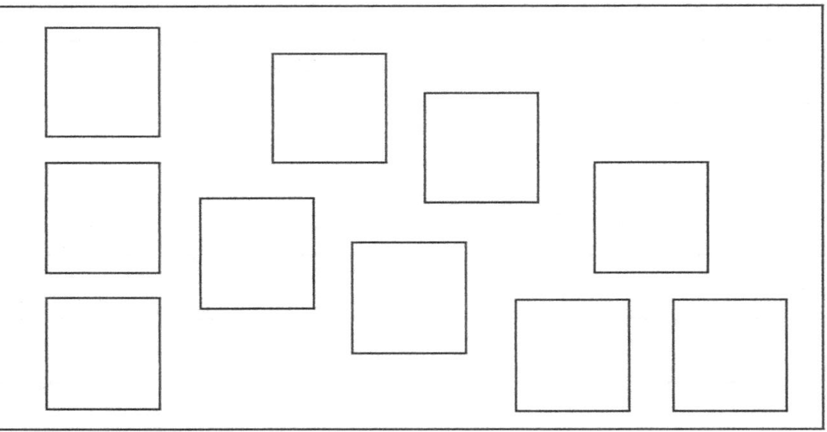

Step 3:

Apply the arrangement of notes to other worksheets.

Worksheet 4.4 Vendor brand arrangement exercise.

Project: ____________________ ___ Benefit ___ Cost ___ Equity Impact

ID	Description	Value	Method
	Total:		

Net Benefit: ____________

Worksheet 4.5 Cost-benefit analysis table.

Project: ____________ In Department: ____________

Objective: ____________ Improvement: ____________

Total Cost: ________ Immediate Cost: ________ ROI Value: ________

Major Benefit(s)	Significant Cost Resource(s)
____________	____________
____________	____________
____________	____________
____________	____________
Implication(s)	**Equity Impact(s)**
____________	____________
____________	____________
____________	____________
____________	____________

Worksheet 4.6 Business case.

Chapter 5

IT Contracting and Outsourcing: Achieving Maximum Value from Vendors

After 5 years, the contractor has reached the end of the performance period of the contract and has finally delivered the Information Technology (IT) system for deployment throughout the agency.

Department Director says: "The software is terrific! What are other people saying?"
Contracting Officer's Technical Representative (COTR) says: "We haven't rolled it out yet."
Director says: "Oh."
COTR says: "That'll be in the next phase."
Director rebuffs: "Next phase? It should be in all departments already."
COTR says: "We don't have any more funds."
Director turns to the Contracting Officer and asks: "Nancy, is that true?"
Contracting Officer responds: "Yes. The contractor has spent all of the money."
COTR says: "We'll need to award another contract to put the system into operation."
Director, feeling exasperated, exclaims: "Put it in operation! What?"
COTR says: "Uhm."
Director sternly but politely asks: "So, what did we actually buy with sixteen-and-a-quarter million dollars?"

Chapter Summary

The government contractor in the foregoing case example can claim that it had delivered an IT system, meeting all of its contractual obligations. But is the IT system successful? That question cannot be answered after 5 years of simply developing the system. Determining success requires that the IT system be in operation and allowed to be used. The end users after all will be the ones who will be using the system in their work. They will say whether they like it or hate it, whether it is useful or not, whether it is acceptable or not acceptable. The use of the IT system can answer the question.

The public manager had taken a lot of time and had expended a high level of effort to do the necessary planning and control as described in the previous two chapters to select and implement the right technology. The cost-benefit analysis will be moot if the IT system (the subject of the analysis) is not deployed and used. The government agency will not be able to observe the benefits that the public manager had estimated. The implementation of computer technology without it being used as intended would mainly be an exercise in spending money.

Any organization when it buys a technological product should be able to use the product and receive value that would result from the product's use. Moreover, the organization should be able to use the product after a reasonable time of developing the product. Whether an internal team or a contracted firm works on the project, the principle remains the same. An IT system must serve a purpose that accomplishes an organizational objective. If the implemented IT system fails to meet its purpose, then the technical team (whoever that may be) must be held accountable.

This chapter describes the difference between contracting and outsourcing and the costs and benefits of each. The chapter explains whether the government agency should build or buy an IT system and when is it appropriate to build a new system. The impact that outsourcing can have on the agency's business process is touched upon. If contracting offers the better option, the chapter further describes various agreements with vendors and how the government agency would be able to maximize relationships with vendors, that is, holding the vendor accountable and receiving value from the vendor's work. This chapter concludes with turning around a troubled contract. Termination can be draconian that leaves hurt feelings. Such a solution should be held off as the last resort, after exhausting all other measures. There are tactful approaches to correcting a difficult situation.

Contracting versus Outsourcing

Upon choosing to acquire a product or a service from a vendor, the government agency needs to ask: Do we contract or outsource? This fundamental question might seem silly, but the difference is no laughing matter. To not understand these two procurement modes, the public manager would be putting their agency in jeopardy of losing a lot of control. A major risk in procurement is that the government agency defers to the vendor's expertise in the way that the acquired product or service is developed and produced. This means that a level of control is given up by the agency.

How much control is retained goes to the heart of who controls the business process inherent in the acquisition. In contracting, the government agency retains control of the business process and provides direction to the vendor in developing a product or delivering a service. In outsourcing, the government agency transfers control of the business process to the vendor, based on the assumption that the vendor can develop a product or deliver a service more efficiently than what the agency can do. Figure 5.1 illustrates a set of tasks that is under the control of the vendor. At some point in the agency's business process, the government agency passes work to the vendor and will have to wait to receive the result from the vendor. The government agency in Figure 5.1 will not have any authority over the vendor's set of tasks (the vendor's business process). The vendor-managed process, moreover, might be a trade secret that gives the vendor a competitive advantage over other organizations.

An example of transferring control of the business process is in acquiring a telecommunication service. The government agency would not have the capacity to manage the telecommunication infrastructure. A specific vendor in this field will have invested in all of the equipment and

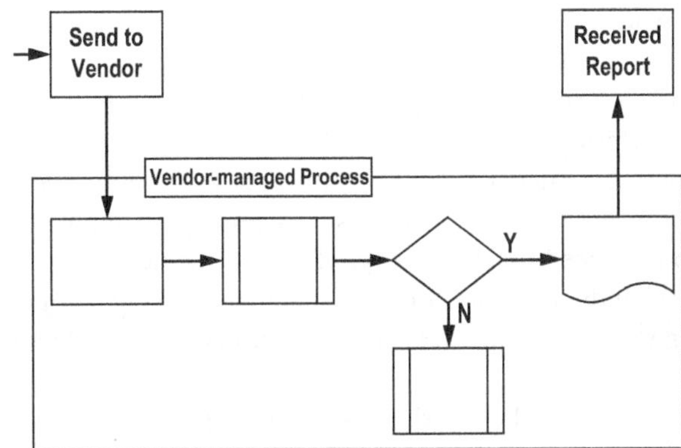

Figure 5.1 Transferred control of a business process.

resources to provide a telecommunication service. This vendor will also have its own business process along with the expertise to provide the service.

Another example of transferring control of the business process is in the area of technical support. The government agency may initially have a support operation, and then it decides to use a vendor to provide technical support. The agency would find that the vendor's process is more efficient. The technical support vendor could handle all of the agency's support cases with better equipment, more support personnel, and at a lower cost.

In both examples where control is transferred, the government agency outsources a specific service to a vendor that is better equipped to provide the service. If anything goes wrong, the government agency would have trust in the vendor that the vendor will handle the problem (e.g., solve a technical issue and discipline a staff member). The government agency would only be concerned that the service is delivered with minimal downtime and at a high level of quality.

There will be cases where control must be held by the government agency. A particular business process is central to a public program that government oversight is essential. The public manager will need to provide direct instruction, guidance, or advice to the vendor. An outsider would not have the same level of knowledge of a particular process with an internal employee. While the vendor has specific expertise, the government agency will need to use the vendor's expertise in a particular way that follows the agency's process.

A common example where control of the business process is typically retained is in hiring an expert for a short-term project or on a temporary basis. The government agency may lack a particular skill at a given moment in time and would need to hire a specialist to fill that gap. The vendor in this case would have a learning curve in the first few weeks to understand how the agency conducts business. The government agency would provide consultations, internal documents, and other proprietary and confidential information to the vendor. The vendor would then be able to apply their expertise in context of the agency's work. Without the provided information surrounding the business process, the vendor could perform work that does not follow the agency's process.

Another example where control of the business process is and must be retained is in the acquisition of a computer software product. A computer program needs to be designed in a particular way that fits into the agency's process. A vendor will have highly specialized skills in software development but may not have any knowledge of the particular process that needs to be programmed. In this respect, the software development vendor is a generalist that would not have technical expertise in a functional domain area such as public health or social security. The Functional Experts in the government agency will have to provide instruction or guidance in how their domain area operates. This instruction will then inform the vendor on programming the computer software in the right way that matches the business process of the functional area. If control of the business process were to be transferred, the vendor could develop a software product that will not follow the government's process and may not be in compliance with applicable law.

In both examples where control of the business process is retained, the government agency contracts a vendor to fill a need that is missing. This missing piece does not mean that the existing process has to change hands. It just means that there is a missing component that could be slowing down or stopping the business process. The government agency does not give up control of its existing process.

Contracting has its costs. Although the government agency can review and advise on personnel matters, the vendor has control on who is hired, disciplined, and fired. The agency depends on the vendor's discretion on the competence of IT personnel. Moreover, the vendor may create their own set of job roles based on different requirements and shifting priorities. The quality then of the acquired product can vary and is susceptible to being lowered. This raises the concern that the agency may not receive a product that is the right one, let alone a high-quality product. Management over the vendor becomes complicated in that the agency needs to find alternative measures other than managing people to control the level of effort. Additional measures such as periodic reporting of activities increase the costs. Not only would the vendor have to bring in a new staff member to prepare and write the reports, the agency would have to allocate the time to read the reports and carry out any follow-up actions. The government agency will have to conduct monitoring, employing additional staff, relying on another team or department, or bringing in a third-party evaluator.

If the costs can be managed, the government agency can realize the benefits of contracting. The lengthy hiring process of the civil service could be difficult to recruit and hire specialized IT personnel. Without a professional development program, the technical skills of existing IT personnel can become outdated. The vendor then can provide the skills and specialized labor that the agency would need to fulfill the demands brought by current technologies. The vendor would be able to introduce the latest computer technology, giving the agency a glimpse of what is possible. The acquired product could then be an advanced IT system that may not have been available through the internal build-it-yourself approach. Through a competitive procurement process, the government agency would be able to choose from a selection of IT project proposals that offer competing technologies at various prices.

Two major benefits from outsourcing could be realized. By offloading a certain part of its business process to the vendor, the government agency could reduce expenses for that particular process. This will improve the agency's budget outlook. As the vendor would carry out the tasks involved, the delivery of service could increase in speed. The people who are eligible to benefit from a public program will receive service faster. This assumes that the vendor has a more efficient business process. It is also assumed that the procurement process for selecting and awarding a contract to a vendor is conducted in a timely manner. A lengthy, drawn-out procurement process, which can involve protests and legal actions by losing vendors and other groups, can undermine outsourcing.

Whether it is outsourcing or contracting, the procurement process itself imposes a cost that can affect the result. Procurement adds an administrative overhead. Aside from implementation, the government agency needs resources and time to solicit ideas, review proposals, award, manage, and close out contracts. All of the steps involved in procurement take a level of effort. Any step in the process could incur an undue delay. Lack of timely appropriations, for instance, can put off the award of a contract for an indefinite time and thus can delay needed work. And then different vendors with varied operating styles and organizational values can change from time to time. A subsequent follow-on contract can introduce a new vendor to succeed where the previous vendor finished. An abrupt end of a contract can bring in a new vendor to make corrections and fix the problems that have resulted from the failed attempt of the previous vendor. Procurement carries its own set of risks and issues.

Procurement risks could be glaring in outsourcing. If the government agency struggles to work with the vendor, the delivery of the service could suffer. The public manager, for example, could receive many complaints from end users in poor and inadequate resolutions to technical support cases. The vendor may not be equipped to handle technical support. In another example, the telecommunication provider-vendor could have too many outages in the provisioned Internet data connection. The possibility of service disruption is a cost of outsourcing that can result in loss of productivity and downtime for affected employees. Recurrence of service disruptions is compounded by the fact that the agency has little to no control on the underlying process to manage the level of service quality. The government agency is dependent on the vendor to make required repairs and to correct problems. During an outage, government employees have to wait, do something else, until the issue is resolved.

Another cost of outsourcing is the possibility of compromised information security. The vendor could be privy to the agency's data. Even with tightened internal security controls, the government agency's information could still be vulnerable to exposure by way of the vendor's inadequate or lack of security controls. The vendor's IT system, which would hold copies of the agency's data, could be broken into.

If the reader is beginning to feel scared, some degree of worry is a good thing. The public manager can be kept vigilant. Further reading of this chapter provides measures to protecting the government agency against the vendor. Chapter 7 provides measures and safeguards for information security in any case regardless of whether contracting or outsourcing is pursued. The main point that must be emphasized is the seriousness with which engagement with an external provider must have. The work that any vendor will do to produce a product or deliver a service must not be presumed as a given assumption.

So, when is it appropriate to pursue contracting or outsourcing? As described in previous chapters, the benefits should outweigh the costs. More important, the public manager needs to examine all the possible costs related to contracting or outsourcing and be cognizant of the issues. The following line of questioning can aid the public manager in making a decision:

1. Does the organization presently have an adequate IT system that meets needs and requirements?
   a. If yes, contracting and outsourcing would not be necessary. There would be no need to acquire a new IT system.
   b. If no, ask the second question.
2. In terms of scope of work: How much of the inadequate IT system must change in order to meet needs and requirements?
   a. If very minor, consider a simple procurement vehicle (e.g., a purchase order) that would be completed in a few days or a few weeks. The IT system may just need replacement parts, some extra supplies, or a fix/repair that would not require a lot of time.
   b. If minor, ask the seventh question. Internal IT personnel may be able to make modifications (e.g., computer software modification).
   c. If major or no system exists, ask the third question.

3. Is there an IT provider that can operate, maintain, and support a comparable product or service on the organization's behalf? In other words, is the organization willing to permit an IT provider to manage the IT system?
   a. If no, ask the seventh question. *The IT system is a candidate for contracting*, but first check if internal IT personnel can perform the necessary work.
   b. If yes, ask the fourth question. *The IT system is a candidate for outsourcing.*
4. How critical is the area of operation or the line of business that which drives the IT system in accomplishing the organization's mission?
   a. If mission critical (highest importance), do not pursue outsourcing and ask the seventh question. The IT system must be managed by internal IT personnel.
   b. If important but not mission critical, ask the sixth question.
   c. If not important, ask the fifth question.
5. Is it a must (an absolute requirement) to retain full and complete control of the business process related to the area of operation or the line of business?
   a. If no, *outsourcing can be pursued.* The organization would permit an IT provider to manage not only the IT system but also the underlying business process as well.
   b. If yes, ask the seventh question.
6. Is it permissible to give up some level of control on parts of the business process related to the area of operation or the line of business *AND* does the organization have adequate resources to conduct monitoring and oversight?
   a. If yes, outsourcing can be pursued to a certain extent as it relates to specific parts of the business process.
   b. If no, ask the seventh question.
7. Does the organization have permanent IT personnel who currently work on the IT system or can be reassigned to work on the IT system?
   a. If no, ask the tenth question. First check if hiring new IT personnel is available before pursuing contracting.
   b. If yes, ask the eighth question.
8. Do permanent IT personnel have sufficient knowledge and adequate skills related to the tasks involved in the IT system?
   a. If yes, contracting would not be needed. Internal IT personnel can perform the necessary work.
   b. If no, ask the ninth question.
9. Does the organization have the approval, funding, and time to train permanent IT personnel?
   a. If yes, carry out training for internal IT personnel.
   b. If no, ask the tenth question.
10. Does the organization have the approval, funding, and time to hire permanent IT personnel?
    a. If yes, go through the HR channel to recruit and hire new IT personnel.
    b. If no, *contracting can be pursued.*

The foregoing line of questioning looks into human resources, scope of work, and level of importance and control to determine whether to pursue contracting or outsourcing. The level of importance and control area indicates a relationship between contracting and outsourcing on a scale. Greater importance on an area of operation or a line of business would tend toward contracting. Diminishing importance on an area of operation or a line of business would tend toward outsourcing. The level of importance somewhere in the middle could go either way. This contracting and outsourcing relationship does not exist in the other two areas. The scope of work can go from a major endeavor to a minor job in either contracting or outsourcing. Unless the organization is outsourcing its human resources (HR) functions, HR deals with contracting.

Some factors highlighted here can compel an organization to pursue contracting or outsourcing. There is a lack of expertise at a given moment in time, and the circumstance does not justify the need for a permanent staff member. In this case, a person would be contracted to provide specific subject matter expertise for a short time period or when needed. There is a budgeting issue or a staffing issue that hinders the IT department from retaining permanent IT personnel. Additional technical staff would have to be hired as independent contractors. In this case, the contracted personnel work as though they are like permanent employees, but they are categorically different in terms of their HR employment record.

There are priorities that make the IT department more focused and leaner. For example, the organization wants to concentrate work on network communications. This places the computer network as a higher priority over information systems and technical support. In this case, the technical support operation would be outsourced to an external organization. The work of information systems would be contracted to one or more vendors.

There is a project that is too large or so complex that the IT department cannot implement alone. An Enterprise Resource Planning system that includes financial management and human resources management, for instance, is a major endeavor that requires involvement from all departments throughout the organization. In this case, an external organization would be contracted to implement the Enterprise Resource Planning system in close cooperation with the IT department.

One factor that can override all other factors is a directive stipulated by law or in a rule that contracting and/or outsourcing must be pursued. In this case, the organization will have no other choice.

Distinguishing a vendor by whether it is handling a contracted activity or an outsourced activity needs to be clear. The term "contractor" is loosely applied to all vendors regardless of the type of work involved. Hence, use of the contractor term can be a source of confusion in understanding the difference between contracting and outsourcing. It would be better to replace the term "contractor" with the term "vendor". And then vendor can be qualified by working as a "contracted vendor" or as an "outsourced vendor".

Build versus Buy

A common question that is often asked is whether an organization should build an IT system itself or buy an IT system from another organization. If the government agency has all the resources (e.g., IT personnel, computer equipment, and software development environment), then the government agency can build its own IT system. But should the agency do so even with all available resources at its disposal? A better question to ask is how unique is the IT system. That is to say, are the requirements so distinctive that no IT system on the market can be found?

Computer software, more broadly, is produced by many companies for a wide range of areas. Commercial software packages exist for business management, business productivity, desktop publishing, antivirus protection, and other subjects. While most packages are designed for individual consumers, some software packages have an enterprise or corporate version that can be efficiently installed and managed on hundreds of personal computers. These computer software programs are fully developed and can be used upon purchase.

The public manager needs to be cautious about the term "Commercial-Off-The-Shelf (COTS) Product". This term is conflated and misused when an IT system undergoes a significant amount of work to customize the software program or to reconfigure any of the system's components. While the core functionality of the software has been developed already, additional software development is required to make the functions work precisely to the organization's requirements. The contracted vendor would bill the organization for the time and labor to customize the software program. It is that non-customized part of the software program that is labeled as a COTS product. A true COTS product does not require additional software development in order to be used. In its purest definition, a COTS software program can be taken off the retail shelf, purchased, installed in a computer, and immediately used.

An IT system with a COTS software component could be less costly than developing a completely new software program. The amount of time is reduced, focused on making needed modifications. Depending on how well the IT provider has made the software program, modifications may not require a high level of technical skill. In other words, a junior- or mid-level Software Developer could perform the work. If the organization already has adequate computer hardware and other equipment, the organization can procure the COTS product alone, modify the software functions, and operate the modified COTS product in its existing IT infrastructure. An example of an IT system with a COTS software component is one that supports a business function that any organization needs (e.g., financial management, human resources management, and inventory management).

There will be a case where no COTS product exists. The government agency would have very specific needs and requirements given its unique mission. Examples would include product inspection, social security/welfare, disease prevention and outbreak, and national identification. The subject matter would be highly specialized that private companies would not develop the product. The market would be too small for private companies to make a profit from. The government agency then would have no choice but to develop an IT system with a completely new software program. With adequate internal resources, the government agency could build a new IT system on its own. If resources are insufficient, the government agency would have to contract an external organization to build a new IT system.

Business Process Analysis for Outsourcing

An important part of deciding to pursue outsourcing is business process analysis. (Refer back to Chapter 4 on analyzing a business process.) The vendor will assume control over the area of operation or the line of business along with the underlying business process. The vendor may adopt the government agency's business process or develop its own process. It is likely that the vendor will develop a new business process that is more efficient. Any changes to the original process could have an effect on service quality and service delivery. The government agency will want to be assured that there are no negative effects.

The public manager then needs to review all of the steps in the business process, examining whether each step can and should be executed by the vendor. Certain steps such as key decisions and document reviews should not be transferred to the vendor. Such steps may have a requirement that they be executed by an agency with legal authority. The vendor (presumably, a private sector company) would not be in a position to carry out such steps, let alone have any legal authority. Those steps must be redrawn so that the government agency continues to have control of those steps. The business process then needs to be redesigned so that only the steps that will be executed by the vendor will be transferred to the vendor.

The vendor can then use the new business process designed exclusively for the vendor. The vendor can adopt the process as is or make further changes as the vendor sees fit. In this new case, the government agency is insulated from any change.

Contractual Agreements

The government agency would have a standard format that it uses for all contracts. But the standardized government contract would not be adequate to provide protection and assurance in acquiring IT-related products and services. The IT industry has a set of contractual agreements described below and should be adopted. As it is relevant to the acquired product or service, any one of the IT agreements should be incorporated into the government contract or included in the appendix of the government contract. The IT contractual agreements are as follows:

- End User License Agreement (EULA)
- Service Level Agreement (SLA)
- Services and Support Agreement (SSA)
- Software Development Agreement (SDA)
- Software Maintenance Agreement (SMA)
- Software Escrow Agreement (SEA)
- Warranty Agreement
- Non-Disclosure Agreement (NDA)

The EULA is an agreement that computer users will have heard about, as this agreement is used in commercial software products – most prevalent in consumer software products. The EULA essentially covers how the computer user can use the software product. The EULA describes the rights and responsibilities of the computer user and the software provider.

The SLA is an agreement that has been traditionally used by a telecommunication provider. This agreement would also be used by a Web host provider or a cloud service provider. Unlike other agreements that cover a product, the SLA is applicable to a service. This agreement provides assurance to the customer that the service will be provided at a specified level of time. For instance, the Internet data connection will be operable 95% of the time for 24 hours per day and 7 days per week. The SLA describes the terms and conditions surrounding the provided service.

The SSA is an agreement that is used by a technical support company. This agreement may be combined with the SLA when support is a part of the provided service. The SSA describes various technical support levels and related services that the company will provide. Any fees would be stated. The SSA outlines the procedures and protocols for contacting technical support.

The SDA is an agreement that is used by a software development company. This agreement provides a summary of the software product, the software features that will be produced, a timeline of activities, milestones, and deliverables. The SDA describes the roles and responsibilities of key personnel in charge of project management. The SDA further describes the terms and conditions surrounding software development.

The SMA is an agreement similar to the SDA. This agreement covers software development work required to maintain an existing software product. The SMA describes the terms and conditions surrounding software updates and modifications.

The SEA is an agreement that is not widely known in comparison to the above agreements. This agreement can mitigate the risk involved in managing a software product provided by a software vendor or an IT provider that operates an online software service. The SEA involves a third-party escrow agent that will protect the computer source code (the first version and the latest updated version) and related software materials from being stolen, tampered with, or otherwise harmed or damaged. The materials are kept in a secured location (e.g., a safe deposit box) where authorized personnel have access to. The SEA describes the terms and conditions surrounding the protected software materials.

The Warranty Agreement is often a section in any of the foregoing agreements to describe the level of warranty for the provided product or service. This agreement describes the risks and liabilities of using the product or service. It may have a limited time period in which the customer can return the product.

The NDA is an agreement that provides assurance to both parties in the agreement that information, which either party may have access to, will not be disclosed to another person or organization. This agreement essentially covers what information is confidential and how such information can be used. The NDA describes the terms and conditions surrounding confidential information.

Development of Vendor Relationships

Differences can make working with vendors difficult. The vendor, which in most cases will be a private sector company, has a motivation fundamentally different from a public sector organization. While the government agency (a public organization) works in the interest of people, a private company works to achieve profit. The government agency does not work to achieve profit. The vendor will have its own organizational structure, strategic plan, and work culture for conducting business that may or may not conform to the government agency. The vendor will have its own objectives that may or may not be aligned with the government agency's objectives. The public manager may not be able to change these differences, but the public manager can and should find ways to narrow the differences, blunt the differences, and turn differences into advantages. An issue that overrides any kind of difference is that the relationship must remain productive. The government agency and the vendor must be able to work together despite their differences. The following points can aid the public manager in developing plans that move beyond differences to develop a strong and productive relationship:

- Find prospective vendors that have identical or very similar objectives and goals.
- Focus on common benefits that both parties see as mutually beneficial.
- Support the other party in assuming a level of risk that the party may be unwilling or unable to bear.
- Develop the scope of work, obligations, expectations, and roles and responsibilities that are direct and unambiguous.
- Develop performance metrics that both parties can agree on.
- Link activities and goals to financial rewards and penalties, creating a system that rewards good work and penalizes bad work.
- Define primary and secondary points of contacts for each party.

The public manager should find prospective vendors that have identical or very similar objectives and goals. Such a vendor will create the ideal partnership. Reviewing each prospective vendor's objectives would be done in the pre-solicitation and solicitation phases of the procurement process. A prospective vendor would have written documents describing their objectives and goals approved by senior management. The public manager should ask for such documents as part of their review. If time permits, a deeper review of each vendor's activities should be checked to see how well the vendor follows through in meeting their objectives. Do the vendor's actions match the vendor's words? The public manager ought to reject a prospective vendor when actual work outcomes tell a story that differs or contradicts the written objectives. The revelation can show a serious concern or even worse.

If objectives and goals are not similar or are divergent, the public manager should focus on common benefits that both parties see as mutually beneficial. The public manager should make it clear in the solicitation request what the benefits will be in the contract. Each vendor's proposal then should respond how the proposed product or service will provide the stated benefits. The awarded contract document would restate the benefits and show the link from the vendor's product or service to those benefits. The government agency will be assured that the vendor will work toward the same benefits.

A major reason why engagement with an external organization is worthwhile is to spread the risk around. A particular activity may just be too risky for a single organization to carry out. This can be in either the government agency or the vendor. For instance, the vendor may not pursue futuristic technology that has little return. The government agency may not invest in infrastructure that it would not be able to maintain. Here is where an understanding of differences can be turned into advantages. Each party can use the other party's difference as a form of leverage. The government agency could support the other party (the vendor) in assuming a level of risk that the vendor may be unwilling or unable to bear, and vice versa. The government agency's long-term planning and outlook and more careful allocation of resources could support the vendor's development of new technology to reach fruition. The vendor's faster pace of improving technological elements could support the government agency's need to keep IT systems updated and secure.

The public manager should develop the scope of work, obligations, expectations, and roles and responsibilities that are direct and unambiguous. Both the government agency and the vendor need to know what each other is responsible for and who is required to do the work. The vendor needs to know what is clearly expected to achieve and what is obligated. The public manager should have the scope of work and all terms written in direct statements as possible and reviewed by a number of people representing the vendor, and ask whether anything is unclear. Reviews by multiple eyes would allow corrections to be made that lead to clearer terms. The direct statements, moreover, will make the work clearer especially when people who speak different languages are involved.

To know whether progress is being made on the implemented work, there needs to be indicators. The public manager should then develop performance metrics that both the government agency and the vendor can agree on. The vendor would likely achieve performance measurement goals with less friction and animosity if the vendor finds the metrics acceptable. In other words, performance metrics ought not to be dictated through one-way communication. The vendor should be allowed to give their input on the formulation of performance metrics. Just as the vendor is allotted time to review the scope of work and related terms, the vendor should be afforded an opportunity to review and comment on the indicators. The public manager would develop work-specific or contract-specific performance metrics that have direct bearing on the vendor.

The following six performance metrics are a few examples that can be used. These are standard in measuring the availability and performance of delivered IT services.

1. Mean Time Between Failure (MTBF)
2. Mean Time To Repair (MTTR)
3. Access Time
4. Response Time
5. Transaction Rate
6. Failure Rate

Mean Time Between Failure

MTBF is the average time in hours that an IT system or a particular component is operational before it stops working due to a malfunction or a component failure. This metric indicates not only performance but also reliability in terms of how the system was designed.

Mean Time To Repair

MTTR is the average time in hours that a technician needs to repair an IT system or to resolve an issue. This metric can be used in combination with MTBF to show how fast a failed system can be brought back to a state of operation.

Access Time

Access Time is the average time in milliseconds that an end user can access an IT system. This metric includes latency time, which is any delay in searching for data or processing a request. The type and speed of a computer network can affect access time, making the IT system appear slower to respond than it actually is. In an online Web software program, from the moment that the end user clicks on submit to send a request, there is some time (i.e., access time) in which the connection is making to reach the system.

Response Time

Response Time is the average time in milliseconds that an IT system can respond to an end user's request. This metric covers the actual processing of a specific request as calculated by the computer server and would provide a more accurate representation of the system's availability.

Transaction Rate

Transaction Rate is the average number of transactions in a specific time period, usually measured by day or by hour. This metric would typically measure database transactions, server requests, Web page requests, or something specific to computing. This metric can be used to measure functional output such as reports per day, registrations per hour, and support cases per hour.

Failure Rate

Failure Rate is the percentage of failed outputs that an organization will accept. This metric is used in relation to transaction rate. For instance, an organization would accept 5% of Web page requests to fail. Another organization would accept only 1% of a specific kind of report to fail. The meaning of failure is specific to the context of the transaction. A report can be deemed a failure by a high number of errors or missing data, for example. A page request can be deemed a failure by one of many Web server response errors.

Progress may be too slow, or it has deviated too far. How then can progress move faster or back on course? The government agency could draw on an instinct that the private sector company knows very well. There needs to be an incentive to do work quickly, ethically, and properly. The public manager should link activities and goals to financial rewards and penalties, creating a system that rewards good work and penalizes bad work. Should the vendor be reimbursed for a shoddy product? The vendor would not have an incentive to produce the highest quality product when it knows that it will always be paid regardless of the quality of output. Payment should be conditional on quality of output. Along with basic payment for performing satisfactory work, the vendor could receive a bonus amount for exceptional work that exceeds the minimum requirement. An additional bonus may be applied for satisfactory or better work completed much earlier than planned. The government agency should have discretion on rejecting any part or all of the vendor's invoice. When a gross mistake or an egregious problem is confirmed, the government agency should have the ability to reclaim a payment in proportion to that mistake or problem. Such a reward-penalty system establishes a performance-based contract.

Whenever any issue – good or bad – arises, both the government agency and the vendor need to be made aware, so that correction can be made earlier than later. Resolving an issue can be increasingly difficult with the passage of time. Both parties must know who to contact from time to time during the period of the contract. And the designated persons should not change. They will have accumulated knowledge about the history and status of the contract and can speak quickly and refer an issue to the appropriate personnel. The public manager needs to define primary and secondary points of contacts for each party. A primary manager and a secondary manager as a backup person are designated to represent the contract on behalf of the government agency. This would be in addition to the contracting officer who manages the financial side of the contract. Primary and secondary managers are designated to represent the contract on behalf of the vendor. The vendor would select its primary manager and secondary manager. Ideally, all four designated persons should be technical managers. If that is not possible, at least one person (either the primary or the secondary) must have technical competence in the subject matter of the contract. At the minimum, each side of the contract should have a technical manager to answer technical questions and to resolve technical matters in a timely manner. This further protects both sides, as each party has a counterweight to check and balance the other, so that neither side can exploit an opportunity to cheat or mislead.

The last area to cover is the structure of the relationship itself, which can affect performance and behavior in both the government agency and the vendor. The contractual relationship can be collaborative or authoritarian. In a traditional structure that is hierarchical, the government agency directs and manages the vendor from a higher standpoint that is superior to the vendor. The government agency focuses on the immediate inputs that the vendor provides. The process of doing business is more important than delivering the final product or service. This naturally leads to an adversarial relationship between the parties. The vendor works at complying with procedures and regulations set by the government agency, rather than focusing on the scope of work. Since the emphasis is not on the output, accountability on the part of the vendor is low.

Figure 5.2 illustrates the result of a hierarchical relationship in a contract. Communication flows essentially one way from the government agency to the vendor. As the vendor works to follow the agency's directions and orders, the vendor can lead to producing outputs that are not exactly what the government agency had planned. The difference may be glaring.

In a modern, contemporary structure that enables partnership, the government agency and the vendor work on building and maintaining trust. Both the government agency and the vendor are seen as standing from a level of equality, where each party cannot dominate over the other.

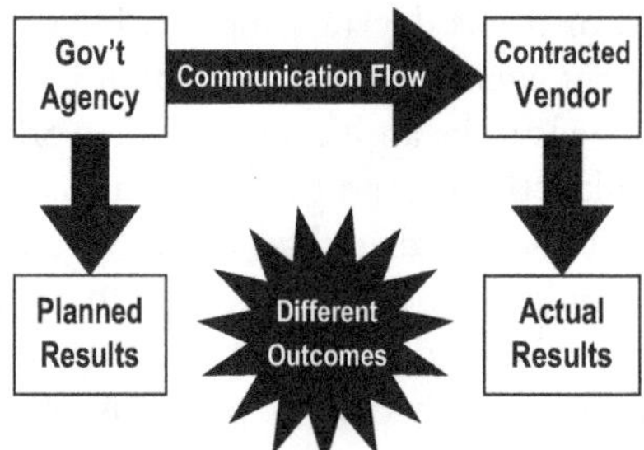

Figure 5.2 Contractual hierarchical relationship.

Figure 5.3 Contractual partnership relationship.

This allows both parties to engage freely with either side having the ability to maneuver without doing harm to the other. The government agency and the vendor become more cooperative and communicative with a focus on achieving results. The vendor understands that it can get paid and will continue to get paid so long as it produces results. In this relationship, accountability on the part of the vendor is high.

Figure 5.3 illustrates the result of a partnership relationship in a contract. Communication flows in both directions (back and forth) between the government agency and the vendor. This allows the government agency to understand the work that the vendor is doing and why a particular approach or technique is used. The vendor can understand the agency's perspective and know more precisely what the agency wants. The final product gets to outputs that are a closer match to what the government agency had planned.

Remedies for a Troubled Contract

Work may not be turning out so well. Outputs are not meeting expectations. The level of effort has slowed down to the point where the number of outputs is fewer. The relationship with the vendor has been strained.

There will be ups and downs in the relationship and highs and lows in ongoing work for a government contract that can span more than a few years. Recognizing that the work may not be as smooth or straight as one hopes, it becomes crucial to ensure that the low points do not overwhelm that lead to a progressively worse situation. Due to the complexity of an IT system, questions and issues can pile up and cascade. It can be difficult to resolve the problems and the contract beyond a certain point in time. But by being proactive in the course of the contract, the public manager can quickly resolve the little issues that pop up before they turn into bigger problems.

The points described above have mechanisms built in to identify issues and to make corrections. The most valuable is to keep up the flow of communication in the contract. The designated points of contacts serve a purpose to exchange information. When one person stops communicating, the other party would start to wonder. If the non-communication goes on for a lengthy duration, one party or both can grow worried. The government agency and the vendor are engaged in more of a partnership, and as such should have open communication. The designated technical managers would be peers who understand that challenges come up now and then. Whenever a problem has been encountered, it needs to be conveyed to the other managers. They could provide advice on how to handle the problem. If the manager keeps the problem a secret and struggles to deal with it, then sooner or later the problem will come out. And at that point, the problem could be large and much harder to solve.

In addition to written reports, the points of contacts should have periodic in-person meetings at least once every 2 weeks. The face-to-face interaction will communicate not only what is said but also *what is not said*. The non-verbal communication that peers transmit in conversation sends useful messages that otherwise can be harder to detect over the phone, through e-mail, and on paper. Subtle cues and hints in people's facial expressions, hand gestures, and body movements provide a richer story that could reveal what is actually happening. A cognizant technical manager would be able to pick up the cues and begin to ask probing questions.

Performance metrics can check on progress. The metrics can show whether the contract is meeting stated goals. If goals are not being met, the metrics will show any shortfall. The designated managers can then inquire about what is going wrong.

If a reward-penalty system is in place, a performance metric that indicates a missed target could trigger a penalty. The vendor would not receive a payment for missing the target goal. The vendor would be notified about the problem and would work to achieve the target by the next reporting period.

If expectations are falling short or obligations are not being met, then the scope of work can change. The government contract can be modified. This approach of making a correction would be suitable when the scope of work starts with broad objectives and ambiguous deliverables. The designated managers will realize mid-way through into the contract that the project is indeed too ambitious. In the course of the contract, designated managers will have observed what is possible. The vendor may have been experimenting with different technologies. The experimentation and observations provide valuable information to the designated managers. The government agency can then use the information to narrow the scope of work and issue a contract modification.

A service credit may be provided. This would be available for a telecommunication service, a data service, and an online software service. In the event that a service is down or inoperable for a prolonged time, the vendor would give credits in the amount equal to the time that the service was down or inoperable. The credits may be in the form of a payment or a voucher. Most IT providers would provide a voucher that can be used for future service. A service credit should be described in the SLA, if not in the government contract.

General damages and liquidated damages may be stipulated in the contract. In the event of a breach of contract, damages may be awarded to the party that has incurred a loss or injury. In the case of liquidated damages, the financial amount must be reasonable and must not be used as a form of penalty, or it can be unenforceable in a court of law. Liquidated damages apply when actual damages cannot be proven or are difficult to quantify.

Contract termination may be used to end the contract. This should be applied when all other remedies have failed to make corrections. Ending the contract could leave both parties bitter. Other remedies described above should be able to bring the contract back on course. The government agency and the vendor can work things out through communication, performance metrics, and contract modification.

Chapter 5 Quiz

Question 1: In which case would outsourcing be appropriate?

A. Hire three IT specialists to work for 24 months.
B. Purchase a replacement part for a computer.
C. Allow a private company to operate a mission-critical IT system.
D. Allow a private company to operate an important IT system.
E. Both C and D.

Question 2: Which product is not a pure COTS product?

A. Computer Antivirus Software Program
B. Computer Operating System Software Program
C. Computer-based Financial Management Information System
D. Laptop Personal Computer
E. Mobile Tablet

Question 3: Your agency is under a directive to outsource. Your business process, however, has critical tasks and decisions that when transferred to the vendor will create problems. What should you do?

A. Do nothing.
B. Develop a standard operating procedure manual and train the outsourced vendor.
C. Ensure that the critical parts are programmed in the software so that the agency can have records of those parts.
D. Adequately monitor and oversee the work of the outsourced vendor.
E. Redesign the business process so that the critical parts are retained by the agency.

Question 4: Which contractual agreement provides assurance that computer source code and related materials are not stolen or tampered with?

A. Software Escrow Agreement
B. Software Maintenance Agreement
C. Non-Disclosure Agreement
D. End User License Agreement
E. Service Level Agreement

Question 5: What are the qualities of a contractual relationship that would lead to a productive relationship and that results in an outcome that is very close to what the agency had planned?

A. Superior direction provided to the vendor.
B. Two-way (back and forth) communication.
C. Focus on the process of doing business.
D. Focus on the end result.
E. Both B and D.

Worksheets

Organization: ____________________ Department: ____________________

Existing: __ Security __ Networking __ Information System __ Support

Lacking: __ Security __ Networking __ Information System __ Support

Strength(s)	Weakness(es)
________________	________________
________________	________________
________________	________________
________________	________________
Opportunity	**Threat(s)**
________________	________________
________________	________________
________________	________________
________________	________________

Worksheet 5.1 **Internal capability, existing and lacking, by department.**

Business Process: ______________ In Department: ________________

Level of Outsourcing: __ Entire Process __ Partial Process __ None

Importance to Organization: __ Critical __ Major __ Minor __ None

Area(s) to Outsource	Critical Decision(s), Affected
______	______
______	______
______	______
______	______
Risk(s)	**Liability**
______	______
______	______
______	______
______	______

Worksheet 5.2 Business process analysis for outsourcing.

Step 1:

Write one specific item (a capability) on a Post-it® note.

Step 2:

Organize written notes on a large board, sorting them in any pattern that makes sense in your operating environment.

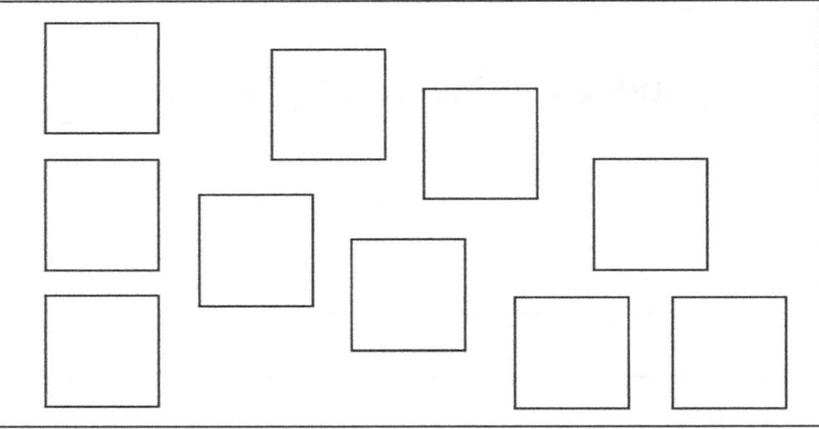

Step 3:

Apply the arrangement of notes to other worksheets.

Worksheet 5.3 Service capability arrangement exercise.

Project: ______________________ In Department: ________________

Need: __ Non-existent or Inadequate Capacity __ Process Improvement

Existing Cost: _________ New Cost (After): _________ % Change: ____

Major Gain(s)	Major Loss(es)
____________	____________
____________	____________
____________	____________
____________	____________
Trade-off(s)	**Critical Decision(s), Retained**
____________	____________
____________	____________
____________	____________
____________	____________

Worksheet 5.4 **Procurement case.**

Chapter 6

IT Execution and Follow-Through: Daily Practice and Improvement

Department Director asks: "Can the software be used in four weeks?"
IT Project Manager replies: "One or two features can be ready. Which features are needed right now?"
Department Director says: "Oh, I didn't know it can be done that way. Won't it cause problems?"
IT Project Manager says: "Not if development is managed properly."

Chapter Summary

There are two general approaches to building an Information Technology (IT) system. The traditional approach can take several months to a year or more to develop the software program and bring together all of the components. The end users would not be able to use the completed IT system until the end of the process. The end users have to wait patiently for a long time. The contemporary approach breaks up the software features of the computer program and the components of the IT system into manageable parts that can be implemented and used. The time needed to develop the individual parts is shorter. IT personnel are more focused on building the components, one or a few at a time, instead of building everything in one long arduous effort. As the parts are developed and tested, the parts are connected and deployed for use in the IT system. The end users can then begin using the incomplete yet evolving IT system.

This chapter describes the process of system development, focusing on important parts of the work to ensure that implementation is managed and controlled while at the same time allowing work to move as quickly as possible. Two general approaches to system development are described along with the costs and benefits of each approach. The public manager will understand scope management and change management – two important areas necessary to manage the development of a computer software program. The chapter highlights a series of documents that are created in the course of developing and operating an IT system. Emphasis is spent on the Software Requirements Specification – the principal document that guides software development. This chapter concludes with a practical approach to keeping team members motivated and involved.

System Development Life Cycle Process

The System Development Life Cycle (SDLC) process is a formal process for implementing an IT system in general and a computer-based information system in particular. This process is also known as the Software Development Life Cycle, since the computer software component is the central focus of the work. The term "system" refers to all of the components in an IT system (e.g., the computer hardware, the computer software, the computer network, and the non-technological elements). In addition to IT personnel, non-IT personnel need to be aware of this process. Everyone from the technical team to Functional Experts to senior executive leaders will understand what is involved and what to expect in every step of the process. The SDLC process goes through the following nine phases:

1. System Assessment
2. System Definition
3. System Selection and Evaluation
4. System Procurement or Development
5. System Testing
6. System Deployment
7. Data Migration
8. System Operation and Maintenance
9. System Disposal

In the first phase, the public manager would have done an assessment as a part of developing the IT Strategic Plan. The public manager would reassess the business needs again when the time is closer to implement the specified IT system. The situation may have changed. What does the government agency or department need?

In the second phase, the public manager translates the business needs into specific system functionalities that will be implemented. The shape of the computer software program will be defined with functional requirements and technical specifications. This is a critical phase.

In the third phase, the public manager uses the functional requirements to review what is currently available in the market. Matching IT systems would be selected and evaluated to check which one will be the right system. Will additional development be required? What kind of technical support is provided?

In the fourth phase, the public manager would procure the selected IT system, or in the case of not finding an available system, the public manager would move forward to build a new system. IT personnel will begin the work of implementation.

In the fifth phase, the IT system is deployed in a testing environment to allow a sample of end users to test the system against the functional requirements defined in the second phase. System testing would undergo real-world scenarios with a set of sample data.

In the sixth phase, the tested and approved IT system moves to the production environment where it is deployed for full operation.

In the seventh phase if applicable, IT personnel would transfer data records from a previous IT system to the new IT system. The data transfer would go through data migration procedures to ensure that older data sets conform to the new database structure. The previous system will then be viewed as a legacy IT system and would be scheduled for disposal.

In the eighth phase, the IT department manages the IT system and maintains it for several years. The completed IT system is used by all end users, providing benefits as estimated to the organization.

In the ninth and last phase, the IT system that has been operating will be disposed of. IT personnel would carry out a plan to archive the data, securely store the software program, stop all related services, and decommission the computer hardware.

Agile versus Waterfall

There are two major approaches to implementing an IT system. The traditional, conventional approach follows the SDLC process in one long linear stream where each phase does not start until the previous phase has ended. Each phase logically follows one after the other, cascading like a waterfall, hence the name given to the traditional approach. The waterfall approach results in a completed IT system that is considered final. This approach provides management controls to manage risks and costs and to ensure a successful outcome.

The modern approach applies a more iterative and adaptive methodology. It is agile. Where the waterfall approach would take several months to a year or more to develop one version, the agile approach would have produced several versions in the same time frame. The agile approach essentially develops one feature at a time to allow end users to begin using the IT system as soon as possible. This assumes that the computer hardware, the computer network, and other elements related to the IT infrastructure are in place. The computer software program then is developed and released within a few weeks per feature. All of the features and functionalities may not have been identified or clearly specified from the beginning. A vision and general requirements are enough to start the project. The actual work of implementing the IT system enables both IT and non-IT personnel to find out quickly what is possible and not possible. If something is not working, the development team can redo the software program. A new idea or feature may arise that the development team will try. The end users are afforded opportunities to provide comments that are more concrete and useful to the development team. Through trial and error, the agile approach delivers the computer software program in a number of iterations.

It is important to note that the agile approach does not dismiss the SDLC process. Every iteration involves the phases where applicable for the feature. Within a shorter period of time, the feature is defined, developed, tested, and deployed. The definition, development, and testing phases are executed simultaneously in parallel. (See the Version Development portion in Figure 6.1.) IT personnel skilled in each phase work together in daily operations, informing each other on progress as work evolves. The Systems Analyst quickly defines the feature and hands it to the Software Developer. The Developer may have a question that needs clarification. The Analyst discusses the question with the Functional Expert, revises the definition, and passes it again to the Developer. The Software Developer completes the feature and informs the Quality Assurance Specialist to test the feature. Quality Assurance carries out testing and reports the result. The Developer then reworks the software program accordingly, fixing any found issue. The work environment is thus engaging and proactive as everyone involved is kept abreast of the latest development.

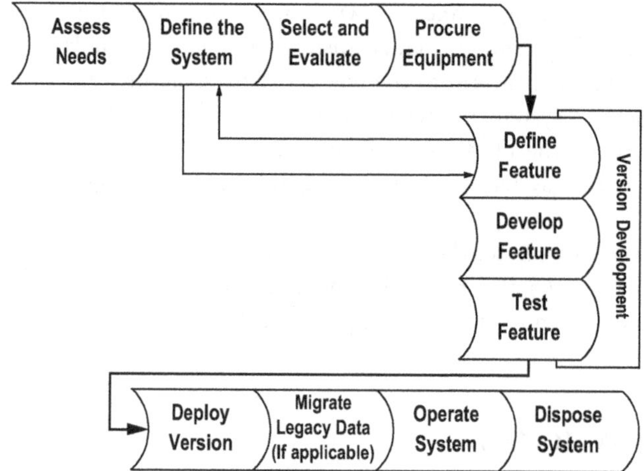

Figure 6.1 Balanced control and flexibility in system development.

A key benefit of the agile approach is that the government agency does not have to wait a year to see and use the IT system. Employees can begin using the system sooner, albeit in parts that are completed in succession. This benefit is also a cost. Implementation feature by feature could lead to ongoing work without a defined end point. In a contracting environment, this could allow a vendor to maintain a contract for as long as possible.

The waterfall approach will have identified all of the features that need to be implemented. It is clear that development will end at a certain point. A cost to this advantage, however, is that the design of the system is no longer open to change. The end of the definition phase puts a control to not making modifications. Anything new that would arise in the course of implementation would have to wait until the next review.

While incorporating new ideas more quickly is an advantage in the agile approach, the risk of introducing problems increases. The addition of a new feature could have a negative impact on existing features already implemented. By not identifying all of the features beforehand, a particular feature that is a prerequisite of another feature could be missed. This missing feature would become evident after the fact when the development team has struggled to resolve a peculiar anomaly. The development team gets that "a-ha moment" in realizing that something was indeed missed. Feature by feature implementation can focus too much on the details while avoiding to see the bigger picture.

A key benefit of the waterfall approach is the ability to manage change. The risk of introducing problems is lower. Because the entire system has been defined with a set of features and components, the addition of a new feature can be done safely. The Systems Analyst will review the original design and analyze how the new feature will have an impact and where it will fit within the design. An appropriate revision can then be made to the design of the system.

While the agile approach starts with a vision, the work could move too far into the details where everyone involved loses sight of the big picture. The waterfall approach, by contrast, can maintain the big picture perspective throughout the course of implementation.

With emphasis on controls and planning, the waterfall approach could move to an extreme end where the design of the system is too constricting to accommodate change. The agile approach, by contrast, keeps the possibility open to make changes whenever needed in the course of implementation.

The public manager can use the strengths of both approaches to create the right balance. Figure 6.1 shows the SDLC process in a slightly different way that combines the two approaches to emphasize specific phases for each approach. The first four phases are executed from one phase after the other (a logical progression). Adequate time spent in the assessment, definition, and selection phases ensures that the right system will be implemented. New equipment will be procured to establish the IT system. All of the components that the developed software program will depend on must be configured and in operation. At this point, software development can proceed at a faster pace. The definition, development, and testing phases are executed in parallel, implementing the software program in a series of managed versions. Each software version consisting of one or a few features and functionalities is completed within a few weeks and deployed.

The definition phase provides the critical fulcrum in which design documents are specific to capture the entire system yet general to make modifications. During version development, the definition phase is repeated to refine the specificity of the design documents even more. This is the distinction that can keep the design of the system open without compromising control.

The deployment, data migration, operation, and disposal phases are executed from one phase after the other to ensure that any new software version and any change, in general, do not disrupt or negatively impact the currently running system. The last four phases must be adequately controlled.

Scope Management

What is the scope of the project? A better question to ask: What needs to be implemented? Answering this question is absolutely critical in software development. Many computer software projects fail due to ambiguous requirements. Both IT and non-IT personnel need to know what exactly will be developed. Drilling down to specific items will avoid having to second guess what an otherwise general or vague requirement means and how it should be interpreted. IT personnel would be able to complete the work faster when the scope has well-defined specific requirements.

The public manager could fall into a dilemma where the government agency has a long list of specific features and functionalities but with limited resources and time to complete the entire list. A solution is to break up the list into smaller lists by which the computer software program can be released in several versions (see Figure 6.2). Instead of waiting for one completed software version

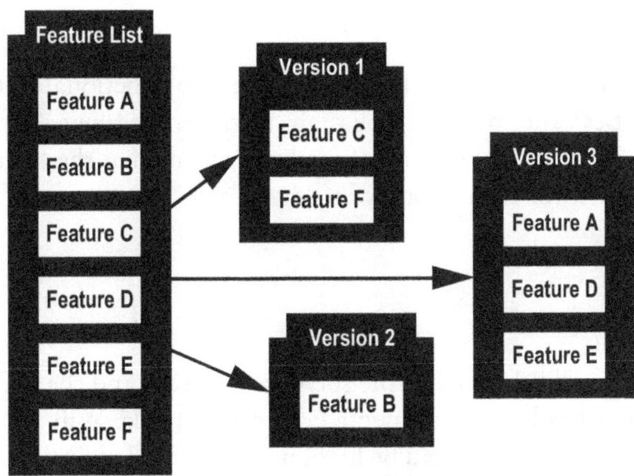

Figure 6.2 Grouped features into versions for system development.

with all of the features, the government agency would receive the software program incrementally with a selected set of features developed in a number of software versions. This will require that the features and functionalities be prioritized. Which features are more important and must be implemented sooner than later? Which features can wait?

Deciding on what will be developed first, second, and so on entails evaluating each software feature on four major factors: priority, effort, risk, and stability. The priority factor is the one where non-IT personnel provide input on. The other three factors involve a level of technical expertise to provide scores that are valid. The IT Project Manager leads and facilitates the process in scoring all of the features and receiving feedback from non-IT personnel. The combined factors provide the basis for selecting which software features will be implemented in one version and in another version.

Each factor has values along a scale. The four major factors are defined as given in the following sections.

Level of Priority

What is the level of priority for the feature or functionality? The values can be critical, important, and useful. A score of critical means that the feature is mandatory. A score of important means that the feature is less than critical but more than useful. A score of useful means that the feature is nice to have but not necessary (i.e., implementation can wait).

Level of Effort

How much work is needed to complete the feature or functionality? The values can be high, medium, and low. A score of high means that the feature requires the highest level of work (most hours). A score of medium means that the feature requires work less than the high score but more than the low score. A score of low means that the feature requires the lowest level of work (least hours).

Level of Risk

How much risk is involved in implementing the feature or functionality relative to all other features and functionalities? The values can be high, medium, and low. A score of high means that the feature poses the highest risk. A score of medium means that the feature poses medium risk. A score of low means that the feature poses the lowest risk.

Level of Stability

How much disruption could there be to the software program and the overall IT system after the feature or functionality has been implemented? In other words: Will the feature create issues in the new software version? The values can be high, medium, and low. A score of high means that the feature has the highest stability (least disruption). A score of medium means that the feature has medium stability. A score of low means that the feature has the lowest stability (most disruption).

The IT Project Manager can manage the scope of the project by evaluating and ranking specific features and functionalities and dividing up the work among a number of incremental versions (see Worksheet 6.1). The transparency of presenting the features with scores would also manage end users' expectations. Non-IT personnel can have a clearer picture of what is going to be developed and when it will be delivered. The public manager is provided assurance of which functions are most important. The factors used to evaluate the features concisely provide a technical summary for how much work is involved and how each feature will have an impact on other features whether completed or still to be developed.

Change Management

As the computer software program is used, the end users will want improvements, enhancements, and new functionalities. Software issues (bugs) would come up and will have to be resolved. All of this work means additional time and resources to modify the software program. Making changes over a running program that is being used, however, has a significant risk. IT personnel must implement changes properly. Non-IT personnel must be aware of when changes will take effect. The IT Project Manager must manage the process of change, and the public manager must be assured that change management procedures are being followed.

The SDLC process provides a road map for change management. The process can repeat over a number of cycles. Test results in the system testing phase would return to the system development phase where the technical team reviews reported issues and makes necessary corrections. The system operation phase would return to the system development phase when end users have reported problems to the technical team. If requirements are completely new, work would return to the system assessment phase where the entire system is reassessed to evaluate the impact of implementing the new requirements. Personnel involved will be informed of where the system currently is in which phase of the process. The public manager will be able to follow the progress of the first version and subsequent versions.

Every version must be controlled for release to the production environment. A final release report, which describes the results of system testing, needs to be issued to show that the version has passed test plans and has been approved for deployment and use. This official report must indicate the version number of the system and whether or not the system should be released to the production environment. A manager or lead representing the quality assurance team and another manager or lead representing the end users both must sign and date the report to indicate their approval. The final release report would show the total numbers of passed and failed test plans. A summary of software issues would show the total numbers of open and closed issues and a breakdown of issues by specific status. Remarks concerning any risks, issues, or caveats need to be included in the report. Unless some problem completely stops the system from operating, the tested version with identified issues could still be released. Such issues must be noted in the final release report.

A formal change request process must be instituted in order to proceed with any system or software change. A request that is made verbally or through some other informal channel should not be accepted. All requests need to be in written form. A change request needs to describe the problem, possible solutions, reasons for the change, affected system and components, date of request, and the name of the person who submitted the request. A small committee should be convened to review and approve all submitted change requests. Each request would be evaluated on cost and technical feasibility and any impact that the change could bring in terms of stability and security. Only approved change requests will be implemented. An approved request will then move to the first phase of the SDLC process.

Version control must be applied in documents, computer source code, exported data, and wherever else an IT system produces outputs that change frequently. Every document produced in all phases of the life cycle process needs to be given a unique version identifier. This could be as simple as an abbreviated document name and the date of last revision. Personnel need to be able to know quickly whether they are reading the most recent document or an older version. An outdated user manual, for instance, may give incorrect information, as the current software program would have changed and may not be the same as the previous version to which the outdated manual refers. The software source code needs to be labeled with the author's name, creation date, last modification date, and version number. IT personnel must know which version of the source code they are using. This becomes critical in a software team environment where multiple Software Developers work on the same version. It is also critical in deploying the completed software program in the production environment where an older version could cause operational problems. The data set whenever the records are exported to a file or backed up to tape needs to be given a unique version identifier. Non-IT personnel need to be assured that they have the most recent data records to do their analysis on a particular subject. Data records that are too old or from an unknown time period could produce inaccuracies or errors in the analytical reports.

Change/revision histories should be added in database transactions, software program versions, and documents. Following the history of what was changed and when provides an audit trail. In any document, a revision history page should be added after the title page. The revision history provides a list of entries of every instance when the document was revised, detailing who made the change, what was changed, when the change was made, and the version number of the document. For any software version, a change history should be provided to end users, describing what is new, what has changed, what was fixed, any new bugs found, workaround solutions for open bugs, and the version number of the software. For any database transaction (e.g., adding, editing, and deleting a record), a set of audit tables should capture every instance of when a user had made a change to the database. Each audit record should show the user name, the user role, transaction date, transaction type, affected data table/record, system code, and error code.

Software bugs should be recorded and tracked. All reported issues in a computer software program need to be organized in a way that allows IT personnel to manage the issues. A software issue table should show the current date, the version number of the software program, the total numbers of open and closed issues, and a disaggregation of the issues categorized by new issues, in-progress issues, resolved issues, and not-a-bug issues. All issues should be listed and briefly described along with a unique identifier of the issue, status, date of issue reported, date of last analyzed, date of closure, expected version number of software release, related support case document number, and the name of the person assigned to resolve the issue.

All of the management practices just described must be overseen by a single authority who is responsible for change management at the daily operational level. The IT Project Manager assigned to an IT project, an IT system, or a specific software development team would be in charge of ensuring that procedures are followed and outputs are checked and verified. The manager, moreover, needs to have the technical knowledge and capacity to review all materials that would entail opening electronic files and navigating the configurations of computer servers. The IT Project Manager needs to maintain copies of all versions (previous and current) in a secured location. Materials should be preferably stored in both a physical, hard copy format and an electronic, soft copy format. Documents that require a signature should have a handwritten signature or a way of attributing and verifying a digitally signed document to a known person.

Design Documents

Two design documents cover the functional requirements and the technical specifications and are written in the definition phase. The first document dealing with functional requirements is the master, guiding document that all other documents will refer to. The second document quickly builds upon the first document to provide overall guidance to the technical team. While non-IT personnel will be able to understand the functionalities by reading the first document, IT personnel will be able to know the general direction of implementation by reading the second document. As a set pair, the two documents complement each other to provide necessary direction for both IT and non-IT personnel.

With regard to change management, the first document as the master document must identify all of the features and functionalities. A brief description of one or two paragraphs will be sufficient for each feature. It is not necessary to describe in length any feature. A Use Case Scenario and other technical documents will provide the details and are written and revised during implementation. It is more important for the master document to capture in broad terms everything that the system will be capable of doing. The IT Project Manager can then evaluate each feature and schedule all of the features for implementation. The features will be divided up among a number of software versions. As the computer software component is developed and released, everyone involved will refer to the master document to ensure that each software version reflects what was originally expressed and approved. IT personnel use the master document to ensure that the work stays on track to meet what was originally expressed. Non-IT personnel use the master document to match the actual result with the expectations described in the document.

Although the contents described below focus on developing a computer software product, the documents can be adapted and modified to suit a particular operating environment. In other words, a document can be adapted to define another component such as a computer network or an IT system in general. Certain sections may be removed if they are not applicable. Section headings may be renamed to suit the context or to conform to an organization's naming convention.

Functional Requirements

Functional requirements are written in the definition phase of the SDLC process. Common terms that refer to the functional requirements are Design Specification, Software Features, Software Requirements Specification, and System Requirements. The actual title of the document may use any one of these interchangeable terms. For an implementation that focuses on development of a computer software product, this book uses and recommends the term "Software Requirements Specification", as it is clear and specific in comparison to the others. For an implementation that does not involve software development but involves the purchase of already completed computer hardware, software, and network products, this book would use the term "System Requirements Specification" to describe all of the components in an IT system. In both cases, the document provides a high-level description of what the IT system or the computer software product will do and accomplish when it is put into operation. In other words, the document describes the purpose and capabilities. Because it will be read primarily by senior executive leaders and non-IT personnel, the document emphatically does not go into much technical detail.

The following business outline provides the contents of the functional requirements document, ordered by section and sub section:

1. Executive Summary
2. Introduction
   2.1. Purpose of This Document
   2.2. Product Overview
   2.3. References
3. User Description
   3.1. User/Market Demographics
   3.2. User Profiles
   3.3. User Environment
   3.4. Key User Needs
   3.5. Alternatives and Competition
4. Product Overview
   4.1. Product Perspective
   4.2. Product Position Statement
   4.3. Summary of Capabilities
   4.4. Assumptions and Dependencies
   4.5. Cost and Pricing
5. Feature Attributes
   5.1. Status
   5.2. Priority
   5.3. Effort
   5.4. Risk
   5.5. Stability
   5.6. Target Release
   5.7. Assigned To
   5.8. Reason
6. Product Features
   6.1. Name of Feature 1
   6.2. Name of Feature 2
   6.3. Name of Feature 3
   6.4. Name of Feature 4
   6.5. Name of Feature 5
7. Exemplary Use Cases
   7.1. Name of Use Case 1
   7.2. Name of Use Case 2
   7.3. Name of Use Case 3
8. Other Product Requirements
   8.1. Applicable Standards
   8.2. System Requirements
   8.3. Licensing, Security, and Installation
   8.4. Performance Requirements
9. Documentation Requirements
   9.1. User Manual
   9.2. Online Help

   9.3. Release Notes
   9.4. Installation Guide
   9.5. Technical Manual
   9.6. Labeling and Packaging
10. Glossary

The Executive Summary section provides an overview in one page, or maximum of two pages. The Introduction section covers the purpose of the document, the purpose, aim, and summary of the product, and any references to other documents. References to applicable laws and regulations would be listed here.

The User Description section describes the intended audience (the end users or the market) for the product. It covers the demographics of the user or market, specific groups of end users differentiated by user profiles, the operating environment of the end users, key user needs, and the alternatives. Market research would have been done to provide information regarding what other products are currently available and what is the competition like in providing the product. The User Description should give information about the operating environment (i.e., working conditions). Do end users work in an office, a warehouse, or in an outside field exposed to weather and the environment? What groups of end users will use the product? Will they be leaders, mid-level managers, and/or specialists? How is each group different? Why is the product needed? What are the key needs requested by end users?

The Product Overview section describes the purpose, shape, and form of the product, a summary of the product's capabilities, assumptions and dependencies, and applicable cost and pricing. Any items or resources that need to be purchased should be listed. The estimated cost for each item should be stated. If the product will be used to generate revenue, the estimated price for the product should be stated. Anything that the product will depend on such as the Internet or another IT system should be listed as a dependency. A summary of capabilities would be a list of product features in a table format wherein a benefit to the end user is concisely described for each feature. In other words, a product feature is intended to benefit the end user in what way.

The Feature Attributes section describes the attributes by which all of the product features will be evaluated against. The factors described above are the main feature attributes. Incorporating this information allows non-IT personnel to understand how the product features are evaluated and scheduled for implementation. Additional attributes named "Status, Assigned To, Target Version, and Reason" would be added. The "Status" attribute refers to where the product feature currently is in the SDLC process; the status of the feature could be proposed, approved, or incorporated (developed). The "Assigned To" attribute refers to which development team or specific person will be assigned to develop the product feature. The "Target Version" attribute refers to the software version in which the product feature will be released. The "Reason" attribute refers to why the product feature will be added and developed.

The Product Features section describes all of the features and functionalities. Descriptions should neither be detailed nor be difficult to interpret. Each feature description must capture the essence of what the feature will do in terms of functionality. Its meaning must be clear and unambiguous. Jargon and references to particular technologies need to be removed from the descriptions. Do not state Artificial Intelligence and Big Data as product features, for instance. A specific aspect of such particular technology needs to be brought out and articulated. What specifically about the technology will be developed? A product feature would indicate its level of uniqueness in relation to other products.

The Exemplary Use Cases section provides illustrations of a few product features. Three features that best represent the product should be selected for this purpose. Each illustration presented as a technical diagram will complement the written description, giving the reader a visual picture of what the product feature will do.

The Other Product Requirements section covers the non-functional requirements. Specific topics include "Applicable Standards", "System Requirements", "Licensing, Security, and Installation", and "Performance Requirements". The Documentation Requirements section also covers the non-functional requirements, related to documents that will be produced. User Manual, Online Help, Release Notes, Installation Guide, and Technical Manual are common documents that would be required and included. If applicable, labeling and packaging as it applies to marketing, distributing, and selling the developed computer software product would be described. The last section provides definitions of key terms.

Technical Specifications

Technical specifications are also written in the definition phase of the SDLC process, after the completion and approval of the functional requirements. This document provides overall technical direction to IT personnel, setting the parameters for how the computer software product will be developed. In the case of an IT system, the document sets the parameters for purchasing the system from available IT providers. Specific technical language and jargon would be used in this document. References to specific computer programming languages, computer software packages, computer manufacturers, and IT providers would also be included.

The following business outline provides the contents of the technical specifications document, ordered by section and subsection:

1. Executive Summary
2. Introduction
   - 2.1. Purpose of This Document
   - 2.2. Scope of This Document
   - 2.3. Definitions, Acronyms, and Abbreviations
   - 2.4. References
3. Functionality
4. Usability
   - 4.1. Training Period for Learning the Software
   - 4.2. Time Frame for Completing Tasks
   - 4.3. Compliance to UI Standards
5. Reliability
   - 5.1. Availability
   - 5.2. Mean Time Between Failures (MTBF)
   - 5.3. Mean Time To Repair (MTTR)
   - 5.4. Maximum Bugs or Defect Rate
   - 5.5. Bugs or Defect Rate
6. Performance
   - 6.1. Response Time
   - 6.2. Output Precision or Accuracy
   - 6.3. Throughput

   6.4. System Capacity
   6.5. Degradation Modes
   6.6. Resource Utilization
7. Supportability
   7.1. Coding Standards
   7.2. Naming Conventions
   7.3. Class Libraries
   7.4. Maintenance Access
   7.5. Maintenance Utilities
8. Design Constraints
   8.1. Software Languages
   8.2. Development Tools
   8.3. Architectural Constraints
   8.4. UI Standards
9. Documentation Requirements
10. Purchased Components
11. Interfaces
    11.1. User Interfaces
    11.2. Hardware Interfaces
    11.3. Software Interfaces
    11.4. Communication Interfaces
12. Licensing and Security Requirements
13. Legal, Copyright, and Other Notices
14. Applicable Standards
15. Internationalization and Localization
16. Physical Deliverables
17. Installation and Deployment

System Testing

System testing must have a formal methodology in order to ensure consistency and quality in the test results. Moreover, the testing methodology needs to be documented so that other teams will be able to understand how the results were arrived at and can conduct their own tests to replicate the results. Similar in purpose to a research methodology for conducting a survey or a scientific study, the testing methodology needs to lay out the plan and techniques for how personnel involved will conduct a number of system tests. The methodology includes the scope of testing (i.e., what will be tested and what will be excluded), who will do the tests, when testing will be scheduled, start and end dates of testing, summary descriptions of test plans, test procedures, and the test plan analysis. If applicable, User Acceptance Testing (UAT) should be described along with the details for how end users will conduct system testing. While this chapter focuses on computer software, test plans should include testing the computer network, information security, and other components linked to the computer software program. All other components in the IT system should be tested to ensure that they work as designed.

Although system testing has an official phase in the SDLC process, preliminary work related to system testing begins in the definition phase. As functional requirements are being written, testing requirements also need to be written and mapped to the features and functionalities. One test plan covers one specific feature. The purpose of testing is to make sure that every feature works as designed. General information about each test plan needs to be defined. An initial set of logical steps involved in the test plan should be developed and written. The steps will be revised and finalized, as the feature is fully developed and completed in the development phase. This initial work to define all test plans creates a smooth and quick transition to the system testing phase. This is especially critical in the agile approach.

Another team of IT personnel provides quality assurance. Specific roles as described in Chapter 2 will develop several test plans, write test procedures, carry out the plans and procedures in a number of trials, analyze the results, and write the final release report. As a separate team, the quality assurance team can remain fairly objective in conducting system testing. The development team, on the other hand, would be biased toward getting positive test results. Although the development team would carry out formal test plans in addition to other tests more technical, the quality assurance team would not have the same level of bias and thus would be able to judge the features and functionalities in a fair manner. The test results from the quality assurance team would provide another perspective that points out issues and potential problems.

An external organization may be contracted to conduct independent system testing. This third party would review the testing methodology and may follow it as is or develop a different methodology with different test plans. A different approach may be implemented. The test results from the external organization would provide a higher level of qualification that reveals weaknesses and possible flaws.

Typically in the waterfall approach, UAT may be carried out to give end users the opportunity to test the features and functionalities for themselves. This is a chance for end users to see what they will be getting. UAT is usually scheduled when the system or software program is about 80% complete, according to the schedule as implemented in the waterfall approach. Within the remaining time in the project schedule, any issues that are found by the end users would be worked on and resolved. The quality assurance team would provide brief training to end users on carrying out the test plans and then administer UAT sessions. The test results from UAT are combined with internal test results and reported in the final release report.

A formal UAT would not be appropriate in the agile approach, since UAT entails another work activity that could place added burden on IT personnel. Moreover, the 80% completion threshold does not apply in an iterative approach to software development.

Under the agile approach, end users can still be given the opportunity to view and test the completed feature in a controlled operating environment. Prior to deploying the new version to production, there is the testing environment that is separate and isolated from the production environment. Another testing environment designated for end users can be set up. This second environment also operates separately from the production environment. The development team will notify end users that a new feature is ready to be viewed. End users can then try out the feature and provide input into what they have observed. The development team receives user feedback and follows up accordingly. The quality assurance team provides guidelines to support end users. End users will accept or reject the newly developed feature and the new version. The final release report for the new version will then be issued. The time frame for testing by end users would be shortened to 1 or 2 weeks.

A computer software program generally has three major classes of software versions to show a particular stage of system testing. The Alpha release software version is for internal use and internal testing. This version has numerous bugs and is highly unstable, since the development team is currently working on and testing the software program. The Alpha release goes through

Alpha testing. The Beta release software version may be distributed to end users, external organizations, and the general public for limited use. This version has most bugs resolved but would still be relatively unstable. Caveats are provided to end users. The Beta release goes through Beta testing and provides end users the opportunity to provide comments and suggestions. The Production release software version is for wide use by all end users. This version is in a stable form with bugs reduced to a minimum or controlled. Bugs may exist, but they would not cause the Production release to be completely inoperable. The Production release goes through a final round of system testing to ensure that end users can successfully use the features and functionalities in the software program. The Alpha and Beta release versions are notated, respectively, with a lower case "a" and a lower case "b" appended to the software version number.

Test Plan

A test plan provides a formal way to test features and functionalities. Other terms that may be used interchangeably with test plan are test case and test scenario. In any case, the test plan must be designed in a way that will ensure consistency, accuracy, and objectivity when the test is repeated numerous times. The testing of a particular functionality must be controlled. The public manager can think of the test plan like designing and conducting a survey on a population. The test plan needs to be rooted in the scientific method.

For any given IT system, there will be several test plans. One plan is meant to test only one feature or functionality in a computer software program. One component or subsystem on which the software depends within the IT system will have its own test plan as well. The quality assurance team needs to check the individual operation of each feature, functionality, component, and subsystem to know that each is working properly. Combining multiple functionalities in a single plan may be convenient, but it would be difficult to know which functionality is causing a problem to occur. In a more controlled environment, the quality assurance team will run each test plan individually to see which functionality produces the problem.

Each test plan needs to have general information about the test. General information includes a unique identifier of the test plan, the name of the test plan, a brief description of the purpose of the test plan, the feature, functionality, or dependent component, the names of the persons who created and modified the test plan, and the creation date and last modification date of the test plan. Any input data that need to be used should be described. A link to a source electronic file that contains sample data would be useful and may be included. The test plan must include placeholders to enter the name of the person who runs the test plan, the instance number of the test plan, and the date and time of running the test plan.

The main section of the test plan includes a list of logical steps and corresponding expected results that will achieve the specified functionality. A person who will run the test will follow the steps and record whether each step passes or fails. The person will mark each step as pass or fail. The person would also provide additional information such as an observation, an issue, or notes regarding a particular step. This will be helpful in an occurrence of a problem. The actual result must match the expected result in each step, or else that particular step will have failed.

True success occurs when all of the steps in the test plan have passed. Partial success may occur with a certain percentage of passing steps. Partial success, however, may not show that the specified functionality was achieved. The quality assurance team would review the execution of the steps to find out what happened. Additional information provided by the person who had run the test will aid in problem identification. A system crash may have occurred, for example.

A transmission error in the computer network may have occurred, in another example. A failure may have occurred in the middle of the test plan which stops the test from proceeding further, and partial success in this case would be deemed a failed test. Another test plan would show that the final step had passed but some intermediate steps did not pass. This second case would indicate that the person who had run the test encountered issues along the way, and partial success in this instance would be deemed passing overall with caveats.

The test plan should be run a number of times and preferably by several different people, if the test result is to be considered valid. A one-time run of the test plan that shows a failed test should not be construed as a true failure. Something independent of the test plan may have caused a problem to occur. It could be the end user's personal computer or network connection or something particular in the end user's operating environment. An anomaly that cannot be explained may have occurred. Computer software is very particular. Running the test plan a second time, a third time, and so on can confirm if the failure occurs over and over. And so, if 50 instances of the test plan show a failed test, for example, then there would be validation of a true failure. The multiple runs would also provide validation of a true success as well.

As a matter of best practice, the test plan should be scheduled to run at different times of the day and on different days of the week. The results could vary between business hours, evening hours, week days, and weekend days. The test plan should run on various computer operating systems. The results could vary between different end-user computers (e.g., Microsoft, Apple, and Android) and with different operating system versions (e.g., different Windows versions and different Mac versions). The test plan should be run in different computer networks. The results could vary between a wired network, a wireless network, and a mobile cellular network. The test plan should be run by more than one person with varied levels of technical skill. The results could vary between a novice end user, an advanced end user, and an expert end user.

Numerous instances of running the test plan are a significant reason why the test plan must be in a standardized format. If every person were to design their own plan or each operating environment ran a different plan, it would be difficult to understand what went wrong when a problem occurs. A different plan could have a different method, approach, or technique. The test plan itself is a variable that has to be controlled. In this way, the test plan as a tool is like a survey questionnaire. Both are instruments to answer a specific question. In this case, the test plan answers whether the specified functionality will work.

System Documentation

Documentation is an important part of IT work. It becomes essential for the government agency, since an IT system can be the subject of an audit. Information in the way an IT system was assessed, defined, selected, procured, tested, deployed, migrated, operated, and disposed would need to be available to an auditor or an investigator for review. The same amount of information makes the work of implementing an IT system easier. IT personnel would benefit the most. The job of implementing a new IT project one after the other would be increasingly easier – and faster as well – when a repository of documents can be drawn upon. Documenting the first system can be tedious and slow, since all of the documents would have to be created from scratch. But documenting the second system would be easier, since now documents from the first time around can be used as models to draw upon. IT personnel can replace specific content with new content while maintaining the same outline and structure. Specific parts in the documentation set could be reused and modified, similar to how blocks of computer programming code can be reused in another software program. System documentation serves as a resource of knowledge that will not only aid in an investigation but also facilitate IT implementation.

Each phase of the SDLC process produces or involves one or more documents. Principal documents have been described above. The first phase produces a brief paper on identified needs, goals, and purpose, based on rigorous organizational and technical assessments. This brief paper would be a project charter or a project inception report.

The second phase produces the functional requirements document, the technical specifications document, and the system testing plan.

The third phase produces a report on the selected IT system, based on an evaluation of available solutions. The third phase would also produce a contract award to procure or develop the selected IT system, setting in motion to start a new contract.

The fourth phase produces numerous technical documents that describe how the IT system is constructed. In the case of a contract, the fourth phase also produces periodic reports to the government agency.

The fifth phase produces the final release report that accepts or rejects the tested IT system. In the case of software development, the final release report accepts or rejects the latest version of the computer software program.

The sixth phase involves a technical guide for installing the latest version of the computer software program and making any necessary configurations to the IT system. A "Read Me" document would be produced for end users to know what is new and what has changed.

The seventh phase involves a technical plan to move existing data from a previously used system to the new system.

The eighth phase involves a systems administrator manual for operating and maintaining the IT system. An end user's manual is involved to guide end users in how to use the IT system. The eighth phase also involves an information security document and a business continuity/disaster recovery plan. In the case of a contract, a final report would be submitted to end the contract at some point after a specified length of time in the eighth phase (e.g., 90 days from the date of operating and using the IT system). The contract's final report would describe the work that had been performed, a summary description of whether agreed objectives had been achieved, and recommendations.

The ninth and last phase produces a certified report that the IT system had been properly disposed.

Although there are more documents produced and involved, key documents are highlighted to illustrate a logical chain that guides and governs implementation from start to end.

Team Motivation

It can be difficult to sustain the momentum and energy of the entire team. Once tasks are understood and members have been oriented in their new environment, team members would settle into a regular routine that could be monotonous. Each specialist will sit in front of their computer and focus on the task at hand. Time will pass by without knowing it. Weeks and then months will have come and gone, finally arriving on the day of completing the project that the team had set out to work on. Certain members would have the high degree of motivation and discipline themselves to see that their tasks are completed according to schedule. Other members would need prodding now and then to keep them energized. Anyone could fall into a rut. Burnout is a particular concern with any IT specialist.

The challenge for the IT Manager is to keep the spirits high of all team members (both IT and non-IT personnel who are involved) and to do it in a way that does not show favoritism for any particular member. The following four practices, which the author has demonstrated in his professional career and personal life, can meet this challenge:

- Leadership by Example: Do It, Don't Just Talk About It
- Potential of Discovery: By Flexible Management, Not by Rigidity
- Individual Respect and Equality: Everyone Learns From Each Other
- Daily Communication: The 5-Minute Brief Meeting

Leadership by Example: Do It, Don't Just Talk About It

The manager in charge should not command orders like a military drill instructor or from a position of superiority and then stand there to watch the team carry out their every move. Team members may obey, begrudgingly, but not without some arguing. The team will appreciate the time taken and value the manager more when the manager shows team members how to carry out the work. Rather than commanding from above, the manager works alongside the team. The manager subjects themselves to the same punishment that team members will endure. The manager will take the full blame in the event of a failure, protecting team members against any repercussions.

By observing what the manager is doing, team members can easily follow along. This is particularly helpful with junior members. The manager does not lead like a dictator but more like a mentor. Based on several years if not decades of experience, the manager provides practical guidance that is rooted in knowing what had been tried in the past. The manager continues to learn and evaluates current technologies against the lessons learnt from previous iterations. The manager then applies this rich background to present work, providing insight and good sense to team members. This style of leadership genuinely motivates people to want to come into the office and do the work. Team members will know that they are not alone. They have a senior specialist who understands them and will help them. The other style forces people to work; they will do the work, but it would not be an enjoyable experience.

Potential of Discovery: By Flexible Management, Not by Rigidity

Rules and procedures should not be so strict and rigid. The ways of operating, if they are very tight, can lose or severely constrain creativity. This would not lead to innovation. The ways of operating should have a degree of flexibility that allows for adaptation into new and unknown situations. While there would be a main path to follow for most situations, a procedure can have an alternate path for a peculiar situation that breaks the mold. A rigid procedure would likely not have taken into account such a possibility. As such, the team could be stuck. A flexible procedure, on the other hand, gives the team room to maneuver.

Flexible rules and procedures are designed to be applied in multiple scenarios. They are generalizable to cover a variety of situations. In contrast, rigid rules and procedures are designed for specific contexts. One rigid procedure will not work in a different situation in which the procedure was not designed to handle.

Rules and procedures that are flexible would stimulate the thought processes of team members. The highly generalizable procedure will have gaps that critical thinking must fill. Team members will apply their critical thinking skills in any given project or system. They will examine a particular system and make adjustments as needed. Adjustments would be made case by case, project by project, and system by system. As they think through a particular situation, team members could generate a new idea. They could potentially discover something new.

It is that potential of discovery that motivates the team. Team members would want to engage more when they know that there is the possibility of finding something that no one else has found – an invention or a breakthrough. Once found and validated as a true discovery, team members will be rewarded with peer recognition, career advancement, or financial compensation. Most important, the manager who follows the first practice will be more than happy to step away from the spotlight, and let the team members have their glory in front of their peers. The manager had done their job to facilitate the process that enabled the team to get to this point. The manager would be satisfied with the job done right.

Individual Respect and Equality: Everyone Learns From Each Other

Every team member including the manager is viewed as a specialist with equal standing. Each person brings to the team a foundation of knowledge and skill sets that contribute to the work. No one person can know everything. Even the manager will have an area that they have no knowledge or skill in. The manager regularly stresses this point. A capacity sheet is updated and maintained, showcasing the knowledge and skills that each team member has. Team members can read what each member is good at and are encouraged to ask them questions and to work with them. By knowing that everyone is viewed as equal, each team member would not feel intimidated or threatened to approach another member. Everyone is given the respect that each person deserves because everyone knows that every team member has something to offer. A working environment is created to motivate team members to grow professionally through collegial engagement.

Daily Communication: The 5-Minute Brief Meeting

Meetings, obviously, are a necessary part of work in any organization. But too many meetings during the day, meetings that are too long, and discussions in meetings that too often depart far from the agenda can lose the interest of team members and make attending meetings more of a chore.

One practice that keeps team members motivated to attend and participate in meetings is to have a very short meeting about 5 minutes, no longer than 10 minutes, as the first order of business every morning of the day. Once every member has arrived in the office and is ready to start the day, team members will meet. Each member will quickly state (1) what they did yesterday, (2) what they will do today, and (3) any encountered issues or problems. The manager will update each member's post-it note with current remarks. As a caveat, this practice may not be suitable for a large team. The daily meeting regime is suited for a small team of 5–10 people.

If a large team does exist, then the large team needs to be broken up into smaller units whose team members are directly engaged on a daily basis. It is unlikely that all members in a large team will be engaged with each other every day. There would be small groups who engage actively on a daily basis. It is those small groups who would benefit from the daily meeting regime.

Having everyone speak will go fast, since each member would have one or two tasks to state. The number of issues would likely be few and stated by a few team members. Statements are limited to a sentence or a phrase. No team member would go into any length to describe a task or an issue at this time. The manager and individual team member can discuss the details in a separate meeting.

The purpose of the brief meeting with everyone is to get a quick status report on progress. All team members involved will know what each member is working on. Any problem that has arisen can be handled and resolved.

By keeping abreast of the latest development every day, team members will be motivated to continue working. Every team member hears what the other member is doing and would be encouraged and maybe gain insight that will allow members to improve their work. The structured series of brief meetings every morning will keep team members fully engaged.

This practice of meeting every day would not be appropriate in a work environment whose nature of tasks does not change much, moves rather slowly, and/or is mundane. A typical office setting where administrative support staff review reports and write letters is an example. A research group whose work entails searching information, reviewing books and periodicals, and analyzing data is another example. Such an environment would not have much new information to give on a daily basis. In this case, weekly meetings will be sufficient.

The nature of tasks in a work environment must be fast-paced and rapidly changing. A consumer retail store where shoppers are moving through the store to buy products is an example of such an environment. A military unit on the front line of battle is another example. The work of software development is a case where various issues can arise during the day in the course of developing a software program. Various factors are involved in software development. In all of these examples, the manager needs to be kept updated on what has happened during the day. Given that things could change at an instant, it becomes that more critical to meet with the team more frequently. The manager does not want to be in a position of being surprised.

Whiteboard of Activities

All of the post-it notes that capture what team members are working on are posted to a large whiteboard in the office meeting room. The team would be able to review activities and follow the sequence of tasks, as the project is implemented day by day. Any issues that arise would be available to read and can be followed through to resolution. The manager would arrange the post-it notes in some manner to monitor progress and track the flow of activities. For instance, all notes specific to one team member would be grouped together. Notes related to a particular software program would be grouped together. Notes related to an issue would be grouped together and placed on the whiteboard in an area that the manager can quickly see every day until the issue is resolved. In accordance with the project schedule, post-it notes would be selected and arranged on the whiteboard to show what is currently the focus. The manager then can effectively follow tasks and issues day by day and week by week. Moreover, the high degree of transparency that this approach affords allows the team to hold every team member accountable.

Chapter 6 Quiz

Question 1: Which phase in the System Development Life Cycle process provides the critical fulcrum?

A. Data Migration
B. System Deployment
C. System Testing
D. System Definition
E. System Selection and Evaluation

Question 2: What is a concern in the agile approach that could be an issue in a contracting environment?

A. Focusing too much on the technical details
B. Ongoing software development work that continuously evolves
C. Changes are relatively easier to make mid-way through in implementation
D. Increased risk in developing new software features without thinking them through ahead of time
E. Incorporation of new ideas as they arise

Question 3: What are the major factors that will aid in selecting all of the software features for implementation and in managing expectations?

A. Critical, Important, and Useful
B. Priority and Risk
C. High Level, Medium Level, and Low Level
D. Priority, Effort, Risk, and Stability
E. Importance and Stability

Question 4: What is the master, guiding document that all other documents will refer to?

A. Business Case
B. Technical Specifications
C. Functional Requirements
D. Final Release Report
E. System Test Plan

Question 5: What should not be done in carrying out a system test plan?

A. Testing a feature only by one person
B. Testing a feature a number of times
C. Testing a feature at different times of the day and on different days of the week
D. Testing a feature in different computer networks
E. Testing a feature on various computer operating systems

Worksheets

Project: ____________________ Manager: ____________________

ID	Feature	Status	Priority	Effort	Risk	Stability	Release

Worksheet 6.1 Software development feature analysis.

Step 1:

Write one specific item (a work task) on a Post-it® note.

Step 2:

Organize written notes on a large board, sorting them in any pattern that makes sense in your operating environment.

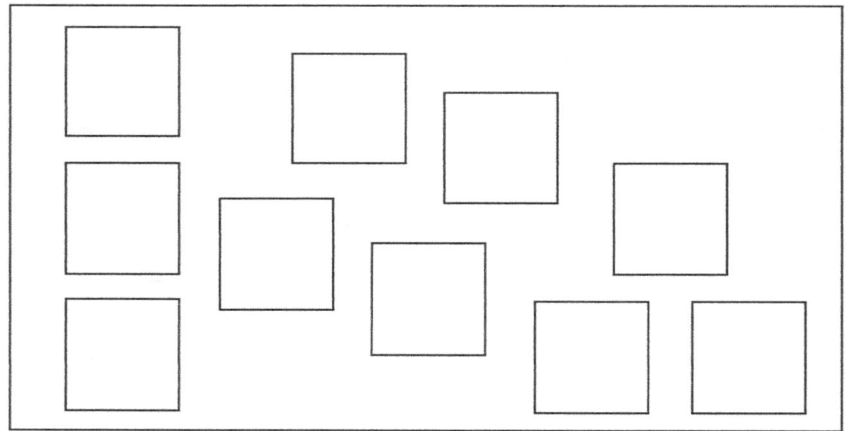

Step 3:

Apply the arrangement of notes to other worksheets.

Worksheet 6.2 Work task arrangement exercise.

Project: ____________________ Manager: ____________________

Est. Total Work Days:

ID	Task	Days	Start	Finish	Predecessor(s)	Resource(s)

Worksheet 6.3 Project schedule.

Chapter 7

Information Security: Protect and Safeguard the IT System

All of the necessary computer technologies had been purchased and developed to secure the agency's Information Technology (IT) systems. Will that prevent a hacker from breaking in? There is one element in the IT ecosystem that if left uncontrolled could still make the systems vulnerable and perhaps could neutralize the implemented technical controls. What is that element?

Chapter Summary

Without stating explicitly what element is being referred to, this chapter will give clues to understanding how that element can be controlled. It is an element that, arguably, can be the hardest to handle. History shows that certain leaders and groups had tried to control it. But it behaves in ways to undermine or work around the measures. Chapter 1 indicated the most important element in the IT ecosystem.

Security broadly defined is vital to governmental operations. With many organizations connected together, security becomes ever more critical for all organizations – both public and private – especially when private companies become engaged in partnerships with government agencies. Various forms of cyberthreats could disrupt business, lose data, and damage equipment. The government agency needs to be assured that its information is protected and safeguarded against potential threats. IT personnel must be able to monitor and assess risks continuously and report and act on serious threats in a timely manner.

This chapter describes the implications and risks of leaving the elements in the IT ecosystem unprotected. A risk assessment method allows the public manager to evaluate and quantify the risk of security threats and the effectiveness of security controls. Based on matching the quantified risk and effectiveness, the public manager can further evaluate one or more controls for each identified threat. A standard three-prong approach (based on managerial controls, operational controls, and technical controls) provides the overall structure for protecting information throughout an organization. The chapter goes into detail in developing an information security program that protects and safeguards an IT system on multiple levels. If one layer is stripped away, the additional layers must be stripped away in order to obtain what an organization highly values. The security program increases the level of difficulty in trying to break into an IT system. This chapter concludes with the development of an Information System Security Policy.

Implications of Security Breaches

A security breach could cause damage to or a loss of an intangible value, a tangible asset, and an intellectual property. Unauthorized access (even access that is duly authorized) could lead to a user-created error, a data or message alteration, a failure in computer hardware or computer software, fraud, or theft. Intentional or accidental disclosure of information could range in severity from a humorous activity that creates an embarrassing situation for a particular department to a secret program that enables an adversary to gain an advantage. Corrupted data in computer hardware or computer software can render information unusable or useless. An Internet connection line bombarded with thousands of bogus connections can cause data to be dropped between legitimate end users who carry out business. The end users involved would find that their communications are extremely slow in such a case of a flooded network. An IT system could be forced to go down for hours or days, and as a result, the government agency would have to halt services or reduce the level of services to the public during the downtime. Any service fees that would be collected or payments that would be made to eligible beneficiaries would not be available for processing in the downed IT system. The forced outage of an IT system, furthermore, could result in a damaged hardware component that would have to be replaced. Trust and confidence can be eroded if not lost by the general public to whom the government agency provides support, if disruption of a service is sustained over a lengthy period of time. As there may be no other organization to provide an equivalent public service, a proportion of the population can be made less well-off or potentially at risk of harm.

Two major problems that could undermine the integrity of an organization are worth highlighting. An IT system would have parts of a business process automated to carry out specific tasks quickly. An automated process engineered in a computer software program could be manipulated to produce a fraudulent user profile or activity, sabotage a system, or create some kind of damage. An end user could inject a script-like command or a seemingly innocuous input to do something in ways that were not intended by the original software development team. Because the work is automated, numerous attempts can be executed in a short period of time without the public manager knowing that the malicious activity is being carried out. The public manager would eventually realize that fraud or damage had occurred but typically after a length of time when the prospect of identifying the suspect is dim.

A computer-based information system critical and important to operations, such as one used for financial management, human resources management, and healthcare management, could be the target for sabotage. Data in the compromised system could be used for blackmail or some other criminal activity. An end user, whether a disgruntled employee or an unknown outsider, could find their way into the system and plant a malicious computer software program that executes at a certain date and time in the future. The execution of the malicious software program could cause data to be deleted or cause some other problem that renders the system useless. Since execution is run at a future date, the prospect of identifying the suspect is very low. The perpetrator would be long gone and forgotten. Moreover, the perpetrator would have removed entries in log files to conceal their tracks in accessing the system. The public manager would be left in a damaging situation where the damaged computer-based information system, which the agency depends on, results in certain functions of the government agency to be inoperable.

Common Weaknesses

Inadequate or lack of technical controls, which are implemented by IT personnel, may not be sources of weakness in information security. An organization could have sophisticated technological elements to harden all of its IT systems and still remain vulnerable to security threats. In other words, an organization can still be very weak after investing in advanced computer technology to keep an IT system secured.

Weaknesses that are often found in organizations are *non-technological* in nature. Such areas do not require implementation or development of computer technology. The areas, moreover, can increase in complexity with the size of an organization. Security risks can be compounded when multiple areas are not coordinated or are left unattended to.

The non-technological weaknesses refer to missing or inadequate managerial and operational controls, which are approved and overseen by senior executive leaders. There could be a poorly designed or haphazardly developed disaster recovery plan that may not offer full protection in a number of different scenarios (e.g., natural disaster, fire incident, and system crash). There could be unclear access policies, which can result in mishandling equipment and information by the wrong persons. Expressed knowledge of who is responsible for a computer-based information system may not be known in documentation. This could lead to an avoidance of accountability in the event of a security issue. There could be no one who is expressly held responsible for a specific security breach. There could be loose to no coordination by various departments when responding to a security event. There could be little to no communication among key personnel about new and emerging threats that may increase vulnerabilities. End users may not be aware of vulnerabilities, as they were not provided security briefs and training. There could be no security-related business process to assess, deploy, and monitor all of the controls for all of the areas. There could be a lack of an information security strategy within the wider organizational strategy.

The non-technological areas fall under the purview of non-IT personnel. IT personnel would provide technical work such as in security training and in carrying out specific technical tasks. High-level policies and guidelines, however, would be provided by non-IT personnel to direct information security in a coherent and organized manner. Senior executive leaders must be assured that all areas that may impact the government agency have been considered and controlled.

Security Threats

A wide range of security threats with various degrees of severity could happen in IT. And a particular threat could occur more frequently than others. A natural disaster would be a rare event that brings intense force to destroy a building and all the equipment inside. A sudden electrical power outage could damage a computer. Foreign particles so small and fine such as dust could get into computer hardware and build up inside, causing a problem in the electrical circuit. Water, soda, coffee, and other liquids spilt over a computer could make the computer inoperable. Several computer servers running continuously in a closed room could overheat, if the room temperature is not maintained at a constant level that keeps the room cooled. Excessive heat creates a hazard in operating computer servers. A computer virus from the Internet or a computer flash drive could infect an end user's computer and execute malicious instructions without knowledge of or permission by the end user, taking control of the computer away from the end user. That infected computer, if it is connected to a computer network, could spread the computer virus to other computers. A Denial of Service (DoS) attack could be sent to a computer server to force it to come down by inundating it with thousands of bogus requests. Legitimate requests from end users would not be processed and would be dropped in such an attack. A Phishing attack could be sent to an individual end user to attempt to get the end user to submit sensitive information such as a password, a credit card number, or a personal identification number. The technique of a Phishing attack could be so persuasive as to look genuine that it can fool an end user. A mistake in data entry could result in a report or some other output that is erroneous or invalid. A peculiar form of data input could be submitted into a computer software program and cause the software program to delete a record or carry out some other task that would not be permitted under normal operating conditions.

A group of security threats relates to unauthorized access. An unauthorized person could physically enter a computer room and gain access into one or more of the operating computers. An unknown user, whether a person or a machine, could gain access electronically into a computer and change the installed software program as an innocent prank or a malicious act. Such an intrusion, whether physical or electronic, could be committed by an internal employee who would have less difficulty in accessing a computer. An internal employee is provided a user account with rights to do certain things in an IT system. Another person could illicitly obtain an employee's password and fraudulently use the employee's user account to gain access into a computer. A network connection could be tapped (similar to a wiretap in a telephone conversation) whereby a third-party user can monitor and record the data as it is transmitted through the computer network. A third-party user could steal a password or some other information or could have knowledge of what document or video had been accessed and viewed.

There could be other types of security threats in addition to the threats described here. This chapter by no means can possibly list all threats. Information security threats can evolve into new forms. As computer technology advances, new types of security threats would likely be created. The public manager then must be vigilant and regularly assess and reassess the IT ecosystem.

Risk Assessment

Some security threats may not apply or can be less important for a particular organization. Geography can determine certain types of threats. A desert region with constant high temperature and dry heat, for example, poses an ongoing challenge to operating electronic equipment. The difference in work culture can emphasize one set of threats over another set. A lax organization, for example, would have to focus on issues related to end users. The number and complexity of IT systems in existence can multiply the effect of a combination of threats. For example, a government agency with several systems in several locations would have a confluence of threats that makes the overall security environment more complicated in comparison to a nonprofit organization that would have a few systems in one or two locations.

Each organization has to evaluate its own security threats to determine which ones pose greater harm (higher risk) and thus would be worthy of increased investment in time and resources to control. It is not possible, financially, technically, and practically, to handle *all* threats. The security threats need to be prioritized. Those threats that would have little impact (low risk) to the organization would be considered a low priority. And those low-priority threats would be allocated a small amount of funds per threat. A high-priority threat would deserve a large amount of funds.

A method for assessing the risk of a security threat is to evaluate its level of severity and its probability of occurrence. How likely will the threat occur? How severe in terms of impact is the threat in a single instance? The product of severity and occurrence gives a "Risk Factor (RF)" score for the security threat. This calculated RF score can then be used to compare one security threat against another in an objective way. The RF score of a hurricane disaster can be weighed against the RF score of a data entry mistake, for instance. Without the calculation, the threat of a hurricane seems obvious that it poses higher risk than the threat of a data entry mistake. But how likely will a hurricane occur in comparison to the occurrence of a data entry mistake? The added occurrence variable could increase the RF score of a data entry mistake higher than that of a hurricane. The equation for calculating a Risk Factor score for a security threat is:

$$RF = V \bullet O$$

where

RF = Risk Factor of a Security Threat
V = Level of Severity
O = Probability of Occurrence

The level of severity is a scale from 0 to 4, with 0 representing no severity (no impact) and 4 representing the highest severity (highest impact). A value of 2 indicates medium level (moderate impact).

The probability of occurrence is a scale from 0 to 1, with 0 representing no occurrence (0% likelihood of occurrence) and 1 representing a 100% likelihood of occurrence. A 0.5 value indicates a 50% likelihood of occurrence.

The estimated values for severity and occurrence will be the opinions of IT personnel, based on experience in dealing with the security threats. Geography, work culture, and other particular factors surrounding the operating environment of an organization can produce risk scores that are different for one organization in comparison to another. The risk assessment is specific to the unique situation in which the organization operates.

In general, a security threat with a low level of severity and a low probability of occurrence can be considered a low priority. A security threat with a high level of severity and a high probability of occurrence is a high priority and will need to be controlled.

Control Effectiveness

Security threats have been analyzed, producing risk scores to indicate their level of priority. Now, it is time to determine what security controls will be most effective in dealing with the threats. The government agency will want to be assured that a security control is mitigating the risk of a security threat and that the investment in the control is paying off. If after several months that it becomes known that a particular control is not working, then another security control should be selected and used. An ineffective security control should be swapped out for a better control.

A method for assessing the effectiveness of a security control is to evaluate its level of security and its probability of protection. How likely will the control provide protection? How secure is the control? The product of security and protection gives a "Control Effectiveness (CE)" score for the security control. The equation for calculating a Control Effectiveness score for a security control is:

$$CE = S \bullet P$$

where
CE = Control Effectiveness of a Security Control
S = Level of Security
P = Probability of Protection

The level of security is a scale from 0 to 4, with 0 representing no security (extremely loose) and 4 representing the highest security (extremely tight). A value of 2 indicates medium level (moderate security).

The probability of protection is a scale from 0 to 1, with 0 representing no protection (0% likelihood of protection) and 1 representing full protection (100% likelihood of protection). A 0.5 value indicates a 50% likelihood of protection.

The estimated values for security and protection will also be the opinions of IT personnel, based on experience in using the security controls. Unlike in the calculation of the risk score, there could be agreement among many organizations in the calculated effectiveness score. Numerous organizations could procure the same or very similar security product from one or a few vendors in the market. A handful of private companies exist that develop an antivirus computer software program, for instance. The opinions for that particular software program to provide effective control would not be wide and divergent.

The CE scores can be used to compare security controls one against the other. The public manager may have a number of solutions to control a particular threat. There may be different vendors providing a solution to the same threat. In any case, the calculated CE scores can provide an objective way to choose a solution.

The quantified security control can be matched appropriately with the quantified security threat (see Figure 7.1). A threat with a low RF score does not necessarily require a control with a high CE score. This may be overkill as the organization would be spending too much money on a particular threat that poses little harm. On the other hand, the organization may not be spending enough on a control with a low CE score to mitigate a threat with a high RF score. A high-risk security threat would warrant a highly effective security control. The RF score and the CE score should be approximately at around the same level more or less, if not equal in an ideal situation. In other words, the amount of control applied should match the amount of risk assessed in a security threat. Why use a hammer to kill a pesky fly when a swatter is adequate?

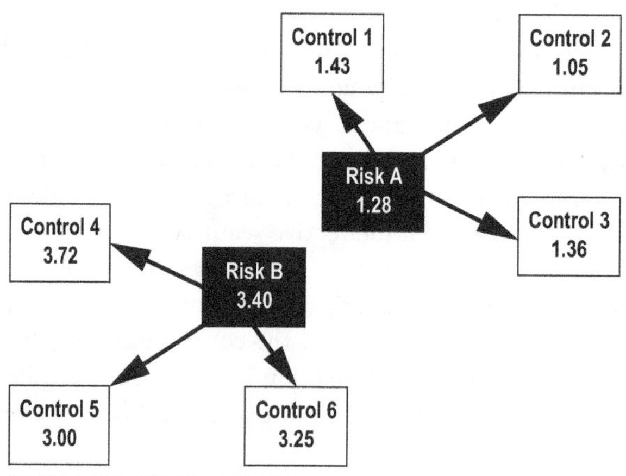

Figure 7.1 Matched security control to security risk.

As a matter of best practice, one security threat should have more than one security control. The public manager should never rely on a single control to counter one particular threat. Even with high security and full protection, a security control could fail or could be neutralized. A security control could be bypassed. At least two alternative controls should be in place to provide backups in the event that the primary control fails. For each security threat then, there should be three security controls (one primary and two alternatives). Among a list of available controls, furthermore, a particular security control may be effective in handling more than one security threat. A number of threats could be countered by the same security control.

Security Controls

Specific security controls are organized into three categories. There are (1) managerial controls, (2) operational controls, and (3) technical controls. Managerial controls include official policies, assigned responsibilities, formal standards, and general guidelines to establish sets of rules related to information security. Three key policies cover the information system, user access, and rules of behavior. Managerial controls are developed by the Information Security Committee and approved by senior executive leaders and are directed with consistent application across the organization. Senior executive leaders must oversee and enforce the managerial controls.

Operational controls include plans, procedures, protocols, and requirements for various areas of IT operations related to information security. Critical areas include user account management, user roles, data integrity, change/version control, physical protection, facility access, and fire safety. Key plans cover business continuity, disaster recovery, incident response, and security training. Operational controls are developed by the Information Security Committee and managed by the IT department. The IT Manager must oversee the operational controls.

Technical controls include implemented technologies, purchased equipment, developed software programs, and specific techniques related to information security. Critical areas include user identification, intrusion prevention, facility surveillance, network monitoring, and data validation. Key controls include a user authentication device/method, a video surveillance camera, a network monitoring tool, a computer diagnostic tool, an antivirus software program, and an audit system to record changes to a computer-based information system. Technical controls are implemented and maintained by IT personnel. These controls can involve time and resources to implement and maintain. The IT Manager must also oversee the technical controls.

All three categories of security controls are not mutually exclusive. The public manager cannot develop and deploy one category of controls without developing and deploying another category of controls. These three categories form a logical structure. Implementing a technical control is guided by a corresponding operational control. An operational control, in turn, is provided direction by a managerial control. The rationale for using a specific technical control has its basis in a managerial control. Granting or denying end users, for instance, starts with an official policy on user access. This managerial control provides direction on what will be needed and why to operationalize user access. Operational controls related to user access (e.g., user account management and user roles) can be planned and developed into procedures. IT personnel will then use the plans and procedures to select the right hardware, software, and other technologies (e.g., all of the parts and apparatus to deploy a user authentication method) to put user access as directed into effect.

Combined together, all three categories of security controls provide meaning to ensure that end users are *willing to follow* and comply with the security controls. End users will have an understanding and awareness of why the controls are needed. Each category serves a particular purpose.

The three categories of security controls provide the three-prong approach (a standard) to implementing information security in an organization.

Security Layers

Another way of seeing security controls is to view them as layers of protection. A set of controls serves as a single security layer that offers protection for an IT system. To use an analogy: A person can protect themselves in cold weather by wearing layers of clothing (e.g., a shirt, a sweater, a light windbreaker, and a heavy overcoat). The outer-most layer would protect a person from snow and wind, while inner layers provide insulation and warmth. The person can remove a layer when they feel it is no longer needed. But it would be harder to add a layer of protection at a moment when an additional layer is needed but would not be currently available. Protecting an IT system follows the same logic. During a crisis, the public manager may realize that another security control (another layer) is needed, but it may be too late, since it was never planned and implemented beforehand. An unplanned control may cost more, since the government agency would be implementing it in a rush in an emergency situation. Implementing layers of security controls will keep the government agency prepared. And the costs can be better managed.

A multi-layered information security program can protect an IT system. In this approach, there will be numerous controls that involve both technology and non-technology. All three categories of security controls are developed. The following five layers provide coverage for an organization's valued asset – information. While each layer carries equal importance, the layers are ordered in such a way as to build successive shields, each one of which serves to protect the layer that lies underneath. Five layers then offer five overlapping shields. If a particular shield is broken through, then the remaining shields can still provide protection. If a certain layer is not needed, then there will still be other layers to provide protection. Figure 7.2 illustrates this multi-layered information security program. The five security layers are as follows:

1. Software Layer
2. Computer Layer
3. Network Layer
4. Physical Layer
5. End User Layer

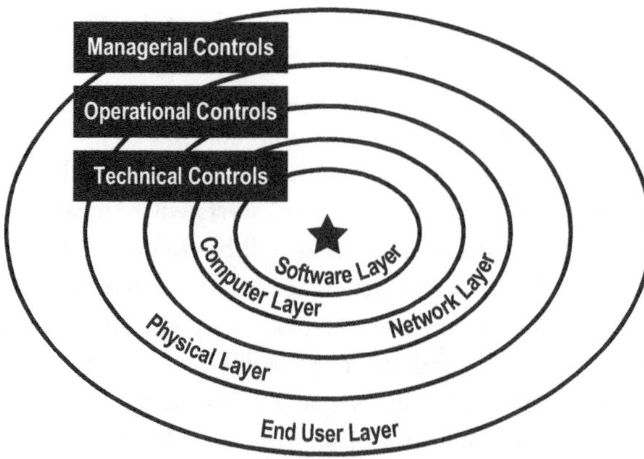

Figure 7.2 Multiple layers of information security.

Software Layer

The Software Layer covers the computer software element in the IT ecosystem. As computer software is the one technological element that directly processes and handles information, the computer software program provides the first line of defense for protecting the information element in the IT ecosystem. Whether it is purchased from a vendor or developed by an internal software development team, the software program must have the three categories of security controls to protect how data are inputted, processed, and outputted. At the point of data entry, an end user could submit information that is a mistake or in error. This can invalidate a particular data record. At the same point of data entry, an end user with malicious intent could submit programming code to try to do harm to the IT system that controls the software program. This is a high risk with online Web software programs. A specific case is known as SQL injection, which is the intentional submission of an SQL command to change or delete records in a database.

A data entry control is to apply constraints on a specific input text field (i.e., an input field used to enter information such as a name, an address, or a product). The input text field should be limited in the number of characters that can be entered. The input text field should also be limited to a specified data type (e.g., a number field, a decimal field, and a date-time field). Additional computer programming should be written to check the format and type of data entered prior to being processed. Any inputted data that do not conform to specifications must be rejected.

Another data entry control is to minimize the number of input text fields that is presented to the end user. A predefined list of items (e.g., a drop-down or pull-down menu) should be presented whenever possible. This provides better security over the input text field and offers convenience for the end user. The end user makes a selection from the list instead of typing in information.

With various types of information, data entry needs to control what types of information will be accepted. If a particular IT system does not require video, for example, then video should not be allowed in the input. Any software program that uses any one of the information types in a self-running executable program should not be accepted as a form of data entry, if it is not absolutely required. Information types beyond text could potentially do harm, since a document, an audio, a video, and a multimedia presentation could be a vehicle that carries malicious programming code. Although rare, an image could potentially be a vehicle for harm; an image is also an electronic file that could be manipulated.

The way in which information is processed and outputted must have controls. Certain information should be limited in how it is displayed to the end user. Information could be constrained to viewing on a display monitor at the time of access with no ability for the end user to copy the information. Information could be formatted in a particular way in a specific document file. In any case, the end user is only permitted to use the information as it is presented.

This gets to the concern in how information is processed. The software program must have the three categories of security controls to protect and manage the processing from input to output. For whatever reason the development team may have (lack of time, convenience, or laziness), there may be parts of programming code that could lead to software issues resulting in information errors or worse. And those parts could potentially be exploited, if known, by a computer hacker. A general software development technique is to throw an exception when specific criteria are not met. In other words, input that does not meet specified rules must be rejected. Additional blocks of programming code should be included to provide various kinds of checks to ensure that the data conform to a certain way as required. Non-conforming data need to be rejected and stopped in the processing flow. Moreover, the software program must have a limit on the number of times that non-conforming data can be processed. Unlimited processing could lead to a problem where the software program continuously executes the process with no determined end (an endless loop), only to be terminated by a system crash when all available computing resources have been exhausted in the computer.

Computer Layer

The Computer Layer covers the computer hardware element, the computer firmware element, and any other hardware-related element in the IT ecosystem. To a certain extent, a computer software program that controls, affects, or interacts with computer hardware is also covered in this security layer. A configured computer system, whether it is a personal computer, a computer server, a mobile device, or some other computerized device, must have the three categories of security controls to protect the installed computer software program that is the subject in the computer software layer. The computer system provides the second line of defense for protecting the information element in the IT ecosystem. If the computer can be broken into, then the installed computer software program can be accessed.

Any computer hardware component that is not needed to run a computer at all hours of the day should be disconnected or disabled. A particular computer does not need to be connected to a display monitor, if it can be managed via a terminal connection or a remote login from another computer. If a computer does not need to be connected in a computer network, then the network adapter can be removed or disabled. With the availability of wireless network connectivity, it should be decided whether a computer needs a wired connection or a wireless connection. Unless redundancy is needed, one or the other network connection type would be sufficient.

The operating system software program has settings that can be configured to enable and disable functions related to the computer system. Changing the settings should only be permitted by an end user who has system administrator rights. The settings can be configured to limit what an end user can see and do in the computer. Installing an unauthorized software program should be denied. A third-party software program should only be installed by IT personnel. Such a software program may be unlicensed, untested, or insecure, creating a problem for the individual computer and/or the computer network. A best practice is to install only those software programs that the end user needs to do their job. Access to a specific folder that contains files related to the operation of the computer should be denied. A person who is not skilled in computers could make their computer system unable to boot up or start up, causing an IT specialist to have to rebuild the computer. Saving a document or a file should be allowed in a number of specific folders, as determined by management. Specific locations of where user files are stored can facilitate the process of backing up and restoring files. In the event that a computer system crashes, user files would be found and restored. Limits on where files are saved, what folders can be accessed, and what software programs can be installed are just a few controls that need to be implemented to keep a computer system secured and stable in operation.

A computer virus, which is a rogue software program containing malicious programming code, could get into a computer system and do damage. The end user could download a software program from an unknown or untrusted source. The downloaded program would appear to look legitimate, but once the program is installed, it will unleash the virus upon execution. An e-mail message could have a software program attached. This attached program also could contain a virus that once installed will execute the malicious code. Even if the computer is not connected to the computer network, a virus could be released from a software program in an external media storage device. A flash drive, which plugs into the computer's USB port, is a common vehicle for transporting a computer virus from one computer to the next.

A number of security controls can reduce the prevalence of computer viruses. Denying the ability to install a software program, as described above, is a control. An antivirus software program is a control that is designed to scan the computer system for any viruses and to quarantine and remove found viruses. As will be described below, controls in the computer network can be implemented to check for viruses and block them before they can hit the computer. Security awareness training is a control that can be provided to inform end users how to detect possible vehicle-carrying viruses and other security threats.

Network Layer

The Network Layer covers the computer network element and the Internet element in the IT ecosystem. As it relates to connectivity to the network and the Internet, the telecommunication infrastructure is also covered in this security layer. The computer network offers a third line of defense for protecting the information element in the IT ecosystem. In order to hit the computer, an attacker will have to get past the security controls in the computer network. The computer network must have the three categories of security controls.

A standard control that is implemented in any organization's computer network is a network firewall. This specialized network device sits at the perimeter edge of the network to protect the entire computer network. As such, it can block specified network traffic coming in from and going out to the Internet and other computer networks. Rules are configured in the network firewall to allow and deny specific network services and network ports. If available, the network firewall may have the capability to scan and quarantine e-mail messages and electronic files for viruses. Not all network firewalls available on the market may have this antivirus capability – an additional feature. In its core purpose, the network firewall can block external end users from accessing the internal network and can also block internal employees from accessing certain services on the Internet.

There may be end users who work remotely at their personal residence or in another location separate from the principal office building. These telecommuters would need to access the government agency's computer network. A Virtual Private Network (VPN) extends the agency's network to the sites where the telecommuters work, allowing the remote end users to access the same services that they would normally have access to if they were working in the principal office with everyone else. A VPN connection is established for each telecommuter and uses encryption technology to encrypt the network connection and all the data that get transferred. The number of VPN connections should be limited in use for individual end users. If a remote site has several end users who require access, then a different network design other than the VPN needs to be implemented.

Hundreds of employees who access Websites on the Internet at the same time can use up the entire data connection. This will slow down the connection speed for some end users or halt the connection completely for others. One way of moderating access to Websites is to install a specialized computer server called a "proxy server" (as a control) in the computer network. End users will connect to this proxy server to retrieve stored copies of Web pages. Unless the requested Web page has expired after a specified date or the proxy server does not have a stored copy, end users are not connected to the Internet to access the original Website. The proxy server can reduce Internet usage and free up resources in the data connection.

The government agency would have computer servers that the general public would have access to. Common examples include a Web server for hosting a Website and a mail server for sending and receiving e-mail messages. If these servers are located inside the computer network, then anonymous end users could potentially use the computer servers as a way to access internal private resources such as computer-based information systems and employees' computers. A control then is to isolate those computer servers available to the public in a separate computer network. Such a network is called a "Demilitarized Zone" or DMZ. The network firewall will have a defined rule that denies access from the DMZ network to the internal computer network. The network firewall will allow everyone, including the public to access the DMZ network, but access beyond the DMZ will be blocked. The general public will not be able to access computers beyond the DMZ network.

A single computer server that operates a Website, an e-mail service, or a computer-based information system can be forced to go down under heavy network traffic. A single computer server may not be able to handle concurrent connections from thousands of end users. A technical measure to ensure continuous service is to replicate the service in a number of computer servers. There would be a control to direct network traffic from one server that is very busy to another server that is less busy. This prevents a computer server from going down as end users are redirected to a computer server that can handle the connections. This type of redundancy can be used in a situation where an online backup of data is required. For instance, a secondary database server contains the most current data set and as it remains online can serve as an immediate fail-over system in the event that the primary database server has to be taken offline for any reason. The redundancy can be used to take down a computer server for periodic maintenance. In this case, IT personnel can regularly keep each server performing at an optimal level, while end users can continuously use the service with minimal downtime.

Given that there will be people intent on trying to access the computer network to do harm, the computer network must be monitored. A key control in this regard is to implement a network monitoring tool that can record and display inbound and outbound network traffic. Such a tool would display network traffic in real time. IT personnel would be able to follow up quickly when they notice a sudden spike in inbound traffic. A possible system crash would be noticed quickly, as the monitoring tool would report very little to no network traffic for a certain period of time immediately after a sudden fall.

An Intrusion Detection System (IDS) provides advanced and sophisticated network monitoring, analyzing activities related to the computer network and IT systems and alerting personnel to possible breaches and attacks. The IDS uses a sensor or an agent to monitor activity at a number of critical points in the network. The analysis could be done on a network connection, a specific network protocol, and a specific host computer.

Physical Layer

The Physical Layer covers the technological elements and the information element in the IT ecosystem, as they relate to their protection in physical forms. All such physical forms, including the data center and operating practices described below, must have the three categories of security controls. Any computer equipment (e.g., a personal computer, a mobile device, and a network device) must be kept clean and maintained and in good working order. A copy of any computer software program must be kept on a storage medium that is stored in a secured location. Documentation of computer software licenses, computer hardware purchases, and other related documents must be stored in a secured location. All types of information should be archived in physical forms and stored in a secured location. Similar to computer software, copies of electronic files of documents, video, etc. would be kept on a storage medium.

An inventory system provides a control to organize and track all computer equipment. The product name, the manufacturer name, the product serial number, and other details related to each computer equipment need to be recorded. The software license key, if applicable the software license start date and end date, and other details related to each computer software program need to be recorded. A permanent tag showing the name of the organization, the name of the department or operating unit, and a unique identification number should be created and affixed to each computer equipment. In the event of loss or theft, ownership could be verified by the tag on the computer equipment.

A best practice and a control for securing storage media containing software programs, electronic files, and/or computer-related documentation is to keep them in a fire-proof safe. Data backups stored on magnetic tape would also be stored in the fire-proof safe. If access to these files is infrequent (e.g., once every 3 months), the media and documentation can be stored in an off-site location such as in a safe deposit box at a bank. Materials must be stored in such a manner as to protect them against accidental misplacement, theft, and fire. Most important, only certain personnel as designated must have the authority to access the materials.

All IT systems, the computer servers, the network devices, cables, and equipment related to the IT infrastructure must be housed in a secured facility commonly known as a data center. Another name for data center is server room. The data center must be kept clean (free of dust and fine particles), cooled at a stable and constant temperature, and completely enclosed with no windows. The data center needs its own dedicated circuit for electrical power, separate from other circuits within a larger building. An auxiliary generator should be installed and available in the event of a power outage. A fire suppression system needs to be installed in the data center.

For decades, a raised floor made up of vented tiles was constructed over a concrete slab floor in a data center. The raised floor provided for the space underneath to run cables, install specially designed water-cooling pipes, and allow air to flow. New practices and equipment, however, do not necessarily require the need for a raised floor. Cables can be run overhead and dropped down into cabinets and racks. Air-conditioning units can be mounted on walls, or a central cooling system can be constructed to provide air-conditioning through air ducts in the ceiling. The decision to construct a raised floor or not would be based on the overall design of the data center. In some cases, a concrete slab floor or a hard floor would be fine. In some regions prone to earthquakes, cabinets and racks should be mounted directly to a solid surface for complete stability.

The data center and other areas and rooms deemed sensitive should include surveillance cameras to record activities on video. Since a supervisor cannot be present at all hours throughout the day, video recordings of people in the areas would be used to review incidents of security breaches and issues. Access to all sensitive areas must be secured through a locked entry door that only authorized personnel can enter. Advanced methods of door-entry systems need to be used instead of the basic key. One door-entry system requires a number combination to be pressed. Another door-entry system uses a proximity card. A particular biometric door-entry system requires a person to place their hand flat along guided pins.

End User Layer

The End User Layer covers the end user element in the IT ecosystem. Even with the technological elements controlled and the physical items and areas controlled, there is still a risk if the end users are not controlled. And the risk is high for a security incident to occur with those end users who are internal to the organization. It is therefore critical to have the three categories of security controls. Every person who needs to access an IT system, a software program, a computer, a network, and a physical room must have the proper authorization. Access must be denied for any end user who does not have the credentials and user role. Every instance of accessing a system, whether it is denied or granted, must be logged as a permanent record, detailing the name of the end user, date and time of access, indication of accepted or denied entry, and the purpose of entry.

Giving access to an end user should be guided by the "Need to Know" principle. Not everyone needs access. Only those who have the inherent need to access certain types of information need to be granted access. Determining who has the need to know is based on the end user's job position, job duties, and job rank or level. A senior-level finance specialist, for instance, will have access to more financial management data than a junior-level finance specialist. Both finance specialists will not have access to any other information outside of financial management. The finance specialists' area of need to know is restricted to financial management.

Implementation of the Need to Know principle is done by assigning a user role to the end user. A specific user role indicates what the end user can see and do. It gives the end user specific rights to perform certain actions (e.g., read data, add new information, and delete a record). As a control, a set of user roles is implemented to grant access to an individual computer, a computer network, and in an IT system. Depending on the context and requirements of a particular system, the definitions and names of user roles can vary. For simplification purposes here, user roles can be simplified to two basic roles: administrator and user. While the user has extremely limited rights to limited areas, the administrator has unlimited rights to all areas. Actual implementation of user roles would have a number of roles between these two extremes to provide for various levels of access.

The user role is managed and governed by a user account. Each end user is provided a user account, which consists of a unique user name, a password, and a user role. There will be additional information to indicate the status of the account, date of account creation, and other details regarding the user account. Log entries of all instances of system access would be associated with the user account. An IT system would have its own user management system whereby a new end user can quickly register and an existing end user can manage their user information.

User account management is a control. The three categories of security controls must be developed to determine how user accounts need to be established, managed, and terminated.

A naming convention for how a user name is assigned is a control. The user name is unique and does not change. The following are common examples of creating a user name that follow a standard pattern:

- jdoe (first initial and last name with no spaces)
- john.doe (first name and last name separated by a period)
- jane_doe (first name and last name separated by an underscore)

Web software programs, in recent years, tend to use the e-mail address as the user name. This convention may not be appropriate for certain IT systems. Use of the e-mail address as the user name can expose the e-mail address to outsiders who would use it for other purposes. A person could change their e-mail address like they would change their phone number or home address. Since the user name does not change, the e-mail address as a permanent user name can cause confusion when the end user changes their e-mail address some time in the future. It should not be assumed that the end user will not move from one e-mail provider to another e-mail provider.

For enhanced security and privacy, the user name could be automatically generated and stored. This convention would associate the computer-generated user name to the end user. The user name could be a random string of characters or a scrambling of the person's name, so as to make it hard to discern the true identity of the end user.

Another control is a set of rules related to the end user's password. As it is a key piece of data for accessing an IT system, the end user's password poses a major security issue. Another person could access a system fraudulently, if they know the end user's password and user name, and do things that the end user would not do. With enough time and sufficient resources, a computer hacker could attempt to access an IT system by submitting numerous combinations of password strings until a successful attempt has been reached. To stop the occurrence of multiple attempts to log in to an IT system, a first rule needs to limit the number of login attempts. After a specified number of unsuccessful attempts, the user account will be locked or automatically set in a state in which the account cannot be used. A second rule needs to require a high degree of complexity in the password. This means that the password should be a certain length or longer, should have a mix of letters, numbers, and special characters, and should not be a recognizable word found in a dictionary. Any password that is a common word or phrase could be detected and used for unauthorized entry. The objective of the rule is to make it difficult to crack the password. A third rule needs to require that the password be changed once every 90 days or another specified period of time. A fourth rule needs to restrict knowledge of the password to the end user who created it. Neither the Systems Administrator nor any IT personnel should know the end user's password. Only the end user needs to know their password and can change it. A fifth rule needs to encrypt the password when it is transmitted across the computer network and when it is stored in the computer. An unencrypted password could be intercepted by a third-party user. It could also be visible to another user if seen in a computer or a database.

A real dilemma arises when multiple systems are used in a single organization. Each IT system would have its own method of user account management. For the end user, a unique password will have to be remembered for each system. For IT personnel, every user account will have to be managed across all the implemented systems. This can create heavy overhead on operation and maintenance and frustration for many end users. Chapter 8 will describe how the government agency should avoid implementing too many IT systems.

A number of systems are unavoidable. Here is a typical work environment: The end user logs in to their computer, submitting their user name and password. The end user opens their e-mail software program and is prompted to enter their user name and password. The end user opens the organization's computer-based financial management information system and is prompted to enter their user name and password. In this case, the end user has to remember and use three passwords. If each system implements the controls as described above, the end user will have to remember three complex passwords and know when to change each one. This situation could lead the end user to doing things that create additional security risks. The end user may write down the password on a small slip of paper and hide the paper under the keyboard or mouse pad. The end user may use the same password for all three systems.

Reducing the number of user accounts and by extension, the number of passwords to the minimum should be an operational goal. A "Single Sign-On" (SSO) environment where every end user can access multiple systems with one user account is ideal. A true SSO environment, however, requires a homogenous operating environment. All of the computers will have to be the same, and the IT systems will have to build on the same software development structure. A mix of computers such as Microsoft Windows, Apple Mac, and Google Android all connected to a mix of information systems made by Microsoft, Oracle, and IBM creates a heterogenous operating environment. Technical configurations need to be implemented in a mixed environment in order to integrate different computers and systems. The easier and less riskier route is to implement an operating environment where all computers are the same. This means deciding on a Microsoft Windows environment, an Apple Mac environment, or a Linux environment. Such a decision is made at the strategic planning level.

It may not be practicable to create a true SSO environment. Two or three user accounts would have to be administered for each end user. A hardware token or a biometric device could be implemented as a control to facilitate the process of accessing multiple systems. The end user would be issued a hardware token that is associated with the end user's account. An advanced hardware token such as a SmartCard could store the end user's user name, password, biometric characteristic, and other data in a computer chip on the card. Various hardware tokens produced by different vendors would authenticate the end user to grant or deny access into a system. As a physical item, the hardware token must be in the end user's possession at the time of system access. The SmartCard token would be inserted into or swiped through a card reader attached to the computer. A touchless hardware token such as an NFC tag would be placed in front of a reader device about a few centimeters apart. Another hardware token would display a randomly generated number that the end user must enter in a login screen. A Personal Identification Number (PIN) may be required to be entered by the end user. In all of these implementations of hardware tokens, the end user does not have to enter their user name and password. Those user credentials would be checked through the particular method in each hardware token.

A biometric device could be used to grant or deny access into a system. A biometric is a characteristic that uniquely identifies one human being. A fingerprint, the shape of a finger, the shape of a hand, a face, the iris part of an eye, the retina part of an eye, a voice, a gait, and a signature all can identify one person. Each of these characteristics will have a specific biometric device to read the characteristic. A fingerprint scanner is the most common device. The hand geometry biometric device described above is another piece of hardware. Each biometric characteristic can be stored as data in a hardware token. The end user's biometric characteristic in an electronic format becomes a part of the end user's user account information. The end user can then authenticate themselves by scanning their finger, hand, face, eye, or some other characteristic into a device.

Encryption Technology

Any sensitive information, which would be handled by a limited group of people, should be encrypted as the information is transmitted across a computer network and is stored inside a computer. If funding and resources permit, all of the security layers wherever applicable should apply encryption. User access credentials should be encrypted. Any physical access point in the physical layer that transmits or stores data should encrypt the data. Data transmitted from one computer to another should be encrypted. A computer storage device such as a hard drive and a flash drive should be configured to encrypt stored data. A computer software program should be developed to encrypt data. A database software program should be configured to encrypt data prior to storing the data.

Encryption provides a method of converting human-readable language into a coded format that humans can no longer understand. The coded format must be decrypted back into human-readable language. Conceptually, the encryption process scrambles words, phrases, and sentences so that they cannot be read by a human. This specialized field of encrypting and decrypting information is called "Cryptography". A cryptographer creates a mathematical formula or a novel technique to encrypt and decrypt information. Before use of the modern computer, various techniques were applied. The Enigma machine used during the Second World War was a mechanical device that encrypted military secrets. The U.S. government employed Navajo speakers during the Second World War to use the Navajo language as a coded format to communicate messages through the radio. Early methods of cryptography can be traced back thousands of years to the ancient Egyptian civilization. Common in all implementations requires a codebook or a key that authorized personnel have to use to encrypt and decrypt information. The codebook provides the formula or technique for converting the language into the coded format. Without having the codebook or key, unauthorized persons would have to spend time and resources to try and break (crack) the coded format.

Modern computer technology has advanced to develop stronger encryption methods that can withstand being cracked by an unauthorized person. Encryption methods include the Message Digest Algorithm (MD5), the Secure Hash Algorithm (SHA), the Data Encryption Standard (DES), the Triple DES standard, and the Advanced Encryption Standard (AES). AES is the current method, replacing DES. Triple DES is a method that encrypts information three times using DES. The strength of any method is determined by the length of the key used in the encryption method. A 256-bit AES key is stronger than a 128-bit AES key. The key is an essential part that carries out the process of converting plain text into a coded format. Unlike in past eras, a physical codebook is not needed, since the computer does the processing automatically so long as it can access the key. If the key is lost or missing, then the computer will not be able to encrypt and decrypt the information.

The public manager needs to understand the purpose of the MD5 and SHA methods. These computer hashing functions are fundamentally different to DES and AES. MD5 and SHA do not guarantee that the encrypted information will be decrypted back into plain text. The central purpose for using MD5 and SHA is to verify the source and integrity of the data. A common application for a computer hashing function is to ensure that an electronic file is from an authoritative source. Another application is to ensure that an electronic file was downloaded completely with no corruption to the data. The content of the electronic file may not be encrypted and could be transmitted across an unencrypted network. An example is downloading a computer software program, which is purchased from an online merchant, from one of several Websites or FTP sites that is geographically closer to the end user's location. There would be an associated MD5 or SHA file that can be used to verify that the purchased software program was downloaded completely. In this case, the purchased software program is not encrypted.

Information Security Management and Coordination

An "Information Security Committee" should be established to manage and coordinate all activities related to information security throughout the government agency. This committee develops and oversees an agreed-upon information security process, which entails monitoring and evaluation of security risks and development and execution of security strategies. The Information Security Committee reviews and approves security policies and plans and security training and awareness programs to ensure that all initiatives are aligned with each other. Specific tasks involving development and implementation may be delegated to appropriate technical teams. Committee members meet periodically to review and discuss current security threats and their risk factors to determine whether existing security policies and programs need to be changed. Committee members prepare and submit policy memoranda with specific recommendations for execution throughout the government agency. Committee members should adopt the following security objectives, which would guide the development of strategies, policies, and programs:

1. To maintain confidence to employees, partners, external organizations, and the general public that sensitive information is protected and safeguarded
2. To protect the confidentiality and integrity of sensitive information
3. To ensure that sensitive information is made available through secured channels and media and only to appropriate persons based on the Need to Know principle
4. To ensure that information and IT resources are not misused, abused, or wasted
5. To prevent the occurrence of fraud, IT-related crimes, disruptive events, and acts of vandalism against the organization

The Information Security Committee must include at the very least senior executive leaders, the Chief Information Officer, the IT Manager, and a Senior Information Security Specialist. If each department has an IT Manager, then all of the IT Managers should be included. Department directors should be included as Committee members, as they have a stake in protecting and safeguarding information within their department. Department directors can provide context about the way in which their department functions that would affect security risks and security controls. Department directors would have particular concerns that need to be addressed. The size of the Security Committee should not exceed 25 members. Too many members can make group discussions unwieldy. The Security Committee should have sufficient funding and administrative support staff to ensure effective oversight and management.

An incident reporting system with operating procedures and communication protocols must be established and maintained. In any event of a security breach, appropriate personnel need to be notified. Depending on the level of risk or urgency, a number of managers up to senior leaders would be alerted. The Public Affairs department may be notified to prepare and release a public statement to the news media. The security breach must be handled promptly and resolved in a timely manner to ensure that there would be no further breach. The security breach needs to be documented with the date and time of occurrence, the place of occurrence, the affected system, the impact of the breach, a description of the breach/attack, evidence of the breach and impact, the resolution, and the names of persons who reported, handled, and resolved the breach. Once documented, the security breach should be analyzed to understand how to prevent it from occurring again. Security controls may have to change.

Security awareness is an important part of information security management and should be implemented in a series of briefings and tutorials. Remember, end users pose a significant security threat. If they are not aware of potential risks in entering data, submitting information, and replying to a message, end users could unknowingly make a mistake that potentially does harm or damage. Briefings that describe how to identify attacks and techniques used by malicious persons should be presented and repeated often. End users need to be able to identify an attack quickly and react appropriately. Tutorials that show the links between security risks and security controls and that concisely explain the reasons for security strategies should be developed and presented. End users need to understand the rationale and circumstance of a needed security policy. Their understanding would result in a higher willingness to comply with such security policy.

Once security policies are in place, security controls are active and working, and end users are aware and trained, all of these security measures could be outdated or neutralized. Security threats will evolve and reshape into newer forms. Security measures, likewise, must be revised and reshaped to match ongoing security threats. A security control that was implemented 3 months ago may no longer be effective today. The Information Security Committee and technical teams must continuously monitor and evaluate all security controls to ensure that they are relevant to meet current security threats.

New and emerging methods, techniques, tools, and technologies should be studied to understand how they will impact the organization. IT personnel need to conduct and report numerous tests on implemented controls with different user roles, at different times of the day, on different days of the week including weekends, from different office sites and locations, and through different Internet connections.

There should be a testing environment where a technical team can simulate breaches, attacks, and brute-force attempts and report the results. Such simulation of a security breach *should not* be conducted in the production environment. If it is, the Information Security Committee and senior leaders must be fully aware of the consequences that a failed simulation could bring (i.e., a simulated attack that goes awry). There must be consensus by the Information Security Committee to conduct simulated security breaches.

Announced and unannounced security drills need to be carried out to ensure that security controls will work in various disaster scenarios (e.g., hurricane, earthquake, and fire) and report the results. Similar type drills need to include tests on the business continuity/disaster recovery plan to ensure that the data are backed up and can be restored and that IT systems can be brought online.

End users need to be reminded of their responsibilities to do their part to keep information secure.

Written Policy for Each Information System

Each information system that is designated as mission critical or important must have its own Information System Security Policy. Simply having one policy to govern all information systems is inadequate. The security controls in one system may not be applicable to another system. This is particularly the case with managerial controls. User access and personnel responsibilities can be different. The points of contacts can be different as well. Everything that has been described above, where applicable, should be described in the Information System Security Policy. And the Security Policy must be approved by the Information Security Committee. Any revision must be reapproved. The Information System Security Policy provides assurance that the government agency's information processed and stored in the specified system will be protected and safeguarded, using all security controls as relevant to the system's operating environment.

The following business outline provides the contents of the Information System Security Policy document, ordered by section and sub section:

1. Executive Summary
2. Introduction
    - 2.1. Purpose of This Document
    - 2.2. Organization of This Document
    - 2.3. System Overview
    - 2.4. Major Application or General Support System
3. System Identification
    - 3.1. System Title
    - 3.2. System Description
    - 3.3. System Operating Status
    - 3.4. System Environment
    - 3.5. System Interconnection/Information Sharing
    - 3.6. Sensitivity of Information Handled
    - 3.7. General Protection Requirement Statement

- 3.8. Responsible Organizations
- 3.9. Points of Contacts
- 3.10. Assignment of Security Responsibility

4. Managerial Security Controls
    - 4.1. Risk Assessment and Management
    - 4.2. Review of Security Controls
    - 4.3. User Access
    - 4.4. Rules of Behavior
    - 4.5. Personnel Responsibilities
    - 4.6. Planning for Security in the System Development Life Cycle Process
    - 4.7. End User Layer
    - 4.8. Physical Layer
    - 4.9. Network Layer
    - 4.10. Computer Layer
    - 4.11. Software Layer
5. Operational Security Controls
    - 5.1. Incident Response System
    - 5.2. Contingency Planning
    - 5.3. Data Integrity/Validation
    - 5.4. Change/Version Control
    - 5.5. Security Awareness and Training
    - 5.6. End User Layer
    - 5.7. Physical Layer
    - 5.8. Network Layer
    - 5.9. Computer Layer
    - 5.10. Software Layer
6. Technical Security Controls
    - 6.1. Audit Trails
    - 6.2. User Identification
    - 6.3. User Authentication
    - 6.4. End User Layer
    - 6.5. Physical Layer
    - 6.6. Network Layer
    - 6.7. Computer Layer
    - 6.8. Software Layer
7. Rules of Behavior

Information Security Principles

To end the chapter, any implementation of information security whether in a policy, a program, or an IT system must adhere to three security principles: (1) confidentiality, (2) integrity, and (3) availability. Information must be held such that it cannot be disclosed accidentally or intentionally to any end user who does not have authorization or permission. Information with regard to its source, content, handling, and production must be controlled for in such a manner that the outputted information must remain intact and accurate as it was originally inputted. Information must be accessible in such ways as practicable for certain specific end users to be able to retrieve and review the information.

Chapter 7 Quiz

Question 1: How should all possible security threats be handled?

A. Analyze the threats' risk level and apply control measures appropriate to countering all threats.
B. Deal with threats one at a time.
C. Select and implement a control measure for each threat.
D. Assess the level of risk for each threat.
E. Analyze the threats' risk level, finding the ones that pose highest risk, and apply control measures appropriate to countering those selected threats.

Question 2: What is the three-prong approach to implementing information security?

A. Software Layer, Hardware Layer, and Network Layer
B. User Access, Data Integrity, and Antivirus Software
C. Managerial Controls, Strategic Controls, and Technical Controls
D. Managerial Controls, Operational Controls, and Computer Controls
E. Managerial Controls, Operational Controls, and Technical Controls

Question 3: What are the security layers in order of defense that can protect an IT system?

A. Software Layer, Computer Layer, and Network Layer
B. Managerial Layer, Operational Layer, and Computer Layer
C. Software Layer, Computer Layer, Network Layer, Physical Layer, and End User Layer
D. Software Layer, End User Layer, Computer Layer, Network Layer, and Physical Layer
E. Validation Layer, Antivirus Layer, Firewall Layer, Building Layer, and Team Layer

Question 4: What needs to be included in the Information System Security Policy?

A. Points of Contacts
B. Rules of Behavior
C. Incident Response System
D. Audit Trails
E. All of the above

Question 5: There is one element in the IT ecosystem that if left uncontrolled could still make an IT system vulnerable and perhaps could neutralize the technical controls. What is that element?

A. End User
B. Computer Network
C. Computer Software
D. Business Process
E. Government Law

Worksheets

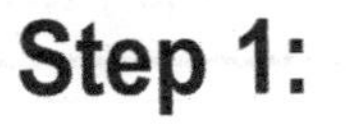

Step 1:

Write one specific item (a security threat) on a Post-it® note.

Step 2:

Organize written notes on a large board, sorting them in any pattern that makes sense in your operating environment.

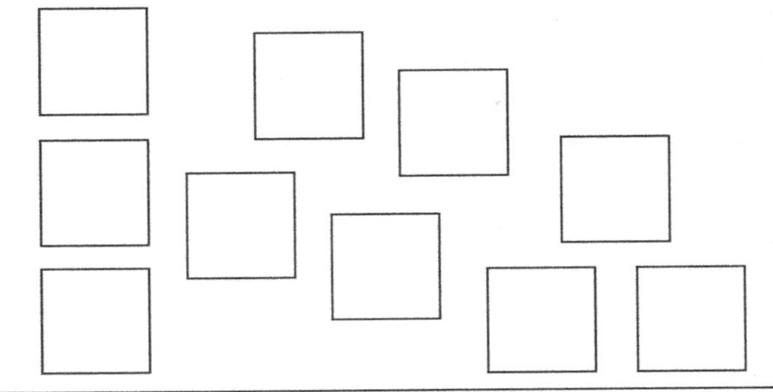

Step 3:

Apply the arrangement of notes to other worksheets.

Worksheet 7.1 Security threat arrangement exercise.

ID	Potential Hazard	Affected	Severity	Occurrence	Risk Factor

Worksheet 7.2 Risk assessment, part 1 of 2.

ID	Control Measure	Est. Cost	Security	Protection Effectiveness

Worksheet 7.3 Risk assessment, part 2 of 2.

Hazard	Affected	Risk Factor	Control	Est. Cost	Effectiveness
		Estimated Total Cost:			

Worksheet 7.4 Risk-to-Control analysis.

	Managerial Control	Operational Control	Technical Control
End User Layer			
Physical Layer			
Network Layer			
Computer Layer			
Software Layer			

Worksheet 7.5 **IT security framework.**

Chapter 8

IT Strategic Planning: Alignment with the Mission

An independent investigation had concluded in its report that duplicated IT systems currently in operation must be consolidated into a single system. The report cited several instances where the five systems had outputted computer-generated reports in which the data from each report contradicted the other report. Management staff had to spend extra person-hours in excess of their regular time to reconcile the discrepancies, making corrections and creating a new final report by hand.

Chapter Summary

In the foregoing hypothetical case example, the efficiency of Information Technology (IT) is undermined by the use of multiple IT systems that are designed to do the same functions. The duplicated IT systems create additional work for the management team to deliver timely reports to senior executive leaders. The organization in this case might have been better off without the computer-based systems, as a manual-based system would produce a similar outcome.

One way that an organization could reach a point of operating duplicated IT systems is where several departments work independently of each other and rather compete more than cooperate. This so-called stovepipe organization would discourage and perhaps obstruct in certain situations the sharing of information between departments. Each department in effect would want its own system to use. With sufficient funds and influence, a particular department could employ its own IT team who works separately from the principal IT department. Other departments would develop strategies to implement IT systems, realizing untapped computer skills in existing staff, contracting out to a vendor, or submitting more IT projects to the IT department.

Another way that an organization could have too many IT systems is through the organic process of growing the IT environment. This is prevalent in many organizations that allow IT to evolve over time with little to no afterthought or critical thinking on what has been implemented. An organization initially has no IT department and no formal IT team. A COTS software program is purchased and used by one department. Another department purchases and uses another software program. A creative team member develops an HR database program to help the HR department in managing employee records. Each of these software programs is added with new features and functionalities over time. Personnel generate new ideas, as they continue to use the software programs. As a result, personnel become increasingly reliant on – and emotionally attached to – their software programs as helping them to be more productive. Eventually, the organization establishes an IT department and hires an IT Manager. The new manager comes in and sees all the variety of IT initiatives that have been in operation. The IT Manager smiles at how personnel have embraced IT with great enthusiasm.

The evolution of an IT system (i.e., improving and enhancing it over time) is a very good thing and should be harnessed in a structured way. Letting IT initiatives grow unfettered brings a set of management issues. The siloed departments create management issues as well. Autonomous departments are not necessarily a bad thing. Independence can provide checks on each department and can introduce a new perspective. The relative autonomy, however, should be moderated.

Unlike a functional domain that is specific to one department and may have little effect on other departments, IT is an area that crosses paths with all departments. As such, the IT department has a high level of knowledge of, if not a high degree of influence on, how every department operates. The IT department can bring to light any overlaps and gaps. IT systems could be deployed to close up those gaps while at the same time allowing each department to maintain a level of control as desired. User roles, encryption, and a generally well-defined system that meets all of the departments' requirements would satisfy every end user. The IT department could enable all end users to work productively and efficiently through the well-defined systems. But it would only be able to do so if it is guided by a high-level plan that is approved by senior executive leaders.

This chapter describes the need for and the role of the long-term IT Strategic Plan. The IT Strategic Plan is the keystone that holds together all of the parts learnt in the preceding chapters. This chapter applies all the lessons of the preceding chapters. The government agency will be able to use all of its IT resources effectively and at a level that controls for all costs – financial, human, material, technological, and security. The process of developing the strategic plan, starting with a strategic planning committee, is explained. Every department is represented to ensure that the strategy can work for all and in perfect alignment to accomplish the agency's mission. IT programs are identified and framed in a coherent plan. The chapter further goes into the execution of the developed and approved plan. Execution succinctly summarizes the workflow described in Chapter 6. This chapter concludes with monitoring and governance of the IT Strategic Plan. Senior executive leaders will be assured that completed IT systems are in place and designed to do what they were originally envisioned to do. If not, senior leaders will be equally assured that proper actions had been made to turn around or cancel failing or failed IT systems.

The Need for and the Role of the IT Strategic Plan

There are many elements in the IT ecosystem. There are many parts in an IT system. There are many specialists to hire and to work with. There are many controls to keep a computer-based information system secured. How can all of this be organized and managed, let alone be financed?

The IT Strategic Plan is an essential instrument that will bring the parts together into coherent programs that are aligned with the government agency's mission. Not everything will be included. Based on organizational needs and limitations, some parts are selected, while others are not. A thorough examination of the agency's current situation would identify the systems that every department needs to do their work better. As every department is included in discussions, the right combination of projects can be found that would minimize if not eliminate duplicated systems. Most important, the discussions will bring department directors together to be fully engaged and motivated to use IT in ways that will accomplish organizational objectives. The IT Strategic Plan unifies all of the departments, through IT, toward one singular aim – the government agency's mission.

Strategic planning, in general, is a process of planning how an organization should use its resources more effectively to achieve its aims. Strategic planning also is a cycle of reviewing the plan to know that what an organization has set out to do is *in fact* being accomplished. A misunderstood perception about strategic planning is that it is a futile, bureaucratic exercise that results in a printed report that sits on a shelf collecting dust. This is not true, of course. Strategic planning, if it is executed correctly and followed up regularly, can ensure that an organization's requests and wishes are fulfilled and in ways that would avoid wasting funds. In fact, it is the manner in which strategic planning is carried out that makes the difference.

The IT Strategic Plan as an instrument plays its role in management and governance to ensure that technological resources are contributing to organizational goals and objectives. It is defined with a long-term horizon of 3–5 years. Within the specified period of time, the government agency will be able to transition from its present situation to a new environment that is hopefully much better and improved than before. To be certain that the future situation has been attained, the IT Strategic Plan sets the course by which the government agency can navigate through. This high-level road map provides alternative approaches and solutions. If one approach or solution is found to be not working, then a decision can be quickly made to change to another approach or solution. Such a pivot may be necessary, as an unforeseen problem may arise. Proper planning ahead of time understands this.

The IT Strategic Plan links the IT projects to public programs. This linkage can be followed and measured through a set of agreed-upon metrics. The IT Strategic Plan defines those metrics as operational goals. These organization-specific IT goals can then be used to measure the progress of how well the projects are moving along in association with broader objectives, which the government agency seeks to accomplish.

Qualities of an Effective Strategic Plan

A strategic plan, in general, can be effective and useful and have greater power if it can

- tell a story;
- communicate to a wider audience;
- speak directly to stakeholders, making it relevant for them;
- set ambitious yet realistic objectives;
- narrow things done from vagaries to concrete specifics;
- cover only what is needed, removing extraneous items and unnecessary information, creating an efficient plan that is easy to read;
- provide measurements by which an organization can use to measure whether or not it is accomplishing what it has set out to do;
- make statements and measurements clear in their interpretation so as others can verify all that are being claimed and proposed and that multiple groups can verify the claims and come to the same conclusion; and,
- come with it an underlying structure of governance that enables leaders and managers to make corrections when necessary and to hold responsible parties accountable, and to do so in ways that are fair, consistent, and transparent.

The Telling of a Story

The IT Strategic Plan should tell a story of how the government agency will get from point A to point B. Over the course of several years, the effort will be like a journey in which personnel would no doubt encounter obstacles, pains, and joys. Aware that the road will not be straight and smooth, the drafters of the plan should develop alternative approaches and describe how those approaches will be employed in any event that one approach does not succeed. In the telling of a story, the IT Strategic Plan will not only inform but can inspire.

Communication to a Wider Audience

The IT Strategic Plan will be read by many people who have different backgrounds and various skill sets. Both IT and non-IT personnel will read it. The general public would also read it too. As such, the IT Strategic Plan should be written in language that all will readily understand. The message needs to be clear and direct. By doing so, the IT Strategic Plan has a greater chance for securing funding to fulfill the plan's objectives.

Relevant to Stakeholders

Among the general audience, the IT Strategic Plan should speak directly to those who have a stake in the outcome. Departments within the government agency need to know what they will be getting. Specific groups within society need to know how they will benefit from the plan's activities. The results need to match what the government agency wants in providing services to the public.

Ambitious yet Realistic

The IT Strategic Plan should reach very high goals, grounded in reality. It should neither be too difficult nor be too easy to achieve. The departments within the government agency should challenge themselves to change or improve, while knowing their constraints and limitations. And precisely because they know their limits, the departments understand what is in their way. The IT Strategic Plan will have been developed to provide the strategy to maneuver around the constraints and limitations. The government agency can move to the next level, if the plan is ambitious yet realistic.

Concrete Specifics

The IT Strategic Plan needs to avoid general statements that refer to abstract concepts and vague technologies (e.g., Big Data, cryptocurrency, digital tools, and anything with the word "Cloud" associated in the term like cloud storage). Doing so is setting up the government agency for trouble. By applying all of the lessons in previous chapters of this book, the drafters of the plan will be able to drill down to specific systems, projects, and activities. The specific items will lead to carefully defined goals. The IT Strategic Plan will then be a document rooted in specifics, which can guide IT personnel in implementing the plan and can guide non-IT personnel in monitoring the plan.

Efficient in Content

The IT Strategic Plan needs to focus on projects that are needed and will contribute to achieving goals. Anything extraneous should be excluded. This includes certain language about technology. Sales and marketing buzzwords need to be avoided. Component parts in the projects and systems need to be easily identifiable as described in Chapter 1. In other words, standard terms should be applied. Descriptions should be concise and readable. The IT Strategic Plan will be read (and read quickly) by many people who have different backgrounds.

Measurable Goals

The government agency needs to determine whether or not it is accomplishing its objectives. To that end, the IT Strategic Plan needs to have measurements. As part of efficiency, the concrete goals that will be defined will serve as key metrics. The level of specificity in the goals is critical. Goals that are too broad, general, or vague are difficult to measure, let alone difficult to realize. Setting specific goals creates for goals that can be measured. Moreover, specific goals can hold the contractor or the implementer accountable. Vague goals, on the other hand, can enable the contractor to escape culpability, since the vagueness is open to wide interpretation. The government agency could lose more than it bargains for when it agrees to overly broad goals.

Verifiable in Clarity

The systems, projects, and activities in the IT Strategic Plan will be reviewed by senior executive leaders, an auditor, and/or an investigator. The general public may also review the substance of the plan. Multiple parties would conduct their evaluation and arrive at a conclusion. If statements, goals, and other content are unclear, the parties will have a hard time to verify the veracity of the IT Strategic Plan. The government agency could end up with differing opinions in the results. The auditor will have a conclusion that can be different from another investigator. Agency personnel can completely disagree with both the auditor's and the investigator's findings. To avoid this situation, the IT Strategic Plan needs to be very clear and not open to wide interpretation. The concreteness, efficiency, and measurement qualities just described will establish claims that can be verified and confirmed with little to no difference in opinions by multiple parties.

Governance Structure

The IT Strategic Plan needs to be monitored and evaluated. And in doing so, the plan needs a structure of governance by which the departments within the government agency can consistently follow. This becomes important when issues arise and corrections have to be made. Personnel, contractors, partners, and others involved need to be certain that decisions were made fairly. Who is to review the objectives and goals, and how often? Who is to follow up on the implementation? How will the plan be executed and overseen? The IT Strategic Plan itself is a tool (a document). In order to be effective, it requires a management system to carry it out.

Strategic Planning Life Cycle Process

The Strategic Planning Life Cycle process is a formal process for developing, executing, and monitoring the IT Strategic Plan. In a similar way, strategic planning requires a deliberate and meticulous process like that in system development. There is a starting point and an ending point. And the completed process will repeat. Over the entire existence of the government agency, which could be several decades, there would be several IT Strategic Plans. The first plan will be just that. The second, next plan would be a product of learning from what had been executed in the first, previous plan. The next plan will show what will be implemented in the next 3–5 years. Given the changing nature of technology, the next plan would incorporate the latest matured computer technologies. The IT Strategic Plan is not a one-off tool that the government agency will develop once and expect to rely on it after the specified period of time had ended. The Strategic Planning Life Cycle process (see Figure 8.1) goes through the following eight phases:

1. Establishment of the IT Strategic Planning Committee
2. Understanding of the Purpose of the Organization
3. Evaluation of Business Needs and Drivers
4. Assessment of Organizational Capacity
5. Development of the IT Strategic Plan
6. Execution of the IT Strategic Plan
7. Monitoring of the IT Strategic Plan
8. Closure of the IT Strategic Plan

Each phase of the Strategic Planning Life Cycle process is fully described shortly. To make it clear how all of the phases relate together, key points are highlighted and emphasized. In the first phase, stakeholders are identified to form a planning committee, the IT Strategic Planning Committee. This sets the stage for all the next phases. In the second phase, the first order of business is to understand the central purpose of the organization. Before any kind of technology can be discussed, stakeholders must know that everyone in the group has a shared interest in accomplishing the overall mission. In the third phase, discussions among the stakeholders will flow from the mission to business and functional aspects, drawing out the organization's core drivers and key needs. In the fourth phase, stakeholders will assess their organization and their departments more specifically to evaluate whether they have the capacity to meet the expressed needs. Current limitations,

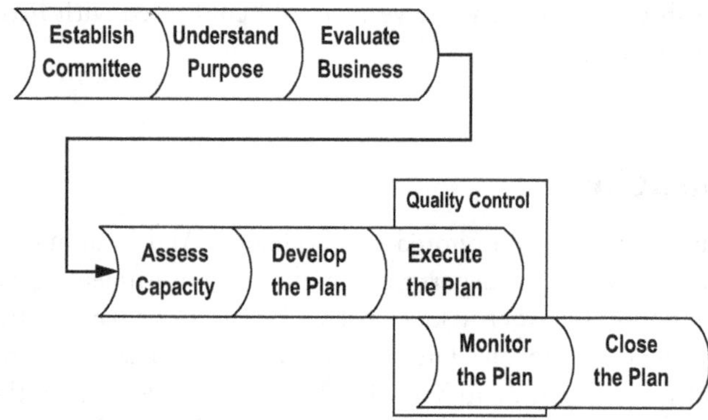

Figure 8.1 Strategic Planning Life-Cycle process.

constraints, risks, and opportunities will become known. Based on all information from previous phases, (in the fifth phase) stakeholders can identify and discuss projects, systems, and activities for implementation. Stakeholders will then have an agreed-upon IT Strategic Plan. That plan will then be executed in the sixth phase. Stakeholders would monitor the plan's progress as it is executed, in the seventh phase, catching any problems as early as possible and making course corrections as needed. There may be other groups who would conduct evaluations related to the IT Strategic Plan. After monitoring has completed, the IT Strategic Plan is officially closed in the eighth phase. Stakeholders will discuss the completed plan, understanding what succeeded and failed. The lessons learnt will then inform the stakeholders on what should be planned for in the next IT Strategic Plan.

Establishment of the IT Strategic Planning Committee

Because an IT program and an IT system will have an impact on the organization for several years, it is necessary to involve a number of leaders and managers to determine how IT will be used throughout the organization. The government agency, therefore, needs to establish the "IT Strategic Planning Committee", made up of senior executive leaders, department directors, the Chief Information Officer, and the IT Manager. Committee members can be the same as with the Information Security Committee. The size of the Planning Committee should not exceed 25 members, for the same reason as described in forming the Security Committee in Chapter 7.

It is particularly critical to have participation by department directors. Department directors will have functional expertise on how their respective department operates and can inform IT personnel on which elements in the IT ecosystem are relevant. If the Planning Committee just involves the Chief Information Officer and the IT Manager, the government agency runs the risk of having a technology-heavy plan that may not be aligned with the mission and that may not be suitable to improving operations. Department directors have a direct stake in IT-related activities to ensure that any IT system can improve or facilitate the work of their department. Thus, the views of the department directors must be represented.

Every member in the Planning Committee is a stakeholder who has a shared interest in accomplishing the overall mission. A "stakeholder" is a person who has a vested interest in some or all of the activities that result in a particular outcome.

The IT Strategic Planning Committee may need to have a legal basis for its establishment, authorized by law for the government agency. In the case of a nonprofit organization, the Board of Directors approves establishment of the Planning Committee. In any case, the Planning Committee must be supported by senior executive leaders. The Planning Committee needs to have sufficient funding and administrative support staff to carry out its activities.

The IT Strategic Planning Committee will be involved in all of the next phases of the Strategic Planning Life Cycle process. Critical attention is on the immediate next four phases to produce the IT Strategic Plan. Committee members need to schedule time to meet and discuss the substance related to each of the four phases. A series of seminar-type planning workshops would enable Committee members to engage more fully. The Chief Information Officer or the IT Manager would serve as the moderator to facilitate discussions and to reach a consensus among all department directors and senior leaders. As the IT specialist, the Chief Information Officer or the IT Manager can inform all non-IT leaders and managers on what is possible and what is not in terms of IT implementation. The planning workshops may span several weeks to several months, depending on time commitments and scheduling. Every Committee member should be afforded enough time to think carefully on all matters. In the end, every Committee member needs to be satisfied that their needs and requests are included in the IT Strategic Plan.

Understanding of the Purpose of the Organization

What is the mission of the government agency? What is the agency's central purpose for operating? What services does the agency provide to the public? How much is the agency's budget?

These questions need to be answered, first and foremost, before implementing anything related to IT. The legislation that established the government agency provides the purpose, mandate, and certain powers. It may have granted rule-making authority. There may be additional laws that have changed the agency's powers and authorities. As part of the budget cycle, a new law is passed that authorizes a specific amount that the government agency can spend in the fiscal year period.

For a nonprofit organization, the Articles of Incorporation and Bylaws provide information about the organization's purpose, mandate, and general rules. Government will have a record of the nonprofit organization's legal existence along with copies of the Articles of Incorporation and the Bylaws. Any changes to the Articles and Bylaws are approved by the organization's Board of Directors and are submitted to government for amendment to the organization's public record. The organization's Board of Directors approves a specific amount that can be spent in each fiscal year period.

For both the government agency and the nonprofit organization, there should be an organization-wide strategic plan that elaborates further on the organization's founding documents. This strategic plan describes what the organization intends to do within a specified period of time, stating the strategic objectives. Typically, this strategic plan does not have details regarding IT. It describes the business and functions formed around specific programs. It would outline specific services to support or aid certain groups within society. It may have cost estimates necessary to operate, broken down by programs. It may include a program to monitor and evaluate the organization's programs and services.

The Planning Committee will gather and review the founding documents. Any additional information relevant to understanding the organization's purpose would be reviewed. Committee members will then be informed to proceed to the next phase.

It will be ideal to have the organization-wide strategic plan in hand. The IT Strategic Plan does not override the organization-wide strategy. It must be an extension of the organization-wide strategic plan, providing the additional strategy specific to the application of IT in the organization. It is distinct in its details and yet is tied to the broader objectives as outlined in the organization-wide strategic plan. As they use the organization-wide strategic plan as a guide, Committee members would be able to ensure that the IT Strategic Plan is perfectly in line with the current direction of the organization.

Evaluation of Business Needs and Drivers

The broad purpose needs to be drilled down further to understand how the government agency essentially operates. An analytical framework can break down the agency's mission into (1) core drivers, (2) key needs, and (3) strategic objectives and then map the relationships between the three parts. This analytical exercise provides the foundation for developing the IT Strategic Plan.

A "strategic objective" is a broad description of some new state or end that the organization wants to reach. It can be the establishment of a specific system. It can be a change in a business process. It can be an improvement in an operating procedure. Committee members would provide objectives that are more specific. For example, the Senior Contracting Officer would add automation of the procurement process as a strategic objective.

A "key need" is a major object or a significant thing that the organization needs or requires to be operationally effective. It is usually something practical. It can be additional staff. It can be computers. It can be data collection standards and protocols. It can be a computer software program. Among the other two parts, a key need is the most tangible.

A "core driver" is some factor that compels the organization to do something or not to do something. It can be voluntary or mandatory, but usually it is the latter. The effect could be positive or negative, creating an opportunity for or imposing a constraint or limitation on the organization. A reduction in funding is a driver that imposes a financial constraint. A law that makes an electronic signature equivalent to a handwritten signature is a driver that creates an opportunity in processing signed documents. A voluntary order that allows personnel to use a hardware token to authenticate themselves when logging in to a computer software program is a driver.

In one or more planning workshops, Committee members will discuss their core drivers, key needs, and strategic objectives. Worksheet 8.2 can be used for this purpose. The moderator will write down everything expressed from all members, creating a master worksheet for the Planning Committee. The result will produce a long list of each part.

Committee members will then analyze how the parts are related. One core driver can be linked to one or more key needs. And one key need can be linked to one or more strategic objectives. It is possible for one strategic objective to be linked to one or more key needs and for one key need to be linked to one or more core drivers. Figure 8.2 illustrates the linkage of the three parts. Here the Planning Committee is mapping out what it will take to achieve the objectives, starting with the drivers. For example, a security law (a core driver) would require (1) a new procedure (a key need) and (2) an update to a software program (another key need). Establishing the new procedure (a key need) and modifying the software program (another key need) would achieve (1) an improvement in security (a strategic objective). Note that the objective is associated to two key needs.

Analyzing all of the relationships between the three parts will help Committee members to prioritize the strategic objectives and consolidate the key needs. Those needs that have many links to drivers and objectives are shared needs. This indicates opportunities for integration or

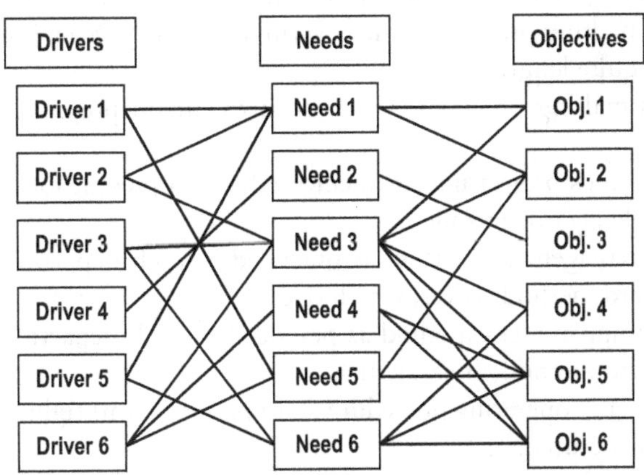

Figure 8.2 Business analysis map, linkage of key needs.

consolidation – areas for lowing costs. A key need with a single link to a core driver and a single link to a strategic objective would indicate a lone item or a stand-alone system.

Those objectives with many links to key needs would suggest higher importance as opposed to those objectives with few links. It shows how multiple key needs can contribute to an individual objective. The same key needs may also be contributing to another objective.

With facilitation by the Chief Information Officer or the IT Manager, Committee members should order the strategic objectives by the amount of links that the objectives have. Objectives with few links would be ranked lower. Those objectives with a single link might be classified as lowest priority and may be excluded, unless the demand of the associated driver dictates otherwise. The driver is a major factor that will readjust the ordering of the strategic objectives. The final ordering will lead to a prioritized selection of projects, systems, and activities.

This analytical exercise deals with the business and functional aspects of the government agency. It is not about implementing or managing any particular computer technology *per se*. It is about getting a handle on what drives the organization forward or holding it back.

The output of this analytical exercise can be further developed and formalized into a standard architectural framework. Enterprise Architecture (EA) and Service-Oriented Architecture (SOA) are two such standards. More information on this is described below.

Assessment of Organizational Capacity

The Planning Committee needs to assess the capacity of the government agency to support the core drivers and to meet the key needs. What currently exists in the present environment? Those Committee members representing the departments (the department directors) will evaluate their respective department in terms of information use and management and operational management. The following 18 questions serve as a guide:

1. What specific information does each department currently use and report?
2. Who currently uses each department's information?
3. Where does each department currently collect its information from?
4. What specific functional application does each department currently use?
5. What specific data set does each department currently collect and analyze?
6. What specific computer technology does each department currently use?
7. Is the decision-making process for the government agency as a whole (in present form) relatively quick or quite lengthy?
8. Is the decision-making process for each department (in present form) relatively quick or quite lengthy?
9. Is each department's project management method (in present form) tightly or loosely controlled or completely uncontrolled?
10. Is the project management method as practiced in each department (in present form) an industry-standard method? If yes, which one?
11. Is the process improvement method as practiced in each department (in present form) an industry-standard method? If yes, which one?
12. Is each department's operating procedure(s) (in present form) tightly or loosely structured or completely unstructured?
13. Is each department's operating procedure(s) (in present form) fully or partly documented or completely undocumented?

14. Is each department's business process(es) (in present form) tightly or loosely structured or completely unstructured?
15. Is each department's business process(es) (in present form) fully or partly documented or completely undocumented?
16. Is each department's information management process(es) (in present form) tightly or loosely structured or completely unstructured?
17. Is each department's information management process(es) (in present form) fully or partly automated or completely manual?
18. Is each department's information management process(es) (in present form) fully or partly documented or completely undocumented?

The Planning Committee should, in addition to the foregoing questions, gauge the level of support and general enthusiasm for IT in the government agency. How receptive are personnel to using an IT system? What percentage of the total work force in the agency would have a hard time doing work in the computer and/or would rather not use an IT system? Answering such questions will reveal how difficult or easy it will be to roll out IT programs across the government agency. The present work culture may reject the deployment of an IT system or may slow down efforts to implement an IT project. Awareness presentations on the benefits of IT and/or basic level of computer training would need to be provided to increase the low level of support.

Skills assessments should be conducted on both IT and non-IT personnel. Two distinct assessments would be given for each group. IT personnel would be assessed on highly specific technical skills such as computer programming, database administration, and network engineering. Non-IT personnel, in contrast, would be assessed on broader computer skills such as word processing, data management in a spreadsheet, information presentation, Website browsing, and Internet access. Non-IT personnel would also be assessed on specific management skills such as accounting, budgeting, contracting, project management, quantitative analysis, and policy analysis. The results of the assessments would show where training is needed in the area of professional development.

Assessments should be conducted in a scientific manner. Personnel should be tested on skills relevant to their job. If it is a self-assessment, the skills assessment should be administered in a formal survey and submitted anonymously.

A survey of a randomized sample of personnel would obtain a more accurate result of the level of support for IT. Moreover, personnel need to submit their answers anonymously, since the survey questions will be asking sensitive questions dealing with attitudes, behaviors, and emotions about technology.

The foregoing 18 questions can be reformulated into a longer list of questions designed in a formal questionnaire. The questionnaire can be given to a number of employees in each department and then collected and analyzed as a survey. The result then would be more accurate and robust, since those who understand how their department operates have submitted their input.

The Planning Committee must obtain a current inventory of all computer equipment and technological resources. Facilities that house and operate computer equipment are included. IT personnel will need to be scheduled to visit all locations where IT resources are in operation and record their existence and status. It is critical at this time to check whether each equipment is in good working order. There should be an inventory list, technical diagrams, and related documentation maintained by the IT department. IT personnel will use existing documentation in their technical assessment and will make any updates to the inventory list and other documents as needed.

The Planning Committee applies the collected information to analyze the government agency's limitations, constraints, risks, and opportunities in each of five resource categories. The resource categories are (1) financial resources, (2) human resources, (3) physical resources, (4) environmental resources, and (5) technological resources. Physical resources refer to buildings, sites, facilities, available space inside buildings, and the like. Environmental resources refer to electricity, cooling, telecommunication infrastructure, environmental factors, environmental effects, and the like. Each category has its own set of limitations, constraints, risks, and opportunities. For clarity, the following questions serve as a guide:

1. What are the limitations, constraints, risks, and opportunities as they relate to IT in the government agency's financial resources?
2. What are the limitations, constraints, risks, and opportunities as they relate to IT in the government agency's human resources?
3. What are the limitations, constraints, risks, and opportunities as they relate to IT in the government agency's physical resources?
4. What are the limitations, constraints, risks, and opportunities as they relate to IT in the government agency's environmental resources?
5. What are the limitations, constraints, risks, and opportunities as they relate to IT in the government agency's technological resources?

Separating the limitations, constraints, risks, and opportunities into the five resource categories *and* then analyzing the categories collectively is key to identifying solutions that could be available. Committee members will be examining trade-offs and implications. A constraint in one resource could be offset by an opportunity in another resource. A human resource opportunity could provide relief to a financial resource constraint. A risk in one resource could be mitigated by a limitation in another resource. A particular limitation in a technological resource could be used to reduce a human resource risk. A limitation in one resource could be overcome by an opportunity in another resource. A technological resource opportunity could be available to overcome a physical resource limitation. The analysis could be applied to more than a pair of resources (i.e., the combination of three or more resource categories). A limitation in one resource evaluated with a risk of another resource and further evaluated with an opportunity of another resource would produce some effect.

The objective of analyzing the resources in combination is to find ways to overcome the limitations, work around the constraints, mitigate the risks, and take advantage of the opportunities. Mixing and matching existing resources could lead to a solution that would not have been possible if the analysis had not been done. The identified solution could be a less costly alternative. In any event, Committee members will be able to analyze how an existing resource would have an effect on another existing resource.

In planning for the future environment, Committee members will use the resource categories to evaluate what could happen if existing resources are left unchanged and when new resources are introduced. The addition of a new technological resource could cause a change to an existing human resource. The existing human resource could then create a limitation, a constraint, a risk, or an opportunity as result. Adding a new resource could create a limitation, a constraint, a risk, or an opportunity in its resource category. Committee members need to analyze the implications that any change of a resource could have both in its own resource category and in relation to another resource category.

Development of the IT Strategic Plan

The government agency will be moving from the present environment (just assessed) to some future environment. Based on all information collected and analyzed in the assessments, the Planning Committee can decide on what needs to be added and changed. In a number of planning workshops in the development phase, Committee members will identify and discuss IT projects, systems, and activities and further discuss solutions and approaches. The moderator (the Chief Information Officer or the IT Manager) should inform everyone whether or not ideas are feasible and viable. The results of the assessments will provide evidence behind the moderator's remarks. Expression of ideas needs to move beyond sales and marketing buzzwords and emerging technologies. Committee members should refer to the elements of the IT ecosystem in Chapter 1 to identify the essential parts and components that will be needed. Getting to the future needs to be attainable.

Architectural frameworks and technical diagrams will need to be produced to represent the present ("As Is") state and the future ("To Be") state. The currently assessed present environment is the "As Is" state. Although several diagrams may be produced, at least three diagrams (EA, SOA, and Network Topology) must be included in the IT Strategic Plan. See Chapter 1 for a description about the computer network and an example Network Topology.

IT personnel will be involved in planning workshops to capture the projects and systems and document them in the architectural frameworks and technical diagrams. Existing documentation of the "As Is" state provides a starting reference point from which existing systems or the parts and components within can be changed. If none exist, then a complete set of architectural frameworks and technical diagrams must be created to show the "As Is" state at this point.

The "As Is" frameworks and diagrams can be modified (reconfigured) to show the future environment. IT personnel will take notes as Committee members discuss solutions. IT personnel will make changes to the frameworks and diagrams and present the changes to the Planning Committee. The visuals inherent in the diagrams can significantly aid in the discussions of solutions, allowing Committee members to see what will be involved and required. Further adjustments will be made to the point of reaching a consensus by the entire Planning Committee. The end result will produce a second set of architectural frameworks and technical diagrams to show the "To Be" state.

The Planning Committee will then have concise graphical representations of where the government agency is today and where the government agency will be tomorrow. In essence, the two sets of frameworks and diagrams will show the change that will occur after implementing all projects in execution of the IT Strategic Plan.

The "To Be" state and all discussions must be framed around a specific period of time in which implementation will take place. Any identified project, system, or activity will need to be implemented within a limited time frame. This inherently excludes certain computer technologies (i.e., emerging technologies) that may not have been proven viable. Such technologies can be reconsidered in the next Planning Life Cycle process.

The Planning Committee must decide on a period of time for the IT Strategic Plan. A plan that is 1 or 2 years long is too short. The level of effort that would be expended in previous phases would not be worth it to develop a 1- or 2-year plan. A plan could be as long as 10 years. Given that technology changes rapidly, however, a 10-year plan would not afford the opportunity to consider and incorporate technological changes. Three years should be the minimum period of time. Five years is a suitable period of time and is the typical length that most organizations would agree on.

The average lifespan of a computer is 5 years, moreover. After 5 years, computer hardware will need to be evaluated and possibly replaced. Every 5 years, the latest matured technology can be evaluated and selected.

The principal part of the IT Strategic Plan follows a logical structure that starts with the organizational mission and ends with primary and alternative solutions. The structure could start with a vision, but given that this plan extends from the organization-wide strategic plan, the vision is not necessary. In perfect alignment, the IT Strategic Plan supports the government agency's vision, which is already defined. Figure 8.3 illustrates the IT Strategic Plan structure. Committee members should take the government agency's mission statement and rephrase it in context of IT. Do not copy the mission statement verbatim. The mission should have bearing on IT. Committee members should avoid the creation of an entirely new mission statement. The mission of the IT Strategic Plan must show that it is aligned with the government agency's mission statement.

The IT mission then links to one or more strategic objectives. A strategic objective is defined above and relates directly to the mission of the IT Strategic Plan. The mission is accomplished through the accomplishment of one or more strategic objectives.

Committee members can use the strategic objectives identified in the assessment phase. Those objectives that members agree are needed and are high priority within the specified period of time would be written into the plan. Members should agree on which objectives to exclude. Each strategic objective needs to be written in a form that expresses an intent to achieve a broad aim or some end. It will start with "To". For example, the establishment of a financial management system can be stated as "To establish a financial management system". Assuming that there will be many objectives identified in the assessment phase, Committee members should consolidate or group the objectives in some manner so as to make the list shorter. Too many strategic objectives in the IT Strategic Plan will make the plan difficult to manage and monitor. The numbers of goals and solutions will increase with each additional objective. Stating an objective in broader terms would capture similar objectives as one group. For example, "To establish information systems for improved financial, procurement, and public health reporting" is a broader objective that covers three types of systems.

Each strategic objective is then linked to one or more operational goals. An "operational goal" is a specific and practical aim that can be measured. An operational goal can be used as a performance metric to show whether or not the associated strategic objective has been accomplished. A strategic objective, because of its broad aim, can be harder to measure and prove. It is through the associated operational goals that strategic objectives can be proven to be fulfilled.

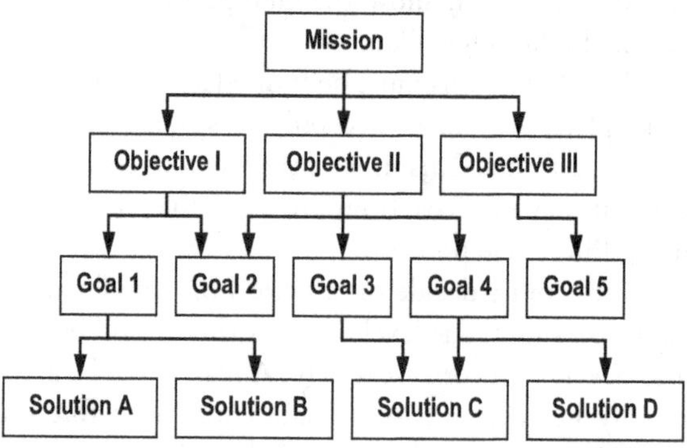

Figure 8.3 IT Strategic Plan structure.

Note: For the purpose of clarity in this figure, not all goals have associated solutions.

Committee members can begin with the key needs identified in the assessment phase as instruction to formulate operational goals. Since the key needs are more tangible, key needs can generate ideas. The language of the operational goal should be written in a form that starts with a verb in the past tense to indicate the goal has been completed. This standard language will inform the IT Review Board, an auditor, and a monitoring specialist to know what needs to be verified and confirmed. For example, "Deployed a computer-based financial management information system" is an operational goal that can be verified. Upon verification, this operational goal will prove that the associated objective "To establish a financial management system" has been accomplished. It is likely that every strategic objective will have more than one operational goal. The example objective would have a second operational goal related to a business process. Committee members will discuss and agree on all possible operational goals.

Each operational goal is finally linked to one or more tactical solutions. A "tactical solution" is a specific project, system, or activity that may be implemented. A selected solution would meet the associated operational goal. For monitoring purposes, the implemented solution provides the evidence to back up the claim of the associated operational goal.

Committee members should definitely decide on two or more tactical solutions for each operational goal. There should be at least a primary solution and an alternative solution. Within the specified period of time, something could happen that would force a change. In such an event, the primary solution would be abandoned, and the alternative would be implemented. Tactical solutions provide backups in cases where the first, second, and so on attempts would not work out. In this development phase, Committee members need to be aware of all possible solutions and select those solutions that would be appropriate for the government agency. The Chief Information Officer or the IT Manager would play an instrumental role if not a decisive one in discussing possible tactical solutions.

Closely related to tactical solutions are the approaches and methodologies. Specific methods and approaches need to be described in the IT Strategic Plan. This will entail gathering details from IT personnel to inform Committee members. Common topics to discuss include the IT operating environment, computer network environment, software development environment, computer manufacturer preference, and computer software vendor preference. A topic would be a discussion on whether the IT operating environment should be homogenous or heterogenous (see Chapter 7). Another topic would be a discussion on whether IT systems should be contracted or outsourced to an IT provider or should remain in operation in internal data center facilities. Another topic would be a discussion on selecting which computer programming languages will be used, and if more than one, what is the order of importance or preference. The discussion and agreement on approaches and methods related to implementation of IT will get the Planning Committee closer to identifying and narrowing down possible solutions.

The IT Strategic Plan needs to have an estimated total cost. The total cost should be broken down by strategic objective. The cost of each strategic objective is the sum total of costs of the associated tactical solutions. The cost of each identified solution needs to be analyzed and calculated (see Chapter 3). Past financial records and IT budgeting plans can be relied upon to obtain specific cost figures. The historical records, moreover, will provide actual amounts previously spent. Research on new cost and pricing would be needed for new solutions.

The calculated total cost of the IT Strategic Plan must include the cost of operating and managing the IT department. While strategic planning inherently focuses on projects and systems, the Planning Committee must not forget about the needs and requirements of the IT department. General IT operations and management will have its own strategic objective with associated operational goals and tactical solutions.

Finally, the Planning Committee must come to a full consensus on the IT Strategic Plan. This will indicate that every senior executive leader and department director has approved of the contents. The final IT Strategic Plan can then be presented for approval by the head of the government agency. It would then be distributed throughout the government agency. It may also be shared with the general public.

The following business outline provides the contents of the IT Strategic Plan document, ordered by section and sub section:

1. Executive Summary
2. Introduction
   - 2.1. Purpose of This Document
   - 2.2. References
   - 2.3. Key Assumptions
3. Mission Statement
   - 3.1. Rephrased Statement from the Organization-wide Strategic Plan
4. Strategic Objectives
   - 4.1. Name of Objective I
   - 4.2. Name of Objective II
   - 4.3. Name of Objective III
   - 4.4. Name of Objective IV
   - 4.5. Given Objective for General IT Operations and Management
5. Operational Goals
   - 5.1. Name of Goal 1
   - 5.2. Name of Goal 2
   - 5.3. Name of Goal 3
   - 5.4. Name of Goal 4
   - 5.5. Name of Goal 5
6. Tactical Solutions
   - 6.1. Name of Solution A
   - 6.2. Name of Solution B
   - 6.3. Name of Solution C
   - 6.4. Name of Solution D
   - 6.5. Name of Solution E
7. Approaches and Methodologies
   - 7.1. Information Security
   - 7.2. Data Center Operations
   - 7.3. Telecommunication Infrastructure
   - 7.4. Internet Access
   - 7.5. IT Operating Environment
   - 7.6. Computer Network Environment
   - 7.7. Software Development Environment
   - 7.8. Computer Manufacturer Preference
   - 7.9. Computer Software Vendor Preference
   - 7.10. Contracting and Outsourcing
   - 7.11. Professional Development
   - 7.12. Funding Source(s)

8. Current Situation
   8.1. Summary of Limitations, Constraints, Risks, and Opportunities
   8.2. Financial Resources: Limitations, Constraints, Risks, and Opportunities
   8.3. Human Resources: Limitations, Constraints, Risks, and Opportunities
   8.4. Physical Resources: Limitations, Constraints, Risks, and Opportunities
   8.5. Environmental Resources: Limitations, Constraints, Risks, and Opportunities
   8.6. Technological Resources: Limitations, Constraints, Risks, and Opportunities
9. Present Environment
   9.1. Summary of Present Environment
   9.2. Enterprise Architecture
   9.3. Service-Oriented Architecture
   9.4. Network Topology
10. Future Environment
    10.1. Summary of Future Environment
    10.2. Enterprise Architecture
    10.3. Service-Oriented Architecture
    10.4. Network Topology
11. Appendices
    11.1. IT Strategic Plan Structure
    11.2. IT Strategic Plan Framework with Estimated Cost
    11.3. Monitoring and Evaluation Plan

A final remark in moving from the development phase to the execution phase:

> The best strategic plan is useless if it cannot be executed tactically.
>
> *Erwin Rommel, Field Marshal*

Execution of the IT Strategic Plan

By the start of the execution phase, the Planning Committee has done the work to complete the IT Strategic Plan. Now, the IT department has to implement the approved activities in fulfillment of the agreed-upon strategic objectives. The length of time to execute the IT Strategic Plan is the specified period of time.

Figure 8.4 illustrates four general areas in which the plan is executed. Following immediately from the IT Strategic Plan is the first area "Business Analysis and Design". The Business Analyst, Systems Analyst, Functional Experts, and others who work on the design part all cooperate to analyze, document, and improve the information flows, business processes, and functional applications. Functional requirements would be a major output in this area.

The results of the business analysis will feed into the next area "Operational Planning". The Chief Information Officer and the IT Manager develop and manage a range of policies and plans (e.g., an annual budget, a multi-year budget, a disaster recovery plan, an Information System Security Policy, and a User Access Policy). The IT Project Manager develops and manages detailed plans to carry out projects. Work plans and project schedules are defined. Specific computer technologies are researched, evaluated, and selected.

The work of planning will feed into the next area "Technical Design and Implementation". The Software Developer, Database Administrator, Network Engineer, and other IT personnel

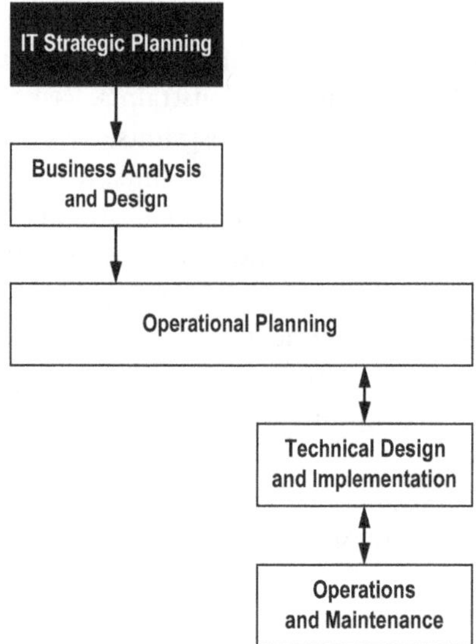

Figure 8.4 Execution of the IT Strategic Plan.

work to design and implement the systems as determined by the previous areas. Technical work is guided by the IT Strategic Plan, the business analysis, and operational planning. In the process of designing the systems, new information can arise and will feed back to operational planning, at which point the IT Project Manager reevaluates plans and makes adjustments. Revised plans will inform IT personnel on changes.

Completed systems are finally deployed, and the work moves to the final area "Operations and Maintenance". The Systems Administrator, Database Administrator, Network Engineer, and other IT personnel are operating and maintaining the computer hardware, the computer software, the computer network, and other components. End users are using the systems. Any changes to the systems will feed back to technical design and will also feed back to operational planning. Plans are further revised to inform technical design again. IT personnel will develop new versions of the systems and deploy them to operation. By this time, operational goals as defined in the IT Strategic Plan will be achieved.

Monitoring of the IT Strategic Plan

The monitoring phase is a phase that overlaps with the execution phase. It would start in 3 months after execution has begun and would end in about 6 months to 1 year after execution has completed. Some period of time is needed to evaluate all of the systems and activities that had been completed upon the end date of the IT Strategic Plan. Monitoring is ongoing during the execution phase. The Planning Committee would meet periodically to review progress and to follow up on issues. The review is based on a monitoring and evaluation plan. After the execution phase, the Planning Committee would review everything that had been done and conclude with whether or not goals and objectives have been achieved. The Planning Committee would prepare and issue internal reports, documenting the reviews and findings.

The IT Review Board conducts independent evaluations. This may be performed on an annual or semi-annual basis. Ad hoc evaluations may be conducted at any time. The IT Review Board would have its own monitoring and evaluation plan. The Planning Committee would be afforded the opportunity to review and comment on the results of the Review Board's evaluations. The IT Review Board would then consider the Planning Committee's feedback and include it in the final reports. The IT Review Board's final reports would be made public.

At any time during the execution phase, an auditor or a third-party investigator may evaluate projects, systems, and activities, individually or collectively. The Planning Committee would be allowed to review and comment on the results of the third-party evaluations. Final reports of the evaluations would be made public.

Closure of the IT Strategic Plan

At the end of the monitoring phase, the IT Strategic Plan can come to an official close. The Planning Committee would have internal reports and formal reports that describe the outcome and performance of the plan. Hopefully, the strategic objectives will have been fulfilled. The reports would show this with evidence to back up the achievements. Some operational goals may have fallen short or failed. The reports would show this as well and may have recommendations for improvement. The Planning Committee convenes a final round of planning workshops to discuss the outcome and performance and to come to an agreement on final conclusions regarding the completed IT Strategic Plan. These final workshops provide the time to learn about the plan's development in light of its execution and to know where the plan succeeded and where it failed. Discussions would provide a sense of direction for the next IT Strategic Plan. The Planning Committee will prepare and issue a memorandum that summarizes the completed plan and lays down broad directions for developing the next plan. The high-level memorandum will then be sent to the head of the government agency.

As a practical matter, all of the documents that had been produced throughout the Strategic Planning Life Cycle process need to be archived and stored for historical purposes. None of the documents can be edited or changed. They all must be preserved. The complete set of documentation would be made available for public review.

Enterprise Architecture

EA was developed in the 1980s by John Zachman. The original form is known as the "Zachman Framework". EA has been applied in the private and public sectors since the early 1990s. The framework has been modified and shaped over the years to fit the particular needs of an organization. Hence, flexibility in its fundamental concept is a credit to its longevity. EA positions itself as being able to align the appropriate technological resources with organizational needs and goals – and ultimately the mission.

Figure 8.5 illustrates an accepted standard of EA as practiced by several government agencies in the United States. At the first, top level before any kind of technology is ever considered, the government agency must have a clearly defined mission, policy statement on why it wants to use IT. This high-level view places the government agency in a position where it can harness the true power of IT. In practical terms, an explicit direction is set by and for the government agency. The first level is "Mission".

The first level brings the agency to the next level of the EA framework. At the second level, the government agency identifies and describes all the types of information that it currently has and will need to fulfill its mission. Information is spread across all departments. This is the essential part that allows personnel to do their work. The second level is "Information".

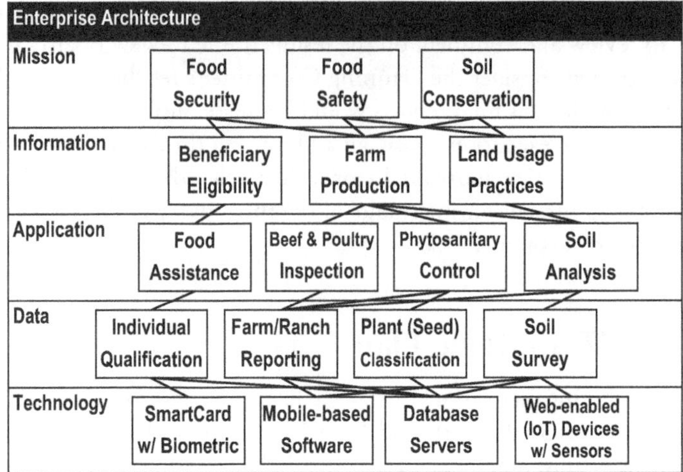

Figure 8.5 Enterprise Architecture. (Structural framework adapted from the U.S. GAO, the U.S. Department of Defense, and the U.S. Department of Treasury.)

Note: This example is not all inclusive. For clarity and legibility, few items are displayed to demonstrate the concept.

The Information level drives down to the next level of the EA framework. At the third level, the government agency can begin to categorize the range of information into several functional applications. All of the possible functional applications can be envisioned. Typically, functional applications will correspond to departments in the agency. The Finance department, for instance, processes financial information. The Human Resources department handles personnel information. Each department would require a functional application through which it can process and handle a specific set of information. The third level is "Application".

As the departments use their functional application, information is processed, and work is carried out. Here is where the need for technology begins to surface. As the departments process their information over time, the results of that work (i.e., reports, studies, and other documents) pile up – literally and figuratively. Eventually, the public manager will realize that they need some efficient way of handling and processing all the mounted up paperwork.

The Application level drives down to the next level of the EA framework. At the fourth level, the government agency breaks up its information into interconnected relationships of numerous data fields to create a systematic way of managing the information. In other words, information is broken down to specific data fields. The end result produces the data architecture of a functional application. Each department's functional application will have its data architecture. And then reviewing all of the departments' data architectures in combination will show where departments have data fields in common. The fourth level is "Data".

The Data level drives down to the last, bottom level of the EA framework. At this level, the government agency can finally decide on which technology will best handle the agency's information. The most appropriate computer technology is determined by the type and amount of data that must be processed. Here is where the public manager will select a combination of computer hardware, computer software, and other technological resources to create an IT system, which end users can input and output data to produce information. Each department can have an IT system, based on its data requirements. The fifth level is "Technology".

EA is a simple framework that explains how any organization can move from strategy to implementation. First, the mission of the organization needs to be known. Second, information that the organization needs to accomplish its mission needs to be known. Third, a range or set of information needs to be identified as belonging to a functional application. Fourth, a functional application needs to be broken up into its essential data fields, which are more precise than information. Fifth and finally, computer technology needs to be selected based on the type and amount of data that a functional application requires. Through this entire flow, the most appropriate technology will be able to process the data in a functional application and produce the information that the organization needs to accomplish its mission. Everything will roll back up from the Technology level to the Mission level.

Service-Oriented Architecture

SOA is an architectural framework designed to deliver services to multiple departments within the government agency and to other agencies and partners in an integrated manner. Conceptually, SOA is not designed to provide computer software programs to end users *per se*, but rather SOA is designed to *integrate business services* across an organization. This framework came about from the many stand-alone IT systems that had been developed. Organizations operated different computer-based information systems with very specific requirements. This resulted in the inability to exchange data between systems. SOA solves this problem by finding ways to integrate disparate IT systems.

The method of SOA can be described in one of two ways. There is the technology-driven SOA that gets into the technical details of how the integrations will be developed. There is also the business-driven SOA that presents the integrations in terms that non-IT personnel can understand. Both methods complement each other. While one is for management, the other is for technical. The technology-driven SOA is a technical representation of the business-driven SOA. This book follows the business-driven SOA.

Linkages between services and data are key to understanding SOA. The formal term is "interface". A specific set of data has an interface (a linkage) to a service. The same set of data can have another interface (another linkage) to another service. The integrations in these two interfaces would be developed in two different forms.

A service is a self-contained business activity. A functional application can be divided into a number of services or business activities. The Human Resources application, for instance, has several business activities. Recruitment, compensation, benefits, and professional development, among others are business activities (services) of Human Resources. Each of these services has a specific set of data. The compensation's set of data can have an interface (a linkage) to a payment service belonging to the Finance application. The compensation's set of data specific to salary and wage can be used by the two services in the different functional applications. There is a logical reason for why a linkage exists in the foregoing example.

When functional applications are divided into services, department directors will be able to see that a particular service in one functional application could be linked to a set of data that belongs to another service in another functional application. The two services could tap into the same set of data. That set of data becomes a shared resource.

Figure 8.6 illustrates the SOA. The framework consists of five layers. The first, top layer is "Presentation". The second layer is "Orchestration". The third layer is "Service". The fourth layer is "Integration". The fifth, bottom layer is "Data".

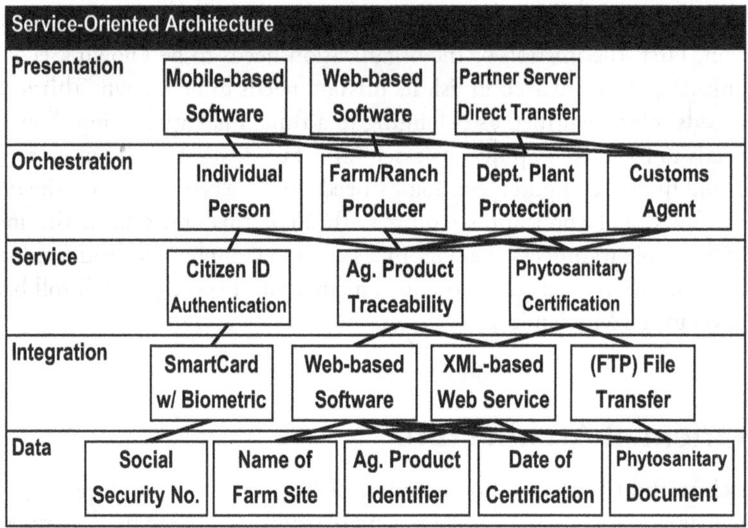

Figure 8.6 Service-Oriented Architecture.

Note: This example is not all inclusive. For clarity and legibility, few items are displayed to demonstrate the concept.

The Presentation layer provides for various forms of presentation that data can be delivered to an end user. Examples include a Web browser user interface, a mobile-based user interface, and an SMS text message.

The Orchestration layer provides for various groups of end users who can have access to certain services via one or more forms of presentation. Examples include a specific department, a specific team, an external partner, and the general public.

The Service layer provides for different business services that can be available to certain groups via one or more implementations of integration. Any instance of a service is a very specific activity that can operate individually regardless of context. Examples include registering a person, sending a payment to a person, and retrieving a particular report.

The Integration layer provides for different technology implementations that can be developed to connect certain services to certain data. Examples include a Web service, a specialized computer software program, and a developed form of embedded computer technology.

The Data layer provides for specific sets of data that can be connected to certain services via one or more implementations of integration. Any instance of a set of data is limited to a few data fields. Examples include a social security number, a person's monthly pay amount and date of payment, latitude and longitude coordinates, and a biometric characteristic.

Monitoring and Governance

A structure of governance needs to be in place to ensure that the IT Strategic Plan is indeed implemented according to what has been agreed upon. The plan itself is just a document. Proper monitoring of the plan will verify and confirm that progress is being made to achieve stated goals. Proper monitoring can uncover problems, bringing them to the fore so that they can be corrected in a timely manner.

A formal monitoring and evaluation plan should be developed. This will entail the development of performance metrics to measure the goals in the IT Strategic Plan. If defined correctly as described, the operational goals can serve in a dual role as performance metrics. Each performance metric needs a detailed methodology for how the metric will be measured and reported. What data will be collected? Who will collect and analyze the data? How will the data be analyzed? What forms of reporting are needed and when? Each metric should be quantifiable, allowing for a numeric value to be set which can be tracked. A target value is given to a performance metric before commencement of any associated activities. On a periodic basis after associated activities have started and are underway, a number of actual values will be reported to check on the achievement of the associated operational goal. The calculated difference between the actual value and the target value will provide an indication of whether or not achievement has been made and the amount of change. The monitoring and evaluation plan must have adequate controls, protocols, and responsibilities defined on how monitoring and evaluation will be conducted with particular controls on how the target values will be set when and by whom.

The IT Strategic Planning Committee should be made permanent to serve as an internal group who will have immediate oversight on execution of the IT Strategic Plan. Committee members would meet periodically, usually on a quarterly basis, to review progress. They would review monitoring and evaluation reports, comparing the reported actual values against the previously set target values in the performance metrics. The Planning Committee would quickly see any difference between what was originally planned and what is actually carried out. Department directors can be informed on the status of their projects and systems. As they meet together, department directors could share information, discuss issues, and make collective decisions. Any potential problems can be caught internally by the Planning Committee.

The IT Review Board independent of the Planning Committee and the IT department needs to be established. This separate body should have had little to no involvement in strategic planning, operational planning, and technical implementation. It needs to be relatively removed, if not completely removed, from any of the work in order for it to have a high degree of objectivity. The IT Review Board is made up of auditors and analysts. The IT Review Board will ensure that all systems are in compliance with quality standards, other relevant standards, organizational policies, and applicable laws and regulations.

Chapter 8 Quiz

Question 1: Who needs to be a member in the IT Strategic Planning Committee?

A. Chief Information Officer and IT Manager
B. Chief Financial Officer
C. Department Directors
D. All of the above
E. A committee is not needed

Question 2: What selected phases in order of progression (one after the other) are in the Strategic Planning Life Cycle process?

A. Assessment of Capacity, Evaluation of Needs, and Development of the Plan
B. Understanding of Purpose, Evaluation of Needs, and Assessment of Capacity
C. Understanding of Purpose, Execution of the Plan, and Closure of the Plan
D. Development of the Plan, Assessment of Capacity, and Execution of the Plan
E. Evaluation of Needs, Development of the Plan, and Execution of the Plan

Question 3: In Figure 8.2, which driver, need, and objective only have one link between the parts?

A. Driver 1, Need 5, and Objective 5
B. Driver 2, Need 1, and Objective 1
C. Driver 3, Need 6, and Objective 4
D. Driver 4, Need 2, and Objective 3
E. Driver 6, Need 3, and Objective 2

Question 4: The assessment of limitations and risks needs to cover what resources?

A. Technological Resources
B. Human Resources
C. Environmental Resources
D. Physical Resources
E. All of the above

Question 5: What is the proper order of levels in EA?

A. Data, Technology, Mission, Information, and Application
B. Application, Information, Data, Technology, and Mission
C. Mission, Information, Application, Data, and Technology
D. Mission, Technology, Data, Information, and Application
E. Technology, Data, Application, Information, and Mission

Worksheets

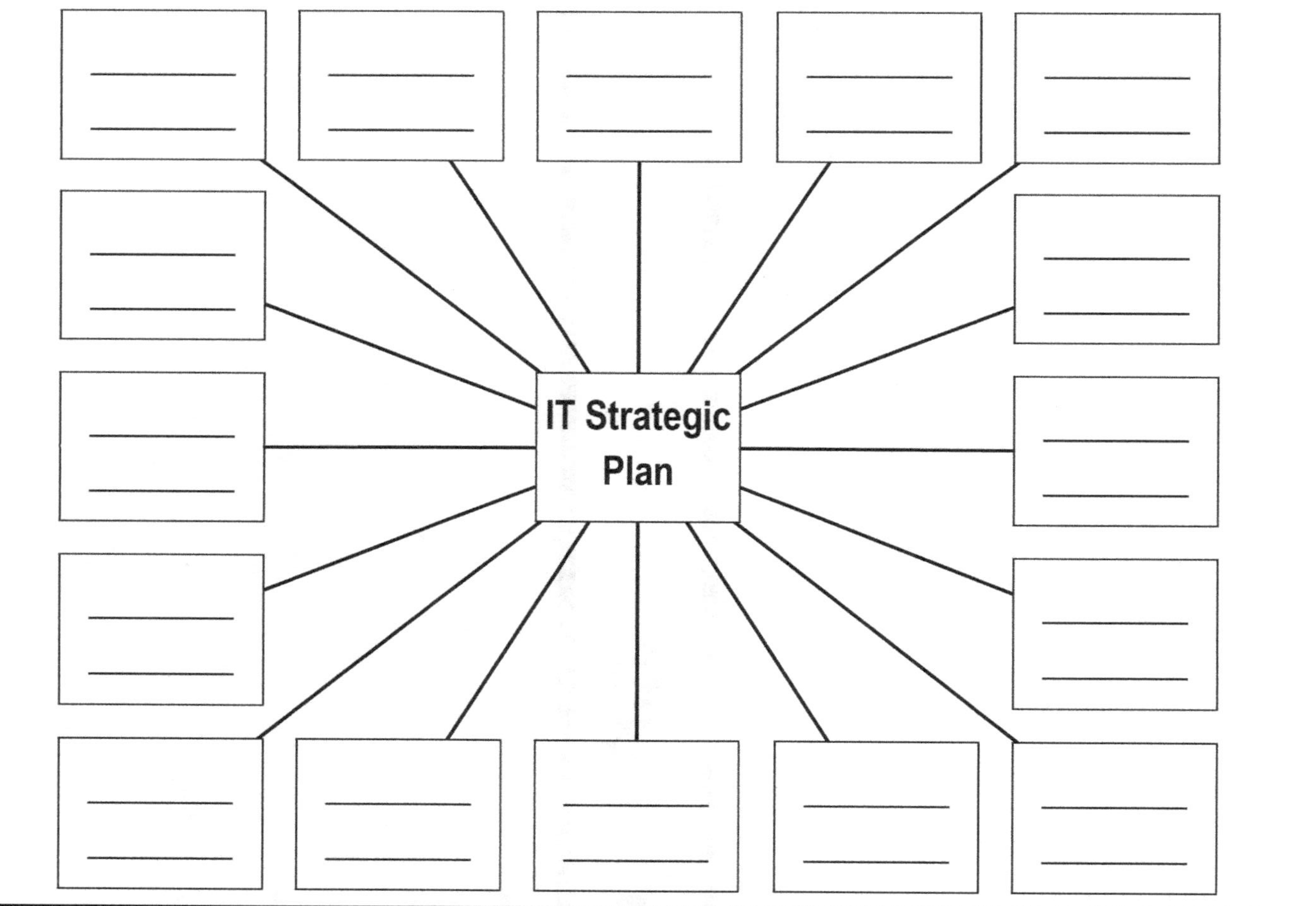

Worksheet 8.1 Planning committee members.

Organization: ____________________ Department: ____________________

Core Drivers	Key Needs	Strategic Objectives

Worksheet 8.2 Drivers, needs, and objectives.

Drivers	Needs	Objectives

Worksheet 8.3 Analysis map of drivers, needs, and objectives.

Organization: ____________________ Department: ____________________

__ Financial __ Human __ Physical __ Environmental __ Technological

Limitation(s)	Constraint(s)
____________________	____________________
____________________	____________________
____________________	____________________
____________________	____________________
____________________	____________________
Risk(s)	**Opportunity**
____________________	____________________
____________________	____________________
____________________	____________________
____________________	____________________
____________________	____________________

Worksheet 8.4 **Current situation assessment.**

Step 1:
Write one item (a tactical solution) on a Post-it® note.

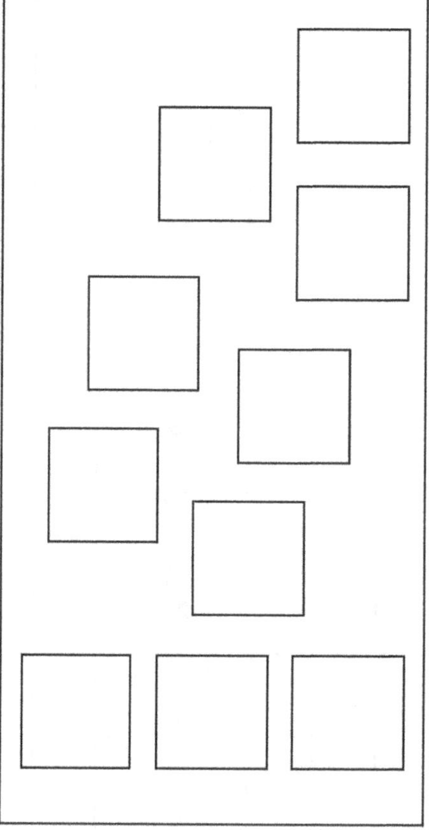

Step 2:
Organize written notes on a large board, sorting them in any pattern that makes sense in your operating environment.

Step 3:
Apply the arrangement of notes to other worksheets.

Worksheet 8.5 IT strategy arrangement exercise.

Enterprise Architecture
Mission
Information
Application
Data
Technology

Worksheet 8.6 Enterprise Architecture.

Service-Oriented Architecture
Presentation
Orchestration
Service
Integration
Data

Worksheet 8.7 Service-Oriented Architecture.

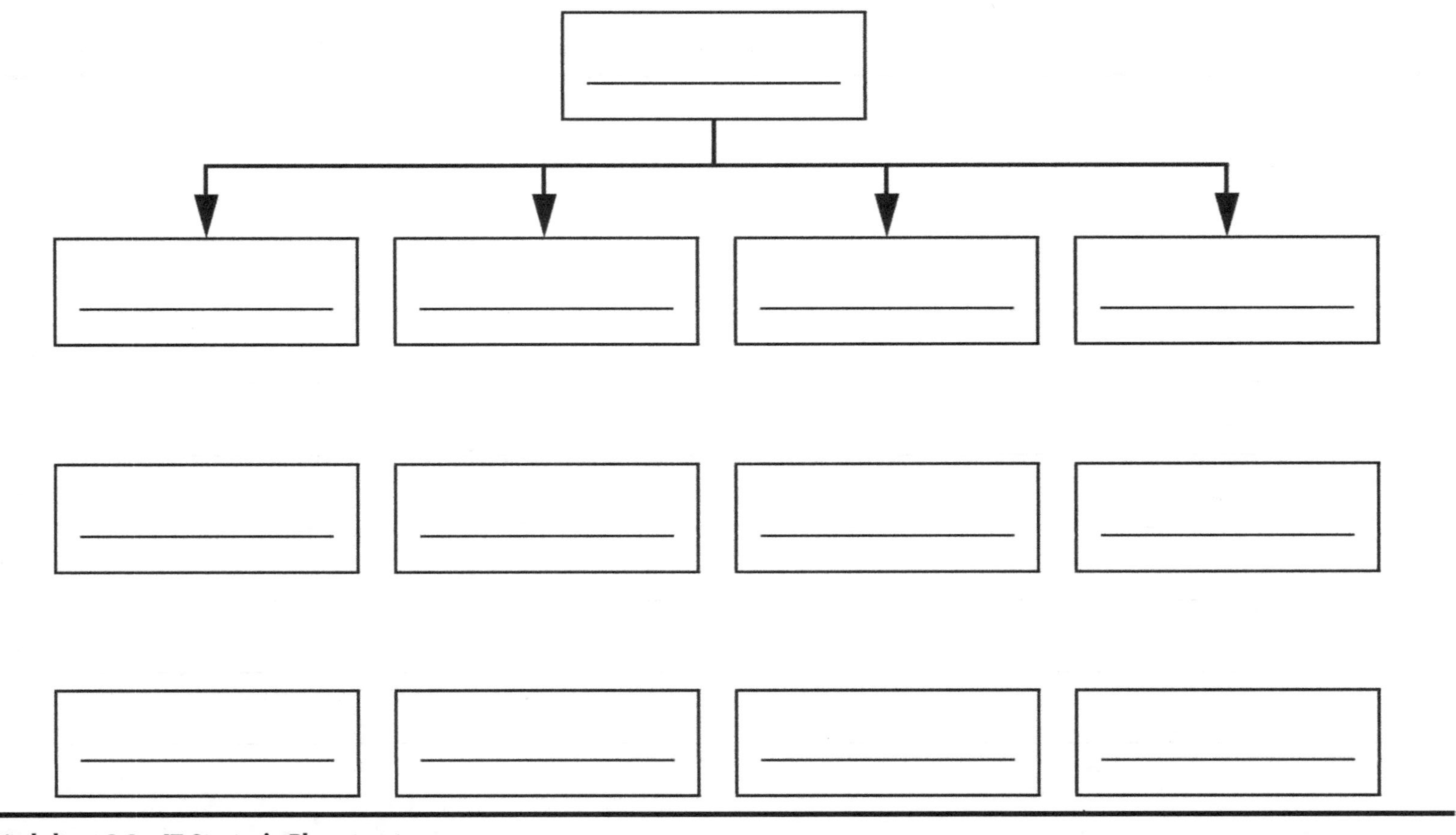

Worksheet 8.8 IT Strategic Plan structure.

Organization: ____________________ Plan From Year 20___ To Year 20___

ID	Objective	Goal	Solution	Principal	Other(s)

Worksheet 8.9 IT Strategic Plan estimated cost and schedule, part 1 of 2.

Organization: ____________________ Plan From Year 20___ To Year 20___

ID	Solution	Start Date	End Date	Months	Total Cost

Worksheet 8.10 IT Strategic Plan estimated cost and schedule, part 2 of 2.

Conclusion

> There's a tendency at the senior and middle-manager level to be too big-picturish and too superficial. There is a phrase, 'The devil is in the details.' One can formulate brilliant global strategies whose executability is zero. It's only through familiarity with details – the capability of the individuals who have to execute, the marketplace, the timing – that a good strategy emerges. I like to work *from details to big pictures.* [emphasis mine]
>
> **Andrew S. Grove, Intel**

The late Andy Grove provides insight in those words. He also captures the essence of this book. Information Technology (IT) and its implementation is too often viewed on a superficial level. Non-IT leaders and managers speak overly broad about technology and in one particular element of the IT ecosystem (computer software). With an awareness of all the elements and how they affect each other, public managers should now be able to speak more concretely. Familiarity with the components of an IT system can aid managers in seeing the larger picture that is realistic. Most important, non-IT personnel will be able to engage constructively with IT personnel on all aspects of IT – from strategic planning to operations and throughout the System Development Life Cycle process. Both groups would come away with feeling more satisfied, as their needs have been met.

IT has been deconstructed to show its organization of people, its budgeting of resources, its selection of systems, its application of contracting, its execution of technical work, its security of information, and finally its planning of all the foregoing topics. The inner working of IT shows one large ecosystem with numerous interactions and relationships. This demystification of how IT operates in an organization gives the public manager the necessary details to manage IT and to use it for proper effect. The public manager can then assemble the methods of operating and the elements of the IT ecosystem to be suitable to their organization.

Like financial management, human resources management, and project management, Information Technology management is a core function in the business of public administration. IT resources must be managed and used properly. Without a management structure in place, technology could lead in a direction that was not intended or anticipated. The public manager can guide technology along a deliberate path that brings results and benefits to the government agency. And as government provides services to the public, the guided technology can support and facilitate the delivery of services to citizens. IT as it is directed and led by public managers can improve the functions of government.

Without proper planning and management, the government agency would be implementing the technological elements of the IT ecosystem blindly with little to no coordination. Issues are likely to come up. The government agency could be spending more money than it needs to.

With many vendors that produce competing products, the government agency could create an environment where several disparate IT systems exist that cannot communicate with each other. This can be problematic when specific data records need to be transferred to other agencies and partners. Inadequate technical capacity in the IT department will make such an environment unsustainable. The environment, moreover, opens up operational and security risks and vulnerabilities.

It is critical that all of the elements in the IT ecosystem be analyzed to know which ones will work together. The technological elements are not the only ones that need to be evaluated. The non-technological elements must also be evaluated. Enterprise Architecture and Service-Oriented Architecture presuppose the analyses of end users, functional applications, business processes, and other non-technological elements. Without the necessary non-technological elements being included, the technological elements could be misaligned. Configured IT systems may still work, but they would not operate optimally or effectively.

The construction of a house is the perfect analogy. Building a house involves different technical disciplines that have to be coordinated. Various aspects such as electricity, plumbing, heating and cooling, flooring, and insulation, among others, have to be planned. A blueprint provides the layout of the house, detailing all the necessary parts. A general contractor then leads construction by ensuring that the house is built according to specifications in the blueprint.

An IT architecture is like a blueprint. The IT architecture shows how an IT program, an IT system, or a specific component of an IT system needs to be developed. One set provides a technology-driven framework for IT specialists to follow. Another set provides a business-driven framework for non-IT leaders and managers to follow.

The Enterprise Architecture provides a concise graphical representation of how IT will be aligned to the mission of the government agency. The public manager will see the logical build-up of steps from the technology level to the data level, to the application level, to the information level, and finally to the mission level. In this way, the value of IT is explicitly clear and known.

The Service-Oriented Architecture provides a concise graphical representation of how specific sets of data can be identified and shared as needed with internal departments, external partners, and the general public, framed under the concept of providing business services. The public manager will see how different IT systems can be integrated by drilling down to specific business activities that get at a more specific set of data. The public manager will further see (through a structure of layers) what selected technology would provide that limited set of data as a service to a certain group of end users via a particular way of accessing and presenting the service. The ability to exchange data between systems and groups becomes easier to comprehend.

The Network Topology provides a concise graphical representation of how various computers and network devices from several locations in which the government agency operates will be connected together in a computer network. The public manager will see how a particular department will be able to access IT systems, shared IT resources, and the Internet. The public manager will further see how departments will be able to connect to each other within a single location and with other operating units in other locations spread geographically across a region or the world. The boundary within which specific technological elements operate is explicitly clear and known.

The Enterprise Architecture, Service-Oriented Architecture, and Network Topology allow the public manager to see "The Big Picture" of a particular aspect of IT from a perspective that is built on a foundation of details. Literally and figuratively, each form of graphical representation provides a clear picture of the whole.

IT is so much more than simply purchasing and using a personal computer and a software program.

Glossary of Terms

Activity: A form of work that uses up resources over time to contribute to the manufacture or development of a product or a service.

Activity-Based Costing: An accounting method used to identify and describe the costs of resources for activities.

Agency Capital Plan: A document that identifies and describes existing capital assets already owned, performance gaps between existing capabilities and organizational goals and objectives, and new capital acquisitions proposed with justification for funding.

Alignment: The placement of structures, systems, processes, activities, and resources that in combination serve to accomplish an organization's mission.

App: An abbreviation of the word "application," and refers to a computer software program.

Backup: A copy of recent data records, electronic files, or computer software programs saved in a storage medium for the purpose of restoring the saved copy in the event that currently operating data records, electronic files, or computer software programs are lost, damaged, corrupted, or otherwise unusable.

Bandwidth: The capacity to transmit data through a physical connection line in a computer network and that is measured at a rate of megabits per second.

Baselining: The action of obtaining data on current programs, processes, and systems to develop metrics against which improvements can be compared.

Benchmark: A previously measured standard that serves as a point of reference against which a new improvement can be compared.

Benefit: A financial or non-financial gain that is received by an organization or a proportion of the population of a particular group in society and that is a result of carrying out activities.

Best Practice: A system, a method, a process, or an approach that is practiced in public and private organizations and that is widely recognized as improving performance and efficiency in a specific area.

Bit: The smallest unit of computer memory.

Bug: A fault, an irregularity, or an unexplained issue that causes a computer software program in part or in whole to operate unexpectedly.

Business Case: A document that lays out the case in a structured format a proposal for why a process improvement project, in general, and a technology-related project, in particular, is needed, summarizing the benefits, costs, equity impacts, and implications, and that functions as a decision package for senior executive leaders and other key decision-makers.

Business Process: A series of steps consisting of tasks, decisions, and documents that together form a path – a structured chain of events – to produce a product or a service.

Business Process Reengineering: A systematic and disciplined approach that examines and redesigns business processes to find and make improvements that result in performance and efficiency gains.

Byte: A unit of computer memory and a form of measurement for storing an amount of information in a computer, expressed in kilobytes (KB), megabytes (MB), gigabytes (GB), terabytes (TB), and petabytes (PB). One byte equals eight bits.

Capital Asset: A tangible property or a durable good that includes land, equipment, a motor vehicle, or a building and that is used over a number of years.

Client-Server System: A particular configuration of an IT system involving a pair of computer software programs designed to work securely to allow a person to use their computer designated as the client to retrieve information from a centralized computer designated as the server.

Cloud: A reference to a symbol that is used in a computer network topology and that is associated with a connection to the Internet, and a further reference to a remote site in which an IT system operates for uninterrupted online service.

Computer: An electronic device composed of hardware and software components in a variety of configurations that is capable of storing, retrieving, and processing data through the execution of programmed instructions.

Computer Case: The physical unit that contains the hardware components of a computer and that creates a single computer system.

Computer-Based Information System: The incorporation of a computer to facilitate, automate, or accelerate specific parts of an information system.

Contracting: A mode of procurement in which the government agency retains control of the business process and provides direction to the vendor in developing a product or delivering a service.

Cookie: A part of a particular technique to maintain the state of an online session in which text is stored in a person's computer by a Website or a Web-based computer software program that the person visits or uses, for the purpose and convenience of remembering certain information, so that the person on subsequent visits to or uses of the same Website or Web-based computer software program can be provided the same or consistent level of service.

Core Driver: Some factor (voluntary or mandatory) that compels an organization to do something or not to do something.

Decision Criteria: A documented set of factors, consisting of screening criteria and ranking criteria, which is used to evaluate and compare the risks, costs, and benefits of a number of IT projects and that serves to aid in the selection of an IT project for implementation.

Direct Cost: A resource that is 100% dedicated to one program, system, or activity and that is not shared with another program, system, or activity.

Domain Name: A unique address (e.g., aphis.usda.gov) that identifies an organization on the Internet and that allows an organization to conduct business or have a presence on the Internet.

Downloading: The action of transferring information from a remote computer to the end user's computer.

Electronic Mail (e-mail): A form of messaging that allows people to send and receive correspondence and a variety of electronic files between computers and that is addressed to a person's e-mail address.

E-mail Address: A unique address that is given to a person for the purpose of sending and receiving e-mail messages and that is composed of a user name followed by the @ symbol and a domain name (e.g., jane.doe@aphis.usda.gov), the entire composition of which points to a specific electronic mailbox belonging to the person.

Emerging Technology: A classification for a group of computer-related technologies that have potential and promise but currently have problems or weaknesses that must be corrected in order for such technologies to be viable for wide, commercial use.

End User: A person or a computer machine that uses a computer-based product or service.

Equity Impact: A concern or an issue that unfairly jeopardizes, creates a loss for, loses, or otherwise harms a certain population of people or a natural resource, and some form of relief or compensation is warranted to the affected persons.

Fixed Cost: A resource whose price (cost) does not change with any given change in quantity.

Flat File Database: A single table of data records that is exported to a plain text file, which can be used to import into a computer software program or can be read by a person.

Functional Application: An organizational activity of significant scope that an organization undertakes, regardless of whether a computer is used.

Handover: The point when an organization accepts that a technology solution is complete and ready to be deployed for operation and use.

Help Desk: A designated department, an operating unit, or a staff group that provides timely support and assistance to people concerning problems and issues related to the operation and use of their computer.

Hypertext: Text that can have a link to another part of a Web page or a document, or to another Web page of a Website, or to another document stored on another computer.

Indirect Cost: A resource that is shared with two or more programs, systems, or activities, apportioning time or capabilities among the different programs, systems, or activities.

Information Engineering: A disciplined approach to plan, analyze, design, and develop a computer-based information system with an enterprise-wide perspective and an emphasis on data and architectures.

Information Management: The planning, budgeting, manipulating, and controlling of information throughout its life cycle.

Information System: The organized collection, processing, transmission, dissemination, and use of information in a complete system that coherently functions in accordance with defined procedures, processes, and requirements, regardless of whether a computer is used. An information system can be based entirely on a manual procedure.

Information Technology (IT): A specialized and disciplined field that applies mechanical and electronic equipment, computer programming, information security, functional applications, business processes, and laws for people to create, store, exchange, use, and manage information that is proper and efficient.

Intangible Benefit: A benefit that makes an improvement on a specific area for an organization or society and can be difficult to express in a figure and hence hard to measure, typically a non-financial or non-monetary gain.

Internet: One global computer network based on a set of standard protocols that enables organizations and persons to communicate and exchange information with anyone around the world.

Internet Protocol (IP) Address: A unique address that is assigned (permanently or temporarily) to a computer and that is required for a computer to connect to a computer network and to communicate with other computers.

Intranet: Like the Internet but it is restricted to the internal computer network of one organization where employees have private access to policies, operating procedures, announcements, and other information that belong to the organization.

IT Architecture: A representative model of an IT system, a computer network, a computer software program, a database software program, or a business-driven framework that shows what is comprised to make the system, network, program, or framework function and that meets organizational needs and goals.

IT Infrastructure: The apparatus comprising equipment, cabling, racks, and related physical hardware that is designed, constructed, and managed to operate a number of IT systems.

IT Management: The area within the field of IT that plans, budgets, organizes, and manages IT-related resources at the strategic and operational levels.

IT System: A system consisting of hardware, software, and network components along with the procedures, processes, and security controls to operate and manage the complete system as a whole.

IT System Functions: A list of specific capabilities that the components of an IT system are designed to do and allow or enable end users to carry out within the boundary and limitation of the system.

Key Need: A major object or a significant thing that an organization needs or requires to be operationally effective.

Life-Cycle Cost: The total cost (estimated and actual) that includes the direct and indirect costs of start-up, development, operation, and closure of a program or system over a period of time that corresponds to the life of the program or system.

Log In (Also, Log On, Sign In, and Sign On): The action of accessing a computer network, a computer software program, or an IT system through a secured method of user authentication, typically by entering user credentials (e.g., a user name and a password) that an authorized person has been given.

Model: A representation of a specific subject that is developed for analysis, improvement or replacement, and overall understanding.

Modular Design: A particular method of project design that breaks the development of a computer software program or an IT system into a number of modules and that reduces risks and shortens the time frame of development on a per module basis.

Multimedia Messaging Service (MMS): A form of messaging that extends the functionality of SMS to send and receive an image file or a very short audio or video file per message between cellular phones (not all phones may support MMS) and that is addressed to a person's phone number.

Multitasking: The concurrent execution of several jobs.

Net Present Value (NPV): A method that is used to analyze cash flow in accounting, converting future costs and benefits into present values (the equivalency in today's terms), and is calculated by subtracting the sum total of present value costs from the sum total of present value benefits.

Offline: The status of being disconnected to or unavailable in a computer network at which point in time the disconnected computer cannot be accessed and cannot make information available to transmit.

Off-site: The status of being located elsewhere in a different location separate from an organization's place of business at which point in time information cannot be accessed and used.

Online: The status of being connected to or available in a computer network at which point in time the connected computer can be accessed and can make information available to transmit.

On-site: The status of being located and available in an organization's place of business where work is conducted and at which point in time information can be accessed and used.

Operational Goal: A specific and practical aim that is measurable and that is associated to a strategic objective.

Operational Requirements: A defined set of specific activities that is required in a tactical solution.

Outcome: A resulting effect (expected and unexpected) of the use and application of outputs.

Output: A thing that is created or generated from the use and application of inputs.

Outsourcing: A mode of procurement in which the government agency transfers control of the business process to the vendor, based on the assumption that the vendor can develop a product or deliver a service more efficiently than what the agency can do.

Performance Gap: The difference between what is expected and what is produced in terms of quality, quantity, time, cost, skill, and overall capacity.

Performance Measurement: The process of developing a set of measurable indicators (metrics) that can be used to monitor and evaluate the progress made in achieving a predetermined set of goals.

Procurement Case: A document that lays out the case in a structured format the rationale for acquiring a product or a service through contracting or outsourcing, summarizing the gains, losses, and trade-offs, and that functions as a decision package for senior executive leaders and other key decision-makers.

Remote Site: A building or a facility located elsewhere in a different location separate from an organization's place of business and that is used to operate and maintain an IT system for uninterrupted online service.

Return on Investment (ROI): A figure of merit that indicates the effectiveness or efficiency of a program, project, or system, showing an amount of tangible or intangible benefit received in relation to an amount of cost invested, and that is a key metric used by senior executive leaders and other key decision-makers to evaluate and decide on a capital investment project.

Security: Protection from potential threats with appropriate control measures designed to prevent and minimize harm or damage to or loss of the equipment, functionality, and contents of an IT system and to ensure that operations can be resumed and continued in any event of an outage or a disaster.

Semi-Variable Cost: A resource whose price (cost) initially starts fixed for a given quantity (a certain number of units) and then changes at each unit change in quantity.

Server Virtualization: A particular approach in IT infrastructure design that allows for a computer server to be deployed, managed, and operated as a configured computer software program, the configuration of which is run with a number of other software-based computer servers in a single physical computer server with substantial computer processing, data storage, and network connection capabilities.

Short Message Service (SMS): A form of messaging that allows people to send and receive very short messages (up to 160 characters per message) in plain text between cellular phones and that is addressed to a person's phone number.

Software Feature: A task or an action that is programmed in a computer software program to make the software program have the capability to carry out the programmed task or action.

Stakeholder: A person who has a vested interest in some or all of the activities that result in a particular outcome.

Steering Committee: A group of persons who meet periodically to discuss and decide on matters that affect the performance, operations, and long-term outlook of their organization, with emphasis on monitoring and evaluating the progress of ongoing activities.

Step-Function Cost: A resource whose price (cost) stays the same for a given quantity (a certain number of units) and then suddenly moves to a new price (cost) at a particular point in a change in quantity and stays the same for another given quantity (a certain number of units) until another sudden move is made.

Strategic Objective: A broad description of some new state or end that an organization wants to reach and that is associated to the organization's mission.

Tactical Solution: A specific project, system, or activity that is planned for implementation and that is associated to an operational goal.

Tangible Benefit: A benefit that is immediately obvious and measurable, typically a financial gain.

Upgrade: The installation of a newer version of a computer software program or additional capacity of a computer hardware component (e.g., increased memory) in a computer that improves on the functionality of the software program or the capacity of the hardware component.

Uploading: The action of transferring information from the end user's computer to a remote computer.

URL (Uniform Resource Locator): A specific form of an address that is used to locate and link to an electronic file or a specific resource on the Internet and that the format of the address is composed of the Internet protocol, the domain name with or without a service prefix, the file path, and the file name (e.g., https://www.aphis.usda.gov/plant_health/plant_pest_info/plum_pox/downloads/plumpox-photos.pdf).

Variable Cost: A resource whose price (cost) changes at each unit change in quantity.

Version: An edition of a computer software program that releases a set of changes (major or minor) to improve or replace a previous edition of the software program and that is notated by two whole numbers separated by a period to denote a major edition in the first number and a minor edition in the second number (e.g., software version 10.3).

World Wide Web (WWW): The most widely used service on the Internet that allows an organization or a person to operate and maintain a Website or a Web-based computer software program to publish, share, and exchange information on the Internet; the WWW is one of many services that uses a standard Internet protocol to transmit information. Other services include e-mail and file transfer.

Answers to Chapter Quizzes

Chapter 1 Quiz

Question 1: E
Question 2: C
Question 3: D
Question 4: E
Question 5: B

Chapter 2 Quiz

Question 1: B
Question 2: E
Question 3: C
Question 4: D
Question 5: E

Chapter 3 Quiz

Question 1: D
Question 2: C
Question 3: A
Question 4: D
Question 5: D

Chapter 4 Quiz

Question 1: E
Question 2: D
Question 3: E
Question 4: D
Question 5: E

Chapter 5 Quiz

Question 1: D
Question 2: C
Question 3: E
Question 4: A
Question 5: E

Chapter 6 Quiz

Question 1: D
Question 2: B
Question 3: D
Question 4: C
Question 5: A

Chapter 7 Quiz

Question 1: E
Question 2: E
Question 3: C
Question 4: E
Question 5: A

Chapter 8 Quiz

Question 1: D
Question 2: B
Question 3: D
Question 4: E
Question 5: C

Bibliography

Aberdeen Group. 2008. "Business Continuity: Implementing Disaster Recovery Strategies and Technologies," February 2008. *Aberdeen Group.*

Adams, C., and S. Farrell. 1999. "Internet X.509 Public Key Infrastructure Certificate Management Protocols," RFC 2510. (March 1999). *The Internet Society*, www.ietf.org/rfc/rfc2510.txt.

Arenaza, Sonia, Eric Kempen, and Guillaume Lechasseur, et al. 2008. Congressional Research Service: Biometrics in the Workplace, Master of Public Administration Workshop Final Report, June 2008. Syracuse, NY: Maxwell School of Syracuse University.

Aron, Jacob. 2015. "Experts doubt Google's claim about its quantum computer's speed." (9 December 2015), *New Scientist*. www.newscientist.com/article/dn28641-experts-doubt-googles-claim-about-its-quantum-computers-speed. (Accessed 13 June 2019).

Aron, Jacob. 2019. "IBM unveils its first commercial quantum computer." (8 January 2019), *New Scientist*. www.newscientist.com/article/2189909-ibm-unveils-its-first-commercial-quantum-computer. (Accessed 13 June 2019).

Badev, Anton, and Matthew Chen. 2014. Bitcoin: Technical Background and Data Analysis, Finance and Economics Discussion Series, 7 October 2014. Washington, DC: Federal Reserve Board.

Beck, Eric A. 2009. "Strategic Planning for BCM." (24 June 2009), *Disaster-Resource.com*. www.disaster-resource.com/articles/05p_044.shtml.

BMC Software. 2007. "BMC Best Practice Process Flow for Release Management," White Paper, October 2007. BMC Software, Inc.

Brayton, Jim, Andrea Finneman, and Nathan Turajski, et al. 2006. "SearchSecurity.com Definitions: PKI." (10 October 2006), *SearchSecurity.com*, http://searchsecurity.techtarget.com/sDefinition/0,sid14_gci214299,00.html.

CA. 2007. "Practical Disaster Recovery Planning: A Step-by-Step Guide," White Paper, January 2007. CA Technologies.

Campbell, George. 2008. "Assess the Probability of Business Loss." (5 March 2008), *Securityinfowatch.com*, http://securityinfowatch.com/print/Security-Technology-and-Design/Stories-from-the-CSO-Executive-Council/Assess-the-Probability-of-Business-Loss/11474SIW2.

CFO Research Services. 2008. "A complete view of the enterprise: Linking operational and financial planning in global organizations," May 2008. CFO Publishing Corporation.

Chen, Lily, Stephen Jordan, and Yi-Kai Liu, et al. 2016. Report on Post-Quantum Cryptography, NISTIR 8105, April 2016. Gaithersburg, MD: National Institute of Standards and Technology.

Cisco Systems. 2007. "Disaster Recovery: Best Practices White Paper," Document ID: 15118, July 2007. Cisco Systems, Inc.

Cresswell, Anthony M. 2004. Return on Investment In Information Technology: A Guide for Managers, August 2004. Albany, NY: Center for Technology in Government, University at Albany, SUNY.

Cresswell, Anthony M., G. Brian Burke, and Theresa A. Pardo. 2006. Advancing Return on Investment Analysis for Government IT: A Public Value Framework, September 2006. Albany, NY: Center for Technology in Government, University at Albany, SUNY.

Cullen, Alex, and Marc Cecere. 2007. "The IT Strategic Plan Step-By-Step: Deliver An Actionable Plan In A Reasonable Timeframe," CIO Roadmap. (10 April 2007), Forrester Research, Inc.

Dawes, Sharon S., and Theresa A. Pardo, et al. 2004. *Making Smart IT Choices: Understanding Value and Risk in Government IT Investments*, Second Edition, April 2004. Albany, NY: Center for Technology in Government, University at Albany, SUNY.

Dubin, Joel. 2006. "One-time password tokens: Best practices for two-factor authentication." (18 September 2006), *SearchSecurity.com*, http://searchsecurity.techtarget.com/tip/0,289483,sid14_gci1216485,00.html.

Durvasula, Surekha et al. 2006. "SOA Practitioners' Guide Part 2: SOA Reference Architecture." (15 September 2006), BEA Systems, Inc.

Dyakonov, Mikhail. 2018. "The Case Against Quantum Computing: The Proposed Strategy Relies on Manipulating with High Precision an Unimaginably Huge Number of Variables." (15 November 2018), *IEEE Spectrum*, https://spectrum.ieee.org/computing/hardware/the-case-against-quantum-computing. (Accessed 13 June 2019).

Federal Computer Security Program Managers' Forum Working Group. 1998. Guide for Developing Security Plans for Information Technology Systems, NIST 800–18, December 1998. Gaithersburg, MD: National Institute of Standards and Technology.

Fowler, Martin. 2004. *UML Distilled: A Brief Guide to the Standard Object Modeling Language*, Third Edition. Boston, MA: Pearson Education, Inc.

Garbani, Jean-Pierre. 2004. "Best Practices For Service-Level Management," Best Practices. (1 December 2004), Forrester Research, Inc.

Greenemeier, Larry. 2018. "How Close Are We – Really – to Building a Quantum Computer?" (30 May 2018), *Scientific American*, www.scientificamerican.com/article/how-close-are-we-really-to-building-a-quantum-computer. (Accessed 13 June 2019).

Hammer, Michael. 2005. "THE CIO ROLE: Creating Business-IT Alignment." (1 August 2005), *CIO*, www.cio.com/article/print/9494. (Accessed 22 October 2008).

Harvard Business Press, Pocket Mentor Digital. 2009. *Preparing a Budget: Expert Solutions to Everyday Challenges*. Boston, MA: Harvard Business School Publishing Corp.

HP. 2007. "Four Starting Points for Effective IT Project and Portfolio Management," White Paper, April 2007. Hewlett-Packard Development Company, LP.

IBM. 2008. "Do More for Less: Build a Cost-Effective, Optimized IT Infrastructure," White Paper, June 2008. IBM Corporation.

IBM. 2007. "Integrated Change and Release Management: A Defect Resolution Use-Case Scenario," White Paper, October 2007. IBM Corporation.

IBM. 2005. "Optimize Change and Release Management for Complex, Dynamically Changing IT Environments," White Paper, April 2005. IBM Corporation.

Kreger, Heather, and Jeff Estefan, ed. 2009. *Navigating the SOA Open Standards Landscape Around Architecture*. San Francisco, CA: The Open Group.

Kroll, Per, and Walker Royce. 2005. "Key Principles for Business-Driven Development." (15 October 2005), *IBM*, www.ibm.com/developerworks/rational/library/oct05/kroll/index.html. (Accessed 29 June 2009).

Leffingwell, Dean, and Don Widrig. 2003. *Managing Software Requirements: A Use Case Approach*, Second Edition. Boston, MA: Pearson Education, Inc.

Leganza, Gene. 2005. "SOA – The Key to Transforming Government Services." SOA for Government Executive Forum, 14 September 2005. Forrester Research.

Leopoldi, Rick. 2002. "IT Services Management: A Description of Service Level Agreements," White Paper, May 2002. RL Consulting.

Lindstrom, Pete. 2005. "Security: Measuring Up." (18 February 2005), *SearchSecurity.com*, http://searchsecurity.techtarget.com/tip/0,289483,sid14_gci1060349,00.html.

Loch, Karen D., Houston H. Carr, and Merrill E. Warkentin. 1992. "Threats to Information Systems: Today's Reality, Yesterday's Understanding," *MIS Quarterly*, 16 no. 2: 173–186.

Maréchaux, Jean-Louis. 2006. "Combining Service-Oriented Architecture and Event-Driven Architecture using an Enterprise Service Bus." (28 March 2006), *IBM*, www.ibm.com/developerworks/library/ws-soa-eda-esb/. (Accessed 10 November 2009).

Markoff, John. 2002. "Vulnerability Is Discovered In Security for Smart Cards." (13 May 2002), *New York Times*, http://query.nytimes.com/gst/fullpage.html?res=9406E4DB1739F930A25756C0A9649C8B63&sec=&spon=&pagewanted=print.

Mauldin, Marcus D. 2016. "No MPA Left Behind: A Review of Information Technology in the Master of Public Administration Curriculum," *Journal of Public Affairs Education*, 22 no. 2: 187–192.

Maxwell School, Department of Public Administration, ed. 2007. PPA 734 Public Budgeting, Summer 2007, *Course Reader*. Syracuse, NY: Syracuse University.

McKeag, Louise. 2004. "The EAP Heap: Wireless Authentication Protocols: Which One is Right for Your WLAN?" (29 March 2004), *Techworld.com*, www.techworld.com/mobility/features/index.cfm?featureid=404.

Meyer, N. Dean. 2005. "IT Mission, Vision and Values Statements," (26 July 2005), *CIO*, www.cio.com/article/print/9311. (Accessed 22 October 2008).

Michelson, Brenda M. 2006. "Event-Driven Architecture Overview: Event-Driven SOA Is Just Part of the EDA Story." (2 February 2006), *Patricia Seybold Group*, http://dx.doi.org/10.1571/bda2-2-06cc. (Accessed 10 November 2009).

National Association of State Chief Information Officers (NASCIO). 2003. NASCIO Enterprise Architecture Maturity Model, Version 1.3. Lexington, KY: NASCIO.

Natis, Yefim V. 2003. "Service-Oriented Architecture Scenario." (16 April 2003), *Gartner Research*, www.gartner.com/DisplayDocument?doc_cd=114358. (Accessed 9 November 2009).

Nickull, Duane, Laurel Reitman, James Ward, and Jack Wilber. 2007. "Service Oriented Architecture (SOA) and Specialized Messaging Patterns," White Paper. Adobe Systems Incorporated.

OASIS Service Oriented Architecture Reference Model Technical Committee. 2008. Reference Architecture for Service Oriented Architecture Version 1.0: Public Review Draft 1, 23 April 2008. http://docs.oasis-open.org/soa-rm/soa-ra/v1.0/soa-ra-pr-01.pdf. (Accessed 9 November 2009).

Osborne, Wilma M. 1989. Software Configuration Management: An Overview, NIST 500-161, March 1989. Gaithersburg, MD: National Institute of Standards and Technology.

Rasmussen, Neil. 2014. "Raised Floors vs Hard Floors for Data Center Applications," White Paper 19, Revision 3. *Schneider Electric*, www.schneider-electric.com/en/download/document/APC_SADE-5TNQYN_EN and www.apc.com/salestools/SADE-5TNQYN/SADE-5TNQYN_R3_EN.pdf. (Accessed 19 April 2019).

Remenyi, Dan, PhD, and Ann Brown, PhD, ed. 2006. *Proceedings of the 13th European Conference on Information Technology Evaluation*. Genoa, Italy, 28–29 September 2006. Reading, UK: Academic Conferences Limited.

Royce, Walker. 2009. "Improving Software Economics: Top 10 Principles of Achieving Agility at Scale," White Paper, May 2009. IBM Corporation.

Schulte, W. Roy 2003. "The Growing Role of Events in Enterprise Applications." (9 July 2003), *Gartner Research*, www.gartner.com/DisplayDocument?doc_cd=116129. (Accessed 10 November 2009).

The Standish Group. 2009. "CHAOS Summary 2009: The 10 Laws of CHAOS." The Standish Group International, Inc.

The Standish Group. 2009. "Solutions for Enterprise Project and Portfolio Management." The Standish Group International, Inc.

Steinemann, Anne C., William C. Apgar, and H. James Brown. 2005. *Microeconomics for Public Decisions*. Mason, OH: South-Western (Thomson Corporation).

Straub, Detmar W., and Richard J. Welke. 1998. "Coping with Systems Risk: Security Planning Models for Management Decision Making," *MIS Quarterly*, 22 no. 4: 441–469.

Symons, Craig. 2005. "IT Strategy Maps: A Tool For Strategic Alignment," Best Practices. (21 November 2005), Cambridge, MA: Forrester Research, Inc.

TIBCO Professional Services Group. 2005. "TIBCO Service-Oriented IT Organizational Structure Best Practices: An Introduction." *TIBCO Software Inc*, www.tibco.com. (Accessed 22 October 2008).

University of California Los Angeles. Undated. "UCLA Corporate Accounting | Principles of Financial Management." www.accounting.ucla.edu/fn_mgmt.asp. (Accessed 20 November 2009).

University of Sussex. 2016. "Construction of practical quantum computers radically simplified." (25 November 2016), *Phys.org*. https://phys.org/news/2016-11-quantum-radically.html. (Accessed 13 June 2019).

U.S. Customs Service, Office of Information and Technology. 1996. Automated Information Systems Security Policy, CIS HB 1400-05, June 1996. Washington, DC: U.S. Customs Service.

U.S. General Accounting Office (GAO). 2003. INFORMATION TECHNOLOGY: A Framework for Assessing and Improving Enterprise Architecture Management (Version 1.1), GAO-03-584G, April 2003. Washington, DC: GAO.

U.S. General Accounting Office (GAO). 2004. INFORMATION TECHNOLOGY MANAGEMENT: Improvements Needed in Strategic Planning, Performance Measurement, and Investment Management Governmentwide, GAO-04-478T, March 2004. Washington, DC: GAO.

U.S. Government Accountability Office (GAO). 2018. FEDERAL CHIEF INFORMATION OFFICERS: Critical Actions Needed to Address Shortcomings and Challenges in Implementing Responsibilities, GAO-18-93, August 2018. Washington, DC: GAO.

U.S. Government Accountability Office (GAO). 2009. GAO Cost Estimating and Assessment Guide: Best Practices for Developing and Managing Capital Program Costs, GAO-09-3SP, March 2009. Washington, DC: GAO.

U.S. National Institute of Standards and Technology (NIST). 2005. Guide for Developing Security Plans for Federal Information Systems, NIST 800–18 Revision 1, August 2005. Gaithersburg, MD: National Institute of Standards and Technology.

U.S. National Institutes of Health (NIH). 2006. "NIH Enterprise Architecture – Service Orchestration Pattern." 24 May 2006. http://enterprisearchitecture.nih.gov/ArchLib/AT/TA/ServiceOrchestrationPattern.htm. (Accessed 10 November 2009).

Van Meter, Rodney, and Clare Horsman. 2013. "A Blueprint For Building a Quantum Computer," *Communications of the ACM*, 56 no. 10: 84–93. https://m-cacm.acm.org/magazines/2013/10/168172-a-blueprint-for-building-a-quantum-computer/fulltext. (Accessed 13 June 2019).

Wailgum, Thomas. 2004. "IT Gets Organized: Introducing The Office of the CIO." (1 July 2004), *CIO*, www.cio.com/article/print/29203. (Accessed 22 October 2008).

Warren, Ken. 2005. "Protecting Smart Cards against DPA vulnerability." (14 December 2005), *Security Park*, www.securitypark.co.uk/article.asp?articleid=24719.

Weinberg, Neal. 2008. "Cutting IT Costs: Gartner Recommends 20 Can't Miss Tips." (16 October 2008), *CIO*, www.cio.com/article/print/455127. (Accessed 22 October 2008).

Weise, Joel. 2001. "Public Key Infrastructure Overview, Sun BluePrints OnLine." Sun Microsystems, Inc.

Wilcoxen, Peter J., PhD. 2004. "Present Value." (29 October 2004). http://wilcoxen.maxwell.insightworks.com/pages/127.html. (Accessed 27 November 2009).

Index

Manager's Notes

Manager's Notes

Manager's Notes

Manager's Notes

Website Address: http://www.PublicServiceIT.org/extra/
Access Code: Lincoln12score4